AMERICAN
INDIAN
CHRONOLOGY

AMERICAN INDIAN CHRONOLOGY

CHRONOLOGIES OF THE AMERICAN MOSAIC

Phillip M. White

GREENWOOD PRESS
Westport, Connecticut • London

Library of Congress Cataloging-in-Publication Data

White, Phillip M.
  American Indian chronology : chronologies of the American mosaic / by Phillip M. White.
    p. cm.
  Includes bibliographical references and index.
  ISBN 0–313–33820–5 (alk. paper)
  1. Indians of North America—History—Chronology.   I. Title.
E77.W47 2006
970.004'9700202—dc22   2006021332

British Library Cataloguing in Publication Data is available.

Library of Congress Catalog Card Number: 2006021332
ISBN: 0–313–33820–5

First published in 2006

Greenwood Press, 88 Post Road West, Westport, CT 06881
An imprint of Greenwood Publishing Group, Inc.
www.greenwood.com

Printed in the United States of America

The paper used in this book complies with the
Permanent Paper Standard issued by the National
Information Standards Organization (Z39.48–1984).

10 9 8 7 6 5 4 3 2 1

For the new generation:
Annabelle Margaret
Anezka Celeste,
Sarah Kaitlyn,
and Bryton Paul

And for my favorites:
Iggy and Marge Russo
and Laura and Lynne

CONTENTS

PREFACE

A chronology is a history book, listing events in order by date. It enlightens students and researchers to key events at particular times. A chronology of American Indians is an orderly way to view the sweeping changes of history, wars and conflicts, government policies, social progress, and cultural changes affecting peoples in the New World.

The purpose of this chronology is to assist researchers in learning about specific events in the history of the American Indians of North America. Students can scan years to see what was happening in American Indian history from the earliest times of prehistory through the beginning of the twenty-first century. Entries include significant events, cultural issues, and influential people affecting the world of American Indians in the area known today as the United States and bordering areas of Canada and Mexico. The arrangement of the chronology is by dates, first, and then within time periods by broad subject categories, designated by abbreviations. The 36 subject categories are: Agriculture and Farming; Animals; Archaeology; Arts and Crafts; Civil Rights and Protests; Contact with Whites; Death and Burial; Economics and Employment; Education and Schools; Environment and Nature; Explorations; Family; Food and Drink; Health and Disease; Hunting and Fishing; Land Cessions and Reservations; Languages; Laws and Legislation; Legends and Storytelling; Migration; Music and Dance; Nature; Politics; Population; Publications; Recreation; Religion and Spirituality; Settlements and Villages; Shelter and Housing; Social Organization; Sports and Recreation; Tools and Weapons; Trade; Treaties; Wars and Conflicts; and Water Rights and Issues. Subject category entries are arranged alphabetically within years or time periods. An index is also provided for further assistance in locating information.

Spellings often vary in the literature for names of Indian tribes, places, ceremonies, and people. An attempt has been made in the chronology to be consistent in identifying tribes and individuals in an effort to eliminate confusion. For example, normally Yakima is used today instead of Yakama (the historical name of the tribe), Ojibwe is used instead of Ojibway, Ojibwa, or Chippewa, and Shoshone is used instead of the alternate Shoshoni. Whenever exact quotes are given from the literature, however, the exact spellings from the sources are retained.

The intention of the chronology is to help students learn more about the significant events in American Indian studies, and to clarify facts, dates, and people in the field. The chronology is a reference source that will supplement studies of the history, political relations, wars, and cultural events of American Indians in North America from prehistoric times to the twenty-first century.

INTRODUCTION

The forward progress of human civilization has been marked by war, conquest, violence, religious conflict, diseases and plagues, and starvation. North America is no exception. When the European explorers and colonizers arrived in the New World they brought diseases and plagues new to the Indians (cholera, influenza, typhus, malaria, measles, bubonic plague, smallpox, tuberculosis, yellow fever, and other infectious diseases), warfare, and radically different religious ideologies. Some historians estimate that up to 90 percent of the American Indian population died within the first century after the Europeans arrived in America (Weatherford, 1988), but historians disagree on how many Native Americans were living when the Europeans first arrived. Estimates range from as many as 100 million to as few as 30 million (Del Testa, Lemoine, and Strickland, 2004).

By the end of the fifteenth century, the expeditions of Christopher Columbus and other explorers had created an intense cultural interaction between the Old World and the New World that profoundly changed Native American culture and society forever. During the late medieval and early modern periods (1200–1800) in Europe, countries such as England, France, Spain, Portugal, and Russia, which had strong centralized monarchies, began to undertake imperial expansion (Del Testa, Lemoine, and Strickland, 2004). The period of 1492–1850 is defined in part by the initiative Europeans took to explore, colonize, and dominate other lands and peoples. Europeans went in search of territories for gold and other resources. Also, this time period was marked by the Europeans' desire to convert as many people as possible in the New World to Christianity. The economic and religious motives of the colonizers led them to interact with non-European cultures, while maintaining a sense of cultural superiority that shaped their perceptions of the natives.

There was also a cultural exchange (now called the Columbian Exchange) of goods, foods, medicines, plants, animals, technologies, knowledge, skills, and inventions that would change the Old World (Europe, Asia, and Africa) and the New World (the Americas) forever. Indians of the Americas gave Europeans such New World crops as potatoes, tomatoes, varieties of beans, sugar cane, maize (corn), peppers, sweet potatoes, cassavas, chocolate, vanilla, a variety of fruits and nuts, turkeys, and new ocean foods (Weatherford, 1988). Indians offered extensive knowledge of plants for medicinal cures (quinine, ipecac, coca, plants for scurvy), as well as tobacco, furs, a better cotton, the rubber tree, and vast quantities of silver and gold (Weatherford, 1988). Europeans brought domesticated animals, guns, and advanced technologies. Until the Spanish arrived, for example, the Navajo did not make silver and turquoise jewelry, nor did they have sheep to shear to make their beautiful rugs. The Plains Indians did not have the horse to hunt buffalo or travel.

Much of the indigenous culture of Native Americans was destroyed after the Europeans arrived. Many of the Indians who survived the epidemics and military conquests adopted European social and cultural practices, converting to Christianity and going to schools. The European conquest of the Americas created an interdependent global market dominated by Europeans for hundreds of years. The wealth pouring in from the American colonies supported the Spanish crown to seek domination in European affairs. And, because Europe controlled the wealth of the Americas, it was able to reposition itself at the center of world trade. The European encounter with the New World marked the beginning of the modern world, resulting in many economic, demographic, political, intellectual, and ecological changes.

In the twentieth century, American Indians were subjected to government policies of allotment, termination, discrimination, and forced education through boarding schools. In the 1960s and early 1970s, American Indian activists staged protests and events that brought awareness to the general population of Indian concerns such as poverty, poor housing, the health crisis in Indian country, lack of job opportunities, high rates of alcoholism and drug abuse, and dismal conditions on reservations. Activists and mainstream Indian organizations fought to reclaim land, establish sovereignty rights, and gain recognition and civil rights. Certainly American Indians have come a long way. The flourishing of Indian casinos and consequent economic wealth has established many tribes as mainstream contributors to cities and states. Many Indians have become leaders, educated and accomplished in their fields. But, the road has been long and hard for America's First Peoples. Is the war won? Has assimilation and acculturation converted Indians into white people? Do Indian traditions, beliefs, languages, ceremonies, and religions still exist? Each tribe, indeed each Indian person, must answer that question individually. The long, sad history of Indian–white relations reflects an attempt at cultural genocide by the Anglo-European newcomers to America. Despite this tragic encounter between two worlds, the rich cultures of Indian tribes persist today.

REFERENCES

Del Testa, David W., Florence Lemoine, and John Strickland, eds. *Global History: Cultural Encounters from Antiquity to the Present. Vol. 3: The Age of Discovery and Colonial Expansion.* Armonk, N.Y.: Sharpe Reference, 2004.

Weatherford, Jack M. *Indian Givers: How the Indians of the Americas Transformed the New World.* New York: Crown, 1988.

ABBREVIATIONS USED TO REPRESENT SUBJECT CATEGORIES

AGRI	Agriculture and Farming	LEGE	Legends and Storytelling
ANIM	Animals	MIGR	Migration
ARCH	Archaeology	MUSI	Music and Dance
ARTS	Arts and Crafts	NATU	Nature
CIVI	Civil Rights and Protests	POLI	Politics
CONT	Contact with Whites	POPU	Population
DEAT	Death and Burial	PUBL	Publications
ECON	Economics and Employment	RECR	Recreation
EDUC	Education and Schools	RELI	Religion and Spirituality
ENVI	Environment and Nature	SETT	Settlements and Villages
EXPL	Explorations	SHEL	Shelter and Housing
FAMI	Family	SOCI	Social Organization
FOOD	Food and Drink	SPOR	Sports and Recreation
HEAL	Health and Disease	TOOL	Tools and Weapons
HUNT	Hunting and Fishing	TRAD	Trade
LAND	Land Cessions and Reservations	TREA	Treaties
LANG	Languages	WARS	Wars and Conflicts
LAWS	Laws and Legislation	WATE	Water Rights and Issues

PREHISTORY

Scholars disagree on the dates that ancestors of Native Americans arrived in North America. What is accepted by archaeologists and scientists is that America's indigenous cultures evolved for many thousands of years before European settlements began. Archaeological evidence now reaches 30,000 to 40,000 years into the past. Some researchers believe that Native Americans have been present in the Americas for 100,000 years or more, while native traditions teach that their people have always lived in their homelands since the beginning of time.

C. 40,000–8000 BC

MIGR. The Paleo-Indian tradition, as determined by most contemporary archaeologists, states that human beings have occupied North America as far back as 40,000 years ago. However, some archaeologists hold that human beings have only occupied North America for the last 8,000 years. The Orogrande Cave in southern New Mexico yields artifacts dating to 40,000 years back.

C. 25,000 BC

MIGR. The Sandia people leave the earliest evidence of human existence in what is now New Mexico.

C. 25,000–12,000 BC

MIGR. At the height of the last Ice Age, the Bering Sea is hundreds of meters below its current level, creating a 60-mile land bridge known as Beringia between Asia (Siberia) and North America (Alaska). Covered with grasses and plant life, it attracts large animals that early humans hunt for their survival. The people who had originally migrated out of Africa through Central Asia probably cross this land bridge in several migrations into North America without knowing they are crossing into a new continent. These ancestors of modern Indians follow animals along the Siberian coast and then across the land bridge. Once in the region known today as Alaska, it takes these peoples thousands of years to work their way down to the present-day lower United States. Some archaeologists believe the first of these migrations into North America from Asia began as long as 40,000 years ago. Most Indian groups have creation stories which hold that their people did not migrate from other lands, but were created in their traditional homelands.

C. 23,000–13,000 BC

TOOL. In 1936, archaeologists found flint knives, scrapers, and other artifacts in the Sandia Mountains of New Mexico that have been dated to this time period. The cultures that evolved in this area at this time become known as the Sandia phase.

C. 17,600 OR 10,000 BC

MIGR. About this time, early Indians begin occupying the Meadowcroft site, near present-day Pittsburgh, Pennsylvania. This is one of the earliest known settlements in North America.

C. 12,000 BC

MIGR. Evidence of early life in North America can be reliably dated to this time around Clovis, New Mexico.

The last Ice Age draws to an end, warming global temperatures, melting glaciers, and raising sea levels. The Bering land bridge is covered with water.

C. 11,000 BC

HUNT. The warmer climate begins to change the Indians' way of life, from simply following herds of large game animals, which they hunt for food, to utilizing new plants and animals that emerge.

C. 10,000–9000 BC

HUNT. Clovis hunters search for mammoth, bison, and other game. By this time, human life is well-established in much of the Western Hemisphere. By 9,000 BC Indians are able to inhabit all reaches of North America. The mammoth and other big game species begin to die out and the bison takes its place as a principle source of food and hides for these early North Americans.

C. 9500–5000 BC

HUNT. The Paleo-Indians emerge as hunters of large mammals. Within this tradition emerge several cultures, including the Clovis and Folsom cultures.

C. 9200–8900 BC

TOOL. The Clovis culture emerges in central North America. Named after an excavation site near present-day Clovis, New Mexico, the Clovis people use flint projectile points on poles as spears to hunt mammoth and other game. The Clovis tradition fades with the disappearance of mammoth and other prehistoric large game.

C. 9000 BC

MIGR. Humans settle all of North America. Around this time, the descendants of the humans who migrated from Asia over the Bering land bridge are found in all regions of North America. They have learned to adapt to all types of environments,

living in small, isolated bands of about 15 to 150 people, gathering wild plants, hunting game, and using simple tools.

C. 9000–5000 BC

SOCI. Early Indians in the Northwest Columbia River Valley of present-day Washington and Oregon develop the Old Cordilleran culture. These peoples are most likely the ancestors of the Cayuse, Chinook, Klamath, and other Indian groups of the region.

C. 8500–8000 BC

TOOL. The Folsom culture flourishes in the Great Plains and in portions of the Southwest based on bison hunting. Folsom hunters develop more refined projectile points than did their Clovis predecessors.

C. 8000 BC

MIGR. Paleo-Indians of the Folsom tradition settle in the region of present-day Lindermeier, Colorado, one of the first early Indian sites to be excavated.

C. 8000–7000 BC

AGRI. Foraging and the first attempts at primitive agriculture begin to appear. Indians in central Mexico lead the way, cultivating corn, squash, beans, and pumpkins. Slowly, this knowledge spreads northward.

C. 8000–4000 BC

ENVI. The climate in North America warms as a result of the end of the last Ice Age, and melting glaciers create the Great Lakes, the Mississippi River, and other waterways. Trees and grasslands appear, and new plant and animal resources develop.

C. 8000–1000 BC

FOOD. The Archaic tradition replaces Paleo-Indian ways. The ecology of North America changes with rising temperatures. Indians gradually replace the hunting way of life with the Archaic tradition, which is characterized by a greater variety of ways to obtain food.

C. 7000 BC–AD 1

FOOD. The Cochise Desert culture emerges in the Southwest. Early Indians in present-day Arizona and western New Mexico develop the Cochise Desert culture, characterized by gathering wild plant foods instead of hunting. Cochise people are the first inhabitants to attempt farming in the American Southwest, cultivating corn, squash, and beans.

C. 6800 BC

SETT. Anangula village becomes the first settlement on the Aleutian Islands.

C. 6400 BC–AD 1200

FOOD. The Koster archaeological site in the Midwest (in Greene County, Illinois) is occupied by people of the Early Archaic tradition, who subsist on a wide variety of game, fish, and plants.

C. 5000 BC

AGRI. Indians in Mexico begin to reap greater harvests by cultivating a hardy hybrid of maize (Indian corn) that changes their way of life significantly .

C. 4000 BC

FOOD. Northwest Coast Indians learn to preserve fish.

C. 4000 BC–AD 300

HUNT. In what is now western Alberta, Canada, buffalo jumps take place off high cliffs, such as at the Head-Smashed-In site. Herds of buffalo are stampeded over the cliffs by bands of Indians.

C. 3000 BC

AGRI. A type of primitive corn is grown in the river valleys of today's New Mexico and Arizona. The first signs of irrigation begin to appear.

C. 3000–2500 BC

TOOL. Archaic Indians in the Great Lakes region develop the Old Copper culture, digging out copper and shaping the metal into tools, weapons, and ornaments.

C. 3000–1000 BC

MIGR. The ancestors of the Aleut and Inuit cross the Bering Strait in boats from Asia to North America. They arrive thousands of years after early peoples traveled across the Bering land bridge.

C. 2500 BC

AGRI. Early Indians of the Eastern Woodlands begin farming, starting with gourds and squash probably brought north from Mexico. Farming marks the beginnings of tribal life and changes the dependency on exclusively hunting and gathering.

C. 2000 BC

SOCI. The ancestors of the Aleut and Inuit who arrived 1,000 years earlier in North America begin to diverge into distinct cultures.

C. 2000–1000 BC

AGRI. Southwestern Indians begin growing maize which was first domesticated in Mexico.

C. 1800–500 BC

TRAD. Poverty Point is settled in Louisiana, a massive settlement with great earthworks overlooking the Mississippi River. This will serve as a major trading center for around 300 years.

C. 1000 BC

SETT. Indians living in the Pacific Northwest make permanent villages, utilizing the plentiful supply of fish and raw materials available.

C. 1000 BC–AD 200

DEAT. The Adena people in the Midwest in the upper Mississippi River Valley are distinguished by clusters of burial mounds. Some of these earthen burial sites and fortifications are in the shape of birds and serpents and probably serve religious purposes rather than defensive purposes. Between 300 and 500 mounds are built, including the Great Serpent Mound. The Adenans are eventually absorbed or displaced by various groups collectively known as Hopewellians.

C. 1000 BC–AD 1600

SOCI. The Woodland tradition spreads through eastern North America with the development of agriculture, manufacture of pottery, and construction of funerary mounds.

C. 500 BC

AGRI. Southwestern Indians begin growing beans, a healthy food that becomes a staple crop.

C. 300 BC

RELI. Peyote begins to be used as a religious sacrament (according to research by botanist Richard E. Schultes). Others believe archaeological evidence shows that peyote was used for religious and other purposes for as long as 10,000 years before the twentieth century.

SETT. Signs of early village life begin to appear.

C. 200 BC–AD 200

SOCI. The Hopewell people who lived in today's Midwest region gradually disappear and give way to a broader group of tribes known as the Mississippians, or Temple Mound culture.

C. 200 BC–AD 400

SOCI. The Great Serpent Mound, the largest effigy mound in North America, is constructed in present-day Adams County, Ohio, by Indians of the Adena or Hopewell tradition. The Hopewell cultural tradition develops throughout the Midwest.

C. 200 BC–AD 750

SOCI. The Basketmaker tradition marks the first phase of Anasazi culture. The Anasazi emerge in the Four Corners region of what is today Arizona, New Mexico, Utah, and Colorado, with the establishment of small villages of underground pit houses. These early Anasazi have limited agriculture with squash and maize, and rely mostly on hunting and gathering. After the year AD 500 they come to rely on agriculture as their primary food source. The Anasazi will enter the Pueblo Period from AD 750–1400.

C. 100 BC–AD 1300

SOCI. The Anasazi culture develops in the Southwest.

1st Century through 16th Century

1st CENTURY AD

SOCI. The Hohokam people are living in settlements near present-day Phoenix, Arizona. They build ball courts, pyramid-like mounds, and canal and irrigation systems. Archaeologists believe the Hohokam lived from c. AD 400 to AD 1500.

2nd CENTURY

AD 1–700

ARTS. Anasazi basketmakers elevate weaving to a high art, creating baskets, clothing, sandals, and utensils.

c. 200

ARTS. Southwestern Indians begin making pottery for cooking food and storing crops.

3rd CENTURY

c. 200–1400

SOCI. The Mogollon culture develops in the Southwest, in present-day east-central Arizona and west-central New Mexico. Farming allows for the development of the Mogollon people, although most of their food comes from hunting and gathering. Farming becomes more important as villages grow larger. Early Mogollon architecture features multifamily villages of subterranean pit houses until the late tenth century when they build aboveground adobe structures similar to modern-day pueblos. They also construct underground ceremonial chambers known as kivas. Pottery grows in its sophistication by the Mogollon, from brown ceramic vessels for cooking and storage to the highly artistic ceremonial pottery with black-on-white designs of the Mogollon of the Mimbres Valley. The Mogollon tradition will die out before the arrival of Europeans in the region, but they are sometimes identified as the ancestors of the present-day Pueblo groups.

5th CENTURY

c. 400–1300

SOCI. The Fremont culture develops in present-day Utah and portions of Nevada, Colorado, and Idaho. These Indians live in scattered villages where they exhibit many traits of Anasazi culture. They have subterranean pit houses, make pottery, and grow maize. The Fremont tradition varies with the natural resources available in the area, but they share religious beliefs as exhibited in their anthropomorphic clay figurines and rock paintings. Their culture fades in the thirteenth century, perhaps due to drought that makes farming difficult, and because of competition from other Indian groups who move into the region.

c. 400–1500

SOCI. The Hohokam culture develops and dominates in the desert Southwest in present-day southern Arizona and northern Mexico. Villages grow over time from several dwellings clustered together to larger settlements of over 500 people which are economically and politically independent of each other. Hohokam villages typically have platform mounds and large ball courts which may be used for rituals. The ball courts may also be used as open-air markets for traders to gather, as archaeological evidence reveals they were a part of a vast network of trade. The Hohokam farm corn, beans, and squash, obtaining most of their food through agriculture. Around the year 800, they begin creating irrigation systems with canals to carry water from nearby rivers into their fields. Eventually, they begin growing tobacco and cotton in addition to staple crops. They also gather mesquite beans and cactus fruit and hunt animals such as deer and rabbits. After 1100, the Hohokam tradition begins to decline and disappears by the year 1500. It is postulated that their disappearance resulted from a series of floods and invasions by outsiders. Today, the Pima Indians, or Akimel O'odham, may be the Hohokam's direct descendants.

6TH CENTURY

c. 500

TOOL. The bow and arrow are used throughout North America. This is the hunting instrument of choice as widely adopted by Indians across the North American continent, replacing the atlatl. The bow and arrow allows hunters to fell their prey at a greater distance and to shoot quickly, and they are easy to make and light to carry. The bow and arrow may have been used by Arctic people as early as 2000 BC.

8TH CENTURY

c. 700

SHEL. Indians in the Southwest begin switching from pit houses to adobe houses. As they depend more on corn and bean crops to feed a growing population, multiroomed adobe dwellings are built which have more space for storing and preparing foods.

c. 700–1300

SOCI. Anasazi culture culminates in the highly developed Chaco Civilization.

c. 700–1550

SOCI. The Mississippian cultural people thrive as mound builders in what is now the central United States. With populations in the millions at the height of this culture, the largest Mississippian settlements are centered along the Mississippi River and its major tributaries from Minnesota to the Gulf of Mexico. Urban areas serve as ceremonial and trade centers, with the largest being Cahokia (c. 800–1400) with a population of around 20,000 residents, located near present-day Collinsville, Illinois. This culture is known for constructing large platform mounds; for trading extensively with other faraway tribes; for farming corn, beans, and squash using the stone-bladed hoe; and for utilizing the bow and arrow. The Mississippian culture Indians continue living into the historic era, having contact with Spanish explorers (Hernando de Soto, c. 1539–1543) and other Europeans who bring infectious diseases that speed the destruction of the culture.

c. 750–1300

SOCI. Anasazi culture enters the Pueblo Period. The Anasazi move from the Basketmaker Period (c. 200 BC–AD 750) to the Pueblo Period with widespread use of adobe dwellings above ground. A form of the underground pit houses is retained as kivas for ceremonial use only. The adobe structures allow the Anasazi more room for storing and milling corn, and for more living space for the growing populations. By the year 1000 some Anasazi villages house as many as 10,000 people, and their total number is as high as 100,000. They maintain a vast network of trade, centered at Chaco Canyon (c. 900–1150). By the fourteenth century, the Anasazi begin abandoning these large villages, possibly relocating to smaller settlements after prolonged droughts or attacks by other Indian groups. The remnants of the Anasazi will become the ancestors of modern Pueblo Indians such as the Hopi and Zuni.

9TH CENTURY

c. 875–1500

SOCI. The Patayan (or Hakataya) culture develops in western Arizona along the Colorado River. These people rely on farming, supplementing their diets with hunting and gathering. Their housing consists of aboveground brush dwellings. The Patayan (the Yuman word for *old people*) make pottery and baskets and may be the ancestors of Yuman-speaking groups such as the Quechan and the Mojave.

10TH CENTURY

c. 900

SHEL. The Anasazi, ancestors of modern Hopi Indians, begin building stone and adobe pueblos.

c. 900–1150

SETT. The "Chaco Phenomenon" evolves in the San Juan Basin, a 25,000-square-mile area in present-day northern New Mexico and southwestern Colorado. The Anasazi here begin to live in large pueblo settlements connected by over 250 miles of roads. Chaco Canyon serves as the trade, administrative, and ritual center for the outlying pueblos. The large population is sustained through this trade network of goods and food. After 1130, the area suffers a prolonged drought, and the population probably grows too large to remain effective in large groups. The people slowly scatter, some forming new, smaller settlements, and others probably returning to hunting and gathering as their main food sources.

c. 900–1500

SETT. The Etowah village site is occupied by the Mississippian people in present-day northwestern Georgia, near the current city of Rome. Etowah becomes one of the largest ceremonial centers covering 52 acres with large plazas, mounds, and buildings serving as temples. This is the center of a chiefdom that controls a large area of what is now northern Georgia and Alabama, eastern Tennessee, and western North and South Carolina. The village declines before the historic period probably due to warfare with the Mississippian chiefdom in present-day Alabama.

c. 900–1600

SOCI. The Thule culture extends across northern Canada and eventually to Greenland. Along the Arctic coast of present-day northern Alaska, groups of native people develop a culture based on whaling as their primary source of food. They create innovations that make it possible for them to survive and thrive in the cold weather—the umiak boat, harpoons and spears, snow houses heated with whale oil lamps, skin tents, sleds drawn by domesticated dogs, and implements from bone, ivory, stone, sinew and copper.

Although this culture will fade in the fifteenth century, many of their cultural elements will be carried over in the modern Inuit way of life.

c. 975–1150

SETT. Near what is now Phoenix, Arizona, the Hohokam site of Snaketown is occupied. This is the largest Hohokam settlement with a population of around 600 people living in over 100 dwellings circling a central plaza.

c. 982–1015

CONT. Norsemen, including Eric the Red and his son, Leif Ericsson, set up outposts in North America, encountering Eskimos, Beothuks, and Micmacs.

11TH CENTURY

c. 1000–1130

ARTS. The Mimbres begin creating beautiful ceramics. Mogollon women of the Mimbres Valley in current-day southwestern New Mexico begin making decorative bowls and pots painted with geometric designs and animal, human, and mythological figures. These vessels are probably used in ceremonies and are often placed in graves over the head of the corpse. In the present-day, Mimbres pottery is treasured and appreciated by collectors.

c. 1001

CONT. Norseman Leif Ericsson (c. 970–1020) lands on the northeast coast of present-day Canada (in Newfoundland or Nova Scotia) when storms drive his ship westward while he is attempting to return to Norway from Greenland. Ericsson and his men explore two islands, identified later by scholars as Baffin Island and Labrador. Then, the Norsemen come upon a land with rich soil, plentiful game and fish, and large patches of wild grapevines. They call the land Vinland (Wineland) where they stay for nearly a year, interacting and trading with the indigenous people of the area (probably Inuit or Beothuk). The encounters with these native peoples are sometimes violent, resulting in Ericsson's men killing some of the Indians. Ericsson's crew will abandon the settlement and return to Greenland, describing Vinland where grapes and wild wheat grow. Several attempts by the Norsemen to settle the new land will be made without success.

c. 1007

CONT. Thorvald Ericsson, the brother of Leif Ericsson, and a crew of 35 men explore the coast of the Atlantic Ocean. According to Norse sagas, they attack nine indigenous people (whom they call Skraelings) on the beach. One of the nine escapes and a party of Indians shoot arrows at the invader's ship, killing Ericsson. His crew returns to Greenland.

c. 1075

SETT. Acoma Pueblo is founded.

12TH CENTURY

c. 1100

SETT. Cahokia, a city of the Mississippian mound-builders just east of present-day St. Louis, Missouri, has a population of about 20,000. This culture depends on a combination of hunting, foraging, trading, and agriculture for their food and supplies.

SOCI. The Sinagua culture develops in present-day central Arizona. After a volcano spreads ash over their lands in the Verde Valley, the crops improve for the next 200 years. These people adopt elements of the Hohokam, to the south, and the Anasazi, to the north.

c. 1100–1200

SHEL. The Anasazi build cliff dwellings at Mesa Verde in present-day southwestern Colorado. The Anasazi at Mesa Verde build large adobe dwellings in alcoves in canyon walls which provide protection from enemies as well as from inclement weather. The largest cliff dwelling is Cliff Palace, with 220 rooms.

c. 1100–1300

SOCI. The Southern Cult Mississippians develop a unique culture. In the current southeastern United States, the people of the Mississippian tradition create what is now called the Southern Cult. The artifacts of this tradition suggest war and human sacrifice were a distinction of this tradition.

c. 1100–1400

SOCI. Indians of the Laurel culture in northern Minnesota build summer villages by the waters. Artifacts will show their use of bones and antlers

Cahokia Mound in present-day Illinois. Courtesy of Library of Congress.

Cliff Palace, Mesa Verde. Courtesy of Library of Congress.

for harpoon points, copper for knives, and beavers' teeth for chisels. They bury their dead under dome-shaped mounds of earth.

1121

CONT. Viking explorations and attempted settlements in North America are recorded in the *Graenlendinga Saga* (Magnusson 1965) and *Islendingabók* (Thorgilsson 1930) and in other Viking sagas in the twelfth and thirteenth centuries. The Norsemen encountered natives and human habitations in the area they called Vinland, which could have been anywhere from Hudson Bay down to Virginia.

c. 1150

SETT. The Anasazi establish Oraibi village in what is now northeastern Arizona. By the late thirteenth century, the settlement will have a population of as many as 1,000. Descendants of the Anasazi, the Hopi, later occupy the village, making Oraibi the longest continually occupied settlement in the present-day United States. (Some would argue that Acoma is the oldest settlement in North America, with a founding date of around 1075.)

13TH CENTURY

c. 1200–1400

MIGR. Ancestral Apache and Navajo bands separate from northern Athabascans and migrate into the Southwest.

c. 1200–1500s

SETT. Pueblo Indians establish villages along the Rio Grande and its tributaries.

c. 1275

MIGR. The Anasazi abandon their settlements in the Southwest due to drought and Athabascan raids. Tree ring dating indicates a period of drought hit the Southwest during 1276–1299.

14TH CENTURY

c. 1300

SOCI. The Middle Mississippian culture of Indians flourishes in the area of present-day Arkansas, Alabama, Mississippi, Missouri, Tennessee, Kentucky, Ohio, Indiana, and Illinois. This culture lasts around 1,000 years (perhaps from 700–1700) with settlements along rivers, cultivation of corn and other crops, hunting with bow and arrow, fishing with bone fish hooks, and construction of temple mounds.

c. 1300–1400

MIGR. The Salado culture is formed from a group of Sinagua people who travel south and settle among the Hohokam in the Gila River valley.

c. 1300–1600

SETT. Indians of the Macon Plateau culture of central Georgia build villages with large circular lodges made of logs.

SOCI. Indians of the Kansas-Nebraska Plains area are today identified as part of the Upper Republican culture. They live in villages of earthen lodges and rely mainly on agriculture, growing corn, beans, and squash.

c. 1300–1700

SOCI. The Caddo Indians live in the area of the convergence of the present-day states of Texas, Oklahoma, Arkansas, and Louisiana. They build large earthen mounds and temples; make pottery, baskets, and woven fabrics; and grow corn and other crops.

15TH CENTURY

c. 1400

SOCI. The Iroquois Confederacy is formed. A Huron prophet known as the Peacemaker advocates the end of warfare associated with the blood feud. The message of peace is promoted by the Onondaga leader Hiawatha to his tribe and also to the Cayuga, Mohawk, Seneca, and Oneida—all from the area now known as New York state and southeastern Canada. The people of the confederacy call themselves Haudenosaunee, meaning the "people of the longhouse." Non-Indians later refer to the organization as the Iroquois League, or the Five Nations. The Tuscarora will join the league in 1722 as a sixth tribe, with the group thereafter called the Six Nations.

c. 1450–1500

MIGR. The Navajo and Apache arrive in the Southwest. The Navajo (Dineh) and Apache are Athabascans who originally lived as hunters and gatherers in what is now southwestern Canada. When they migrate to the Southwest, their way of life contrasts with that of the Pueblo tribes who live in villages and farm, creating conflicts and hostilities. By the seventeenth century, however, a blending of the old Navajo and Apache cultures with the Pueblo farming techniques, ceremonies, and customs will create a hybrid culture.

c. 1400–1650

SOC. Indians of the Nebraska culture live along the Missouri River of present-day Kansas and Nebraska. Their houses are multifamily dwellings, made partly underground, and sometimes entered through the roof by a ladder. Though mainly agriculturalists, they also use bone hooks and harpoons for catching fish.

c. 1400–1700

SOC. Indians of the Mille Lac region of central Minnesota live in dome-shaped houses built with

---

Thomas Jefferson is said to have studied the Constitution of the Iroquois when it came time to frame the U.S. Constitution. Earlier, in 1751, when Benjamin Franklin was pleading the cause of political union of the American colonies at Albany, New York, Franklin referred to the Iroquois Confederation: "It would be a strange thing if Six Nations of ignorant savages should be capable of forming a scheme for such a union, and be able to execute it in such a manner as that it has subsisted for ages and appears indissoluble; and yet that a like union should be impracticable for ten or a dozen English colonies, to whom it is more necessary and must be more advantageous, and who cannot be supposed to want an equal understanding of their interests" (Johansen 1982, 56).

saplings covered with skins. They exist primarily through hunting and gathering, and build earthern mounds over their buried dead.

c. 1450

RELI. The Southern Death Cult in current-day central Georgia exists among Indians of the Etowah culture. They build a large temple mound as a ceremonial center and perform rites that probably include human sacrifice.

c. 1492

MIGR. A band of Arawak Indians emigrate from the present-day Greater Antilles in the Caribbean to Florida, where they settle a town they name Abaibo.

1492

CONT. Christopher Columbus (Italian) leads the three ships *Santa Maria, Pinta,* and *Niña* across the Atlantic Ocean to make the first known European landing in the Western Hemisphere since early in the eleventh century. He disembarks on October 12 in the Bahamas on an island he names San Salvador, thinking he has reached the outlying islands of Asia and will soon discover the ports of India, China, and Japan. Believing he has reached the East Indies, he names the islands the Indies and calls their inhabitants Indians. The local inhabitants of the island are the Taino people, a subgroup of the Arawak ethnic group of the Greater Antilles islands. They call their island Guanahaní. According to Columbus's diary, these people are friendly, willing to communicate, and eager to exchange goods with the strangers. In a letter written in 1493 to King Ferdinand and Queen Isabella of Spain regarding this first voyage, Columbus writes that the inhabitants of the islands are timid, friendly, generous, and simple people, and they are convinced that he and his men came from the heavens. Columbus claims the islands and peoples for Ferdinand and Isabella. Columbus never saw the mainland of North America.

Columbus's group explores several bays of Cuba on October 28.

Columbus and his men explore the islands in the area, landing on Quisqueya, on December 6, which he renames Hispaniola (now comprising Haiti and the Dominican Republic). From their ships anchored off its coast, the men conduct an active trade with the Arawak.

On December 24, the *Santa Maria* ship runs aground. With the Indian's help, they are able to save the supplies on the sinking ship. Columbus returns to Spain in his two remaining ships, leaving 39 men behind at a fort built from wood salvaged from the wreckage of the *Santa Maria* (the men later disappear, probably killed by the Tainos).

FOOD. Columbus discovers foods unknown in the Old World: maize, sweet potatoes, capsicums (peppers), allspice *(Pimenta officinalis),* plantain *(Musa paradisica),* pineapples, and turtle meat.

LANG. When Columbus arrives, Native American groups in North America speak around 250 mutually unintelligible languages. In Mexico and Central America they speak around 350 different languages, and in South America there are around 1,400 different languages.

1493

CONT. In his second voyage to the New World, Christopher Columbus brings horses and livestock to the island of Hispaniola (modern Haiti and the Dominican Republic). Hispaniola became known under Spanish dominion as Santa Domingo. This is the first time these animals are seen in the New World. (The horse originated in the Western Hemisphere and migrated to Asia before becoming extinct in its continent of origin at the close of the Ice Age.)

Columbus finds a Carib Indian settlement on the Caribbean island of Guadeloupe. He takes six Arawak women on board, freeing them from captivity by the Caribs. Columbus claims many territories for Spain, and returns to the Old World on March 4. He presents Isabella with several "Indians" whom he has captured (some of the Indians die in route to Spain), as well as parrots, strange animals, and gold. He introduces the Atlantic slave trade by bringing many Native Americans back to Spain. Columbus will make two more voyages to this new land in search of a passage to the mainland of China. He leaves a legacy of mistreatment, disease, warfare,

Christopher Columbus landing at San Salvador, October 12, 1492. The print depicts a welcoming and happy group of natives. Courtesy of Library of Congress.

enslavement, and cruelty to the Indians he encounters.

Christopher Columbus attempts to subjugate the Arawak. On Hispaniola, the Spaniards storm the Arawak villages using European weapons to capture 500 and kill hundreds more. Columbus sends these 500 Arawak slaves to Spain. In 1507, the Arawak population of Hispaniola is around 60,000. The military attacks and epidemics brought on by the Spanish bring about the complete extinction of the Arawak. In 1511, the Arawak Indians of Cuba will be the last of their race to succumb to the Spanish.

1497

CONT. Italian navigator John Cabot (Giovanni Caboto) and his brother Sabastion explore the northern Atlantic coast of North America on a mission for the British king. On June 24, they arrive on the coast of what is now Labrador. For six weeks they explore the coasts of Nova Scotia and Newfoundland southward. They encounter Massachuset Indians, and kidnap three Micmac men. Their journey is later the basis for British claims to North America under the doctrine of discovery.

EXPL. The Italian explorer Amerigo Vespucci (sponsored by Spain) begins a six-year exploration of the coasts of the West Indies and the southern Atlantic Coast (South America). He is later given credit for discovering the great land mass between Europe and Asia, although he probably never set foot on the land named after his first name, or encountered any of its natives.

16TH CENTURY

c. 1500

ARTS. American Indians in the Northeast have been traditionally using copper and brass sheet metal for thousands of years before the Europeans arrived. They use copper and brass to make utensils and tools including pots, spoons, arrow points and pipes, as well as jewelry including tinkling cones, beads, bracelets, and rings. Large copper deposits exist in present-day Virginia, North Carolina, Tennessee, Arizona, New Mexico, Nova Scotia, and around Lake Superior.

EXPL. The Spanish, English, Italian, Dutch, Portuguese, and French begin explorations of the New World.

HEAL. European diseases begin killing North American natives, who have no natural immunity to them.

1500–1501

CONT. Portuguese explorer Gaspar Corte Real explores the coasts of Newfoundland and Labrador. He takes 57 Indians (Beothuk or Micmac) captive and attempts to take them back to Portugal with him. However, his ship sinks in 1501 on the homeward voyage and Gaspar Corte Real and his crewmen, along with the slaves chained in the ship's hold, all drown.

1501

EXPL. Amerigo Vespucci (Italian navigator) disputes the idea that Columbus had found a back route to Asia. He is the first to call the Americas a "New World." European mapmakers come to know both continents of America as "the land of Amerigo," or America.

1501

EXPL. Spanish settlers import African slaves to the New World.

1502

CONT. On his fourth and final trip to North America, Columbus and a crew of 115 are shipwrecked on the coast of present-day Jamaica. The Europeans demand food from the local Indians, but after several months the Indians resist. Columbus knows of an upcoming lunar eclipse and tells the Indians that his God will make the moon disappear unless they give his crew what they need. The Indians, frightened by the eclipse, decide to help the foreigners until they are rescued in 1503.

1512

LAWS. Spanish law allows Spanish land grantees the right to make slaves of Indians under the *encomienda* system. Spanish colonists in the New World are given grants of land in trusteeship with the inhabiting Indians required to work as serfs. In return, the *encomenderos* are required to clothe, feed, Christianize, and civilize their Indians. This system was supposed to help alleviate some of the extreme

mistreatment of the Indians by the Spanish. Spain will abolish the *encomienda* system in 1721.

The debates over the Spanish governance of the Indians confirm that Spain has a legitimate claim to its lands in North America and to authority over the Indians living there. Spanish intellectuals agree that wars waged against non-Christian Indians in order to force them to convert are just.

RELI. Also in 1512, the Catholic Church in Rome declares that Indians are descended from Adam and Eve and have souls. These declarations reinforce the obligation of Spanish conquistadors and colonists in North America to try to convert the Indians to Christianity.

1513

CONT. Juan Ponce de León (Spanish) lands on the Florida coast near the present city of St. Augustine. He has extensive contact with Indians before Calusa Indians drive his ships away in a fleet of about 80 war canoes along the Florida peninsula near present-day Fort Myers. The Spaniards continue on, in search of both gold and a fountain that can restore a person's health and youth. This is the first exploration of the continental United States since Columbus claimed the land for Spain. Ponce de León finds neither gold nor the fountain of youth and returns to Spain.

EXPL. Vasco Nuñez de Balboa (Spanish) becomes the first European to see the Pacific Ocean. He crosses Central America, climbs a mountain crest on the Isthmus of Panama and sees the Pacific, realizing the vast distance between the New World and Asia.

1514

LAWS. A royal Spanish decree called the *Requerimiento* is made that requires that the Indians have to be warned (in Spanish) before they are attacked. The Indians must acknowledge submission to the crown and church or take the blame for any consequences.

1519–1521

EXPL. Ferdinand Magellan (Portuguese) is spurned by his king and turns to Spain for support of the first circumnavigation of the globe. Blessed with unusually peaceful weather across the new ocean, he names it the Pacific. He is killed in the Philippines while fighting in a local war, and only 18 members of his crew return home.

1521

CONT. Juan Ponce de León attempts to establish a Spanish colony in Florida after his initial trip there in 1513. His party of 200 lands on what is now Sanibel Island, where they are attacked by Calusa Indians. The Spanish retreat to Cuba, and Ponce de León dies from a wound he suffered in the attack.

1524

CONT. Giovanni da Verrazano (Italian sailing for France) explores the Atlantic coast from present-day North Carolina to Newfoundland seeking a route to the Pacific Ocean. He encounters Wampanoag, Narragansett, and Lenni Lenape (Delaware) Indians in the present-day Delaware and Chesapeake Bay areas. The Indians' response to Verranzano ranges from generally friendly, to refusing to communicate with the visitors, to open hostility by Indians in Maine. Some Indians may have been attacked by previous European visitors to their shores and have strong suspicions toward the foreigners.

1528–1536

CONT. Spanish explorer Alvar Nuñez Cabeza de Vaca and his men are the first Europeans to explore and cross the continental United States. His story is a remarkable and sensational one that has been retold in books, novels, films, and stage. How much is true is debatable, but he evidently survived one disaster after another during an 8-year exploration from Florida to the Gulf of California. He is intent on colonizing Florida for Spain and leads a sailing expedition of several hundred men in 1528 to the Gulf of Mexico. Beginning in Florida, according to the published account of his adventures (*Naufagios,* 1555), Cabeza de Vaca's ships are destroyed in a storm. He and two Spanish noblemen and a black slave named Esteban survive and are taken captives by Indians. Eventually, they embark on foot toward Spanish-held lands in what is now Mexico, their journey takes them 6,000 miles through the Southwest, across present-day Texas and northern Mexico, making them the first non-Indians to travel through the region. Some historians believe he traveled to Lake Michigan, and through Missouri, Tennessee, and Kansas, as well as throughout the Southwest. By accident, he and three others become the first Europeans to cross the North American continent. The explorers have many stories of adventure and daring and relations with Indian tribes. They eventually reach Mexico in 1536, and tell stories related to them by the Indians of fabulously wealthy cities to the north—especially the Seven Cities of Cibola. These stories lead other explorers, such as Coronado, on expeditions for treasure-seeking. Cabeza de Vaca's writings are the earliest stories on the region's Indians, geography, and animal and plant life.

1532

POPU. The Indian population of Mexico falls tremendously due to the Spanish conquest and the introduction of diseases such as smallpox, measles, influenza, and typhoid. In 1532, the Indian population of Mexico is estimated to be a little over 16 million, and by 1568 it will drop to around 2.65 million.

1534–1542

CONT. Jacques Cartier (French) explores the St. Lawrence River area in eastern Canada in three voyages. He intends to claim land for France and to find a Northwest Passage—a water route between the Atlantic and Pacific. When he arrives, he kidnaps two Huron men to serve as guides for the expedition. He makes contact with Algonquian and Iroquoian-speaking tribes. The Indians tell them about great Indian settlements in the region, which excites the Europeans with visions of enormous riches like those discovered by the Spanish in Mexico. However, after Cartier explores further without finding any riches, the oncoming winter compels him to return to France, and he takes his Indian captives with him. Cartier will return to the St. Lawrence River region for further explorations in 1535 and 1541. When he returns, Cartier and his party of 110 men encounter a town of around 3,600 Iroquois Indians at Hochelaga (Montreal). He reports that there are 50 lodges, each 50 paces in length and 50 paces in breadth. The upper areas of the lodges are used to store corn, dried fruit, beans, peas, and smoked fish. The Frenchmen fall prey to scurvy, and are nursed to good health by the nearby Huron Indians.

The area colonized by France in North American from 1534 through 1763 becomes known as New France; it extends from New Foundland to Lake Superior and from the Hudson Bay down to the Gulf of Mexico.

1536

CONT. Jacques Cartier returns to France from New France with a Huron chief (Donnaconna) and his two sons, three adult Hurons, two little girls, and two little boys—all of whom soon die. Before he dies, Donnaconna entices the French king, Francis I, with stories of mines of gold and silver in his native land.

1539

CONT. Franciscan missionary Marcos de Niza explores territory that will later become Arizona and New Mexico. He and his guide, the black slave Esteban (from the Cabeza de Vaca expedition of 1528–1536), lead an expedition to find Cibola and reach the Zuni village of Hawikuh, where Esteban is killed. Marcos de Niza returns from the Zuni pueblo with claims of having found one of the legendary Seven Cities of Cibola.

1539–1543

CONT. Hernando de Soto (Spanish) lands in Florida at Tampa Bay with more than 600 men, 200 horses, and 13 hogs. He claims Florida for Spain. He explores the southeastern United States from Florida to Texas in search of gold, encountering and alienating tribes including the Creek, Hitchiti, Chickasaw, Chakchiuma, Choctaw, Tunica, Yuchi, Cherokee, and Alibamu with his aggressive and hostile style of conquest. His horses and men require food which he extorts from Indian villages. De Soto conducts dawn raids on unsuspecting villages, scaring natives with his dogs and horses, capturing chiefs, and demanding food. In 1541, he and his Spanish expedition become the first Europeans to see the Mississippi River as they explore westward from Florida.

1540

CONT. Hernando de Soto visits the Chickasaw Indians in the northern area of what is now the state of Mississippi. Beginning in December, de Soto and his forces make themselves guests for the winter in one of the Indian towns. But on March 4, the Chickasaws attack the Spaniards and burn the town, forcing de Soto and his men to retreat.

EXPL. Spanish explorer Hernando de Alarcón discovers the Colorado River. Hopi Indians guide a detachment of Spaniards, led by Garcia Lopez de Cardenas, to the Grand Canyon of the Colorado. The detachment formed part of the Spanish expedition of Francisco Vasquez de Coronado, seeking the fabulous land of Quivira and the Seven Cities of Cibola.

WARS. On October 18, a fierce battle takes place between the forces of the Spanish explorer Hernando de Soto and the Alibamu Indians in their town of Mabila in the central Mississippi area. The Alibamu lose at least 2,500 men, women, and children. The Spanish lose 20, with 150 wounded.

While traveling through the lands of the Choctaw Indians, Spanish soldiers under Hernando de Soto threaten the Choctaw leader Tuskaloosa, and demand he turn over some of his tribal members for the Spaniards to use as slaves. But the Choctaw leader tricks de Soto, telling him to meet at the village of Moma Bina (near present-day Mobile, Alabama) to collect the captives. When de Soto and his men arrive, they are met by a huge army of Choctaw warriors. Many Spaniards are killed and wounded, including de Soto who is wounded by Choctaw arrows.

1540–1542

CONT. Spanish explorer Francisco Vazquez de Coronado, 30, arrives in the American southwest in 1540 with the first horses, mules, cattle, sheep, and hogs in the region. Accompanied by 300 Spanish soldiers and about 1,000 Indians, Coronado explores the Southwest in search of the Seven Cities of Cibola, from present-day New Mexico to Kansas. His lieutenant, Lopez de Cardenas, discovers the Grand Canyon in December, 1540.

Instead of gold and fabulous wealth, the group finds seven adobe pueblos of the Zuni Indians, and further north they encounter the Hopi, Lipan, Jicarilla, Mescalero, and other tribes before reaching Quivira (Kansas). Although no mythical city of gold is found, a very significant thing happens on this expedition: enough horses escape from Coronado's party to transform life on the Great Plains. Within a few generations, the Plains Indians become masters of horsemanship, expanding their range and activities greatly.

1541

EXPL. Hernando de Soto dies on May 21 en route to Spanish territory. After two years of exploring the American Southeast, de Soto and his men are exhausted from constant fighting with Indians, and are disappointed by not finding gold and other riches. As the Spaniards head for Florida, de Soto falls ill and dies. The expedition continues to search for riches for six more months until they give up, and raft down the Mississippi River and along the Gulf Coast, reaching Spanish settlements in present-day Mexico.

1542

EXPL. Juan Rodriquez Cabrillo and Bartolome Ferrelo (Spanish) explore the California and Oregon coasts.

1559

CONT. Around 1,500 Spanish colonists land at Pensacola, Florida, but are turned back by hostile natives. They move to Port Royal Sound in what will become the English colony of South Carolina.

c. 1560–1570

SOCI. The Iroquois League of Five Nations (or Iroquois Confederacy) which includes the Mohawk, Oneida, Onondaga, Cayuga, and Seneca, is formed by Deganawida, a Huron (Wyandot) Indian prophet and statesman, and Hiawatha, his Mohawk disciple. Deganawida and Hiawatha persuade the five tribes to form a league with a common council, each tribe having a fixed number of delegates. The Ho-De-No-Sau-Nee is the most democratic nation of its time and will be a strong power in the 1600s and 1700s up until

Coronado marches west. Although he never discovered the fabled Seven Cities of Cibola, enough horses escaped from his party to transform life on the Great Plains. Courtesy of Library of Congress.

the American Revolution. It becomes the most powerful of all the North American Indian confederacies, numbering about 16,000 people in 1677. When the Tuscarora Indians join the Confederacy in 1722, it will become known as the Six Nations.

1564–1565

SETT. René de Laudonniére founds a French Huguenot colony on St. Johns River in Florida, until they are driven out by the Spanish.

1565

ARTS. French artist Jacques Le Moyne paints the first known European depictions of Indians from life. To escape persecution, a group of French Huguenots migrate to North America and establish settlements in present-day South Carolina and Florida. Jacques Le Moyne is among them. He paints images of the Timucua Indians, who are often positioned in poses and given proportions of classical sculpture, a convention that will be emulated later on by European artists.

1565

SETT. St. Augustine, Florida, is founded by the Spanish under Pedro Menéndez de Avilés with 3,000 Spanish colonists. This is the first permanent European settlement in North America. (The second will be Santa Fe, New Mexico in 1607.) To eliminate French presence in the area, they attack Fort Carolina, near present-day Jacksonville, Florida, and kill all of its male inhabitants. A military post is also established to the south of St. Augustine.

WARS. Tribesmen in the region that will later be called Virginia kill Juan Bautista Seguar and other Jesuits, thus ending Spanish efforts to colonize the region.

1571

WARS. Don Luis leads a revolt against Jesuit missionaries. Don Luis is an Algonquian Indian who had converted to Christianity, and even led the missionaries to his people on the York River in present-day Virginia a year earlier. Around 1560, Don Luis was picked up by a Spanish ship

"How the Natives collect gold in the streams," by French artist Jacques Le Moyne, who painted the first known images of Native American life. Courtesy of Library of Congress.

traveling the river. He then spent the next decade receiving "instruction" in Cuba and Spain. In 1572, a retaliatory force will invade the homeland of Don Luis's tribe and kill around 40 Indians.

1576–1578

CONT. English explorer Martin Frobisher sails on three expeditions to the Canadian Arctic in search of the Northwest Passage between the Atlantic and Pacific Oceans. He encounters various Inuit (Eskimo) groups along the way, and captures a few Inuits on the coast of Baffin Island. He takes them to London for exhibition, where they all soon die, most likely from foreign diseases.

1578–1579

CONT. Francis Drake (English adventurer) explores the Pacific coast, anchoring off the coast of present-day northern California where he and his crew encounter the Miwok Indians. The English spend five weeks with the tribe, exchanging gifts, and being friendly together. The Miwok may have been awed by the visitors who sailed to their lands from the west where the Miwok believe the land of the dead is located.

1580–1581

CONT. Fray Agustin Rodriquez leads an expedition to New Mexico. Four members of the party are killed by Indians.

1581

EXPL. Francis Drake (English) glimpses the Pacific Ocean in Panama, like Balboa did 60 years earlier. His voyage around the world as a privateer was instrumental in breaking Spain's control of the high seas. Later, he will be knighted by Queen Elizabeth.

1582–1583

EXPL. Fray Bernardino Beltran and Fray Antonio de Espejo lead an expedition to New Mexico to search for survivors of the ill-fated Rodriquez mission (1580–1581).

1583

EXPL. A British expedition explores the coast of North Carolina and Florida.

1584

CONT. The first British colony in North America is founded on Roanoke Island, off the coast of present-day North Carolina, under the sponsorship of Sir Walter Raleigh. This is 22 years before the Jamestown Colony, and 34 years before the Pilgrims land in Massachusetts. The Indians in the area welcome them and assist them in planting crops. However, the colonists antagonize the Indians and disputes arise between the two groups. The colony is a failure. Most of the English return home in late 1585. Another group of 113 or so colonists arrive in 1587. The leader of the colony, John White, returns to England in 1587 to obtain more supplies. Due to the English fighting the Spanish Armada in 1588, John White does not return to Roanoke until 1590. When he arrives, the settlement is deserted. Few signs are visible of the colonists, except the word "Croatoan" carved into a tree. Some historians believe the "Lost Colony" was absorbed into the nearby Lumbee Indian tribe and the colonists intermarried with the Indians, while others theorize they were killed by the Powhatan Indians of present-day Virginia. It will be several years before the British will succeed in establishing colonies in North America, at Jamestown (Virginia) in 1607, and at Plymouth (in Massachusetts Bay) in 1620.

1590

MIGR. Jesuit missionary José de Acosta theorizes that Indians crossed a land bridge between Asia and North America and populated the continent before the birth of Christ. De Acosta's speculation is the first idea of the Bering Strait theory to appear in print.

1598

SETT. Don Juan de Oñate establishes a new Spanish colony north of the Rio Grande River called San Gabriel del Yunque (present-day San Juan Pueblo) in New Mexico. His soldiers and families succeed in establishing the first permanent European settlement in the region, creating the first Spanish capital of San Juan de los Caballeros at the Tewa village north of present-day Espanola, New Mexico. Oñate sends messengers to other pueblos telling them they are now subjects of Spain and must obey Spanish law. If the Pueblo Indians agree to submit, they will obtain benefits such as new trade goods and the Catholic religion.

1598–1599

WARS. Acoma Pueblo Indians (New Mexico) attack a party of 30 visiting Spanish troops in December 1598, killing 13 men, including several Spanish officers. In 1599, a Spanish retaliatory force under Oñate kills up to 800 Acomas, and takes 80 men and 500 women and children into captivity. Oñate punishes the survivors by sentencing them to servitude, and cutting one foot off of men older than 25 years of age in a public ceremony. The Spanish also amputate one hand of two Hopi who had been at Acoma at the time of the rebellion and send them off to tell others of the serious consequences of rebelling against the Spanish. Although this extreme punishment quells any other pueblo revolts for a long time, it also sows the seeds for the Pueblo Revolt of 1680.

17TH CENTURY

C. 1600

MIGR. The early 1600s see the beginning of a great tide of emigration from Europe to North America. Colonists come in overcrowded ships from England and other European countries, suffering meager rations, diseases, and storms. Many die along the way. European emigrants leave their homes to escape political oppression, to seek religious freedom, to pursue economic opportunities, and for adventure. By 1640, the British will have colonies established along the New England coast and the Chesapeake Bay. This region also draws Dutch colonists and a small colony of Swedish immigrants. Early colonial-Indian relations are an uneasy mix of cooperation and conflict.

SOCI. The Dismal River culture exists with the prehistoric Athabascan Indians of western Nebraska. Living in circular earthen lodges, these Indians live primarily by hunting buffalo, deer, elk, beaver, and turtle. Dogs are domesticated and perhaps used sometimes for food. Some corn and squash are grown, and various fruits and berries gathered.

1602–1615

CONT. Samuel de Champlain, sailing for France, begins exploring the Northeast in the region of the Atlantic coast of present-day southern Canada and the northeastern United States. These travels lead to encounters with many Algonquian and Iroquoian tribes with attempts to establish friendly relations with them. In 1602, Champlain visits the site of present-day Montreal. In 1605, he founds Port Royal with Sieur de Monts in Micmac country. In 1608, he founds Quebec City, which is the first permanent French settlement in North America. In 1609, Champlain discovers the lake that now bears his name. In 1609 and in 1615, Champlain joins the Huron in attacking their Onondaga enemies, supplying the Huron with muskets. These actions turn the Iroquois League tribes against the French.

1604

TRAD. The Micmac Indians and the French begin a close trading relationship at Port Royal on the Bay of Fundy in present-day Nova Scotia. French traders offer the Indians an array of European goods, but the Indians are most interested in muskets and steel arrow points, which will help them defeat their enemies.

1605

TRAD. English ships begin trading with Algonquian tribes along the coast of New England.

1606

SETT. The Plymouth Colony and the London Company are authorized by a Virginia charter to establish settlements in North America.

1607

SETT. The English establish their first permanent settlement in North America at Jamestown, Virginia. Jamestown Colony (in present-day Virginia), is founded by approximately 100 English

Pocahontas saving the life of Captain John Smith. Courtesy of Library of Congress.

colonists arriving in three ships on May 14, 1607, under Captain Christopher Newport of the London Company, and is left under the direction of Captain John Smith. The colony is established on a site along what is now called the James River, in the lands of the Powhatan Confederacy of Indians. This is the first successful British colony in the New World. However, during the first winter about two-thirds of the colonists will die. The colonists come into extensive contact with the tribes of the Powhatan Confederacy. In December, Captain John Smith travels up the Chickahominy River to explore and trade corn with the Powhatan Indians, and is captured. Smith believes his life is spared by the intercession of the Powhatan chief's daughter, Pocahontas, who is 11 or 12 years old. Between 1607 and 1624, hundreds of people will migrate to the Jamestown colony, but only 1,132 are left living there in 1624 due to the death rate from disease and Indian attacks.

Santa Fe is established on the site of ancient Indian ruins by Pedro de Peralta, the Governor of New Mexico (after the removal of Oñate). Santa Fe will become the new capital of the Spanish province of New Mexico and will serve as the most important trading center for the Spanish and the

Indians in the American Southwest for more than 200 years. Construction begins on the Palace of the Governors, completed in 1610. Santa fe will become the official capital of New Mexico in 1610, the Territorial capital in 1851, and the state of New Mexico capital in 1912.

1607–1699

POPU. From the time of the founding of the English colony of Jamestown (Virginia) to the close of the seventeenth century, the population of the surrounding Indian tribes of coastal Virginia declines from 12,000 to around 3,500, due to disease and warfare.

1608

POLI. Powhatan (Wahunsonacock), chief of the Powhatan Indian confederacy of about 30 tribes, controls the area surrounding the colony of Virginia. He is crowned king by the English soldier Captain John Smith, with regalia sent from England. Powhatan, however, soon loses his friendly feelings toward the English and is only deterred from destroying the Virginia colony by the kidnapping of his daughter Pocahontas and her subsequent marriage to John Rolfe, an Englishman of the Jamestown colony.

Oñate is removed as governor of New Mexico and sent to Mexico City to be tried for mistreatment of the Indians and abuse of power. A decision is made by the Spanish Crown to continue settlement of New Mexico as a royal province.

SETT. Samuel de Champlain and French colonists found a settlement at Stadacona, which will become the city of Quebec. Champlain later pushes west to Lake Huron, establishing alliances with Indians and opening what becomes a vital fur-trading route through the wilderness.

1609

CONT. Henry Hudson (English navigator working for the Dutch India Company) anchors off Manhattan and trades with Indians. Two canoes of the Manhattan band of Lenni Lenape (Delaware), or Wappinger Indians, attack his ship as it sails down the Hudson River in what is now New York state. Hudson explores the river named for him in search of a Northwest Passage to India. Other Dutch settlers soon follow Hudson, and the Indians who had been living along the coast of New Jersey, such as the Delawares and Mahicans, are driven westward by the expanding European settlements.

EXPL. Samuel de Champlain (first governor of French Canada) explores the area that will later be called Vermont as lieutenant to the owner of the French fur trade monopoly. With a Huron and Algonquian war party, Champlain discovers the lake that will later bear his name, and participates in an attack on a party of Mohawks of the Iroquois Confederacy. This is the first Mohawk experience of firearms, and they are badly defeated. It is thought that the Iroquois never forgave the French for the defeat and the Iroquois Confederacy tribes thereafter allied themselves with the English against them.

1610

CONT. The Virginia colonists and the Powhatan Indians begin warfare that will last for four years. The colonists are on the brink of starvation when ships from England arrive,

bringing provisions and 300 more settlers. As the English expand their colony and the Indians defend their territory, war breaks out between the two groups. Only 150 of the 900 colonists brought to Virginia in the last three years have survived.

1611

TRAD. Champlain builds a fur post at Montreal.

1612

AGRI. The English colonists begin to cultivate tobacco. Virginia planter John Rolfe (who will marry Pocahontas in 1614) develops a new strain of tobacco for export to Europe. The American Indian tobacco is too strong for Europeans. By 1620, tobacco will become Virginia's largest cash crop.

1613

CONT. In the spring, Pocahontas is captured by an English captain after luring her onto his ship with offers of gifts. As the teenage daughter of the Indian leader Powhatan, the English try to use her to force the Indians to surrender their guns. Powhatan refuses to meet the demands of the English and Pocahontas is taken to Jamestown where she will be educated in the English language and white customs, and will be baptized a Christian.

HEAL. Smallpox kills over half of the Timucua Indians in the area of present-day northern Florida in a four-year epidemic.

WARS. In today's Newfoundland, Canada, Beothuk Indians kill 37 Frenchmen after a Frenchman shoots a Beothuk man. The French retaliate by arming the Micmac, traditional enemies of the Beothuk, and offering bounties for Beothuk scalps. With the assistance of the French, the Micmac nearly exterminate the Beothuk tribe.

1614

CONT. Virginia colonist John Rolfe, a widower, is married on April 5 to Pocahontas, the favorite daughter of Powhatan chief Wahunsonacook. Pocahontas was seized by colonists in 1613 and held for ransom where she met Rolfe. Now, at age 18, she has become Europeanized, adopted Christianity, and changed her name to Rebecca. She will not see her father again. In 1616, Pocahontas and Rolfe will visit England to raise funds for the Jamestown colony, where she will be received at the royal court as a "princess." She will die of smallpox in 1617, however, while preparing to return to America.

1614

CONT. Wampanoag Indian Squanto (or, Tisquantum) from Patuxet is kidnapped along with about 20 Wampanoag Indians along the coast of present-day Massachusetts by English slaver Thomas Hunt, who attempts to sell the Indians into slavery at Malaga, Spain. When priests stop Hunt from selling his captives, they take over the care of the Indians, who they attempt to convert to Christianity. Squanto is taken in by the priests, and during the next five years will travel to London, become fluent in English, and knowledgeable in English ways. When he returns to North America in 1619, his experiences allow him to help colonists at Plymouth to adapt to their new environment.

TRAD. The United New Netherland Company is chartered by Dutch merchants in Amsterdam and Hoom to colonize New Netherland and develop the fur trade. Dutch traders arrive in present-day New York state to get involved with the lucrative fur trade with Indians. The New Netherland Company erects Fort Orange on Castle Island near Albany (New York) and begins trading with the Indians for furs. This is the beginning of bringing Dutch colonists and establishing Dutch settlements in the region.

1615

POPU. Samuel de Champlain reports that the Huron Indians along the St. Lawrence River number about 30,000, divided into 18 towns. They grow large quantities of corn, squash, beans,

tobacco, and sunflowers. Champlain goes with the Huron on raids against the Iroquois.

1616

CONT. Pocahontas visits England with her husband John Rolfe and her infant son, Thomas.

HEAL. A massive smallpox epidemic strikes New England tribes during a three-year period. As many as 90 percent of the Indian population of the region between Narragansett Bay and the Penobscot River dies, with some tribes virtually ceasing to exist.

POLI. Samuel de Champlain visits a confederacy of Indian tribes near Lake Erie in Ontario which he calls the Neutral Nation because they remain neutral in the wars between the Iroquois Confederacy and the Huron. The Neutrals number around 4,000 warriors at this time.

1617

EDUC. British King James endorses the establishment of Indian churches and schools in Virginia, ordering the archbishops of York and Canterbury to raise funds for this cause.

HEAL. Pocahontas dies in England at age 21 of smallpox.

WARS. About this time, the Narraganset Indians of present-day Rhode Island assert their authority over the neighboring tribes of the Nipmuc, Niantic, Shawamet, Wampanoag, and Massachuset.

1618

HEAL. Smallpox is introduced by European explorers and colonists and rages though New England and south to Virginia, where it kills Chief Powhatan and many others in his tribe.

POLI. Opechancanough, the brother of Chief Powhatan, becomes the leader of the Powhatan tribes after the death of Chief Powhatan at the age of about 70. Land-hungry British colonists are demanding more and more of the Indians' territory. Opechancanough's rage at the English will erupt into open warfare in 1622.

WARS. Etienne Brulé, a French adventurer, arranges to sell furs to French traders. He arrived with Champlain at Quebec in 1608 and went into the western wilderness where he lived with the Hurons. The Hurons will kill him and eat him in 1633.

1619

SOCI. This year marks the beginning of slavery in Anglophone America, being the first date historians know that servants of African descent are living in Virginia.

1620

LAWS. A royal order is issued by the viceroy of New Mexico to regulate the use of Indian labor in Spanish New Mexico. Tensions have been growing between the Spanish authorities and priests in Pueblo territory over the use of Indian labor. The *Royal Order of 1620* attempts to regulate the exploitation of Indians by limiting the number to two percent of Indians at any pueblo who can be pressed into working for the Spanish as herders and tillers, and that these laborers must be paid for their work. The Order also discontinues the practice of allowing Spanish livestock to graze on or near the Pueblos' fields.

SETT. Pilgrims arrive in Plymouth. English Puritans (separatists from the Church of England, also known as Pilgrims) land on December 21 on the coast at present-day Cape Cod, Massachusetts, and establish a colony on Indian lands. The area is already occupied by several Indian groups, including the Wampanoag, Massachuset, Pawtucket, and Nipmuck tribes. The Pilgrims immediately start farming plots. The Wampanoag Indians provide information that helps sustain them, such as teaching them how to grow maize. However, of the 101 men, women, and children who arrive in Plymouth harbor, nearly half will soon die from disease and exposure.

1621

AGRI. Squanto (or, Tisquantum), the Wampanoag Indian kidnapped by slaver Thomas Hunt in 1615, has made his way back from Spain to the Plymouth colony on Cape Cod Bay in March. The Plymouth Pilgrims have had a very difficult and cold winter with little food, resulting in half of them dying from disease. The Wampanoag leader Massasoit shows compassion to the survivors and sends an Abenaki Indian named Samoset to the English settlement. Samoset had learned a little English from coastal fishermen, and greets the Pilgrims in English, and is warmly received. In a few days, Samoset brings Squanto to the settlement. Squanto, who speaks fluent English, shows the Pilgrims how to plant maize, beans, squash, and pumpkins, how to fish in area rivers, and how to build shelters. Squanto also acts as an interpreter for the Pilgrims in their dealings with Indians. On March 22, he helps Massasoit and the Pilgrim leaders negotiate a treaty to establish friendly relations between the Wampanoag and the English. The Wampanoag grant the Pilgrims land, and the two groups forge a defensive alliance against the Narragansett, who are the enemy of the Wampanoag.

RELI. The first Thanksgiving is celebrated. In autumn, the Pilgrims and their Wampanoag guests celebrate the first Thanksgiving together. The English of the Plymouth colony invite the Wampanoag leader Massasoit to a feast in appreciation for the help his people have provided in teaching the Europeans how to farm in their new land. Massasoit arrives with about 90 of his men. When it becomes clear that the colonists do not have enough food for everyone, Massasoit orders his people to contribute to the feast. The event follows the Indian tradition of thanking the Creator for a plentiful harvest. In 1863, President Abraham Lincoln will declare an annual commemoration of the Thanksgiving feast as a national holiday.

Also in this year, new religious leaders appear among the Powhatan Indians who promise a return to the old Indian world before the white man arrived, and the diseases and warfare came about. Among these revitalization prophets is Nenmartanaw, who tells his followers that he possesses an ointment that will make them invulnerable to the bullets of the colonists. Rumors go around that this Indian is planning a rebellion against the British. When Nenmartanaw kills an Englishman and then walks into the man's village, he is shot dead by the colonists. Many of the prophet's followers will avenge his death the following year by joining Powhatan leader Opechancanough in his surprise attack against the villages of the English.

TRAD. The Dutch West India Company is formed in the Netherlands and is designed to have a monopoly on Dutch trade in North America and Africa. The Company quickly gains in the fur trade business with northeastern Indian groups such as the Mahican and the Mohawk. Within ten years the firm will have over 15,000 employees. The Company will be instrumental in encouraging Dutch colonists to come to North America by offering large tracts of land to Dutchmen who bring 50 settlers or more to the Dutch colony of New Netherland.

1622

HEAL. Disease takes a heavy toll among Virginia colonists and their Indian neighbors.

WARS. On March 22, Opechancanough, chief of the Powhatan Indians, leads an attack on the English colony of Jamestown killing about 350 colonists, almost a quarter of Virginia's population, and destroys the first American ironworks. The attack mobilizes the colonists to organize a campaign to exterminate the Indians living in their area. Nine years of warfare will follow.

1623

WARS. Miles Standish leads the Plymouth militia against the Massachuset Indians, killing eight of the tribe who were formerly friendly to the British.

In May, a peace conference is set up between Powhatan chief Opechancanough and other Powhatan leaders and the Virginia colonists. The Powhatan were beaten down by the continual military campaigns against them by the colonists, and the Indians agree to release a few English prisoners and discuss terms of a truce. At the end

of the meeting, the English offer the Indians wine tainted with poison. As the effects take place, the English shoot the groggy Powhatan Indians, including Opechancanough, who nevertheless manages to escape and survive.

1624

SETT. Virginia becomes a royal colony of England.

TRAD. Dutch settlers found Fort Orange (Albany, New York) in New Netherland. This is their first trading post in North America, and the Dutch will develop prosperous trading relationships with the Mahican, Mohawk, and other local Indian tribes.

1626

POLI. On May 6, Manhattan Island is purchased by Dutch colonists under Peter Minuit, the Dutch governor of New Netherland (now New York) from Canarsee Indians (a band of Lenni Lenape, or Delaware, Indians) for 60 Dutch guilder's worth of trade goods. Although the folklore today says that the Canarsee received the equivalent of two cents per acre (or $24 or $39, varying with the estimates of economists) the actual price translates into today's dollars at about $10,000 to $15,000. However, the Canarsee have sold land that belongs to the Manhattan band of Lenni Lenape (or Wappinger Indians), and they probably thought they were accepting a gift to share the land, not sell it, because they did not buy and sell real estate as Europeans did. The Carnarsee only used the island for hunting and fishing. The Dutch will later have to pay the Manhattan Indians of the Wappinger Confederacy, actual occupants of Manhattan Island. The Dutch name the town on the island New Amsterdam. The town will soon have a population of 270, complete with forts, homes, farms, and government buildings.

RELI. The Spanish Inquisition is established in New Mexico.

WARS. The Dutch usually followed a policy of neutrality in wars between Indian tribes.

However, this time four Dutch traders join the Mahicans in a raid against their Mohawk enemies and are defeated and killed by the Mohawk.

1627

TRAD. The Company of New France is created to colonize New France and develop the fur trade with Indians.

1628

SOCI. The small British colony of Merry Mount, led by Thomas Morton, infuriates the nearby Plymouth Colony by trading gunpowder and liquor to local Indians. These Puritans also stage dances around a maypole. A group of Plymouth colonists, led by Miles Standish, attack Merry Mount, arrest Morton, and send him back to England in an effort to remove his immoral influence from the colonies.

1629–1633

RELI. The Spanish found Catholic missions at Acoma, Hopi, and Zuni pueblos.

1630

HEAL. Infectious disease epidemics in the decade ahead will reduce America's Huron tribe to a third of its estimated 30,000 population.

SETT. A new wave of immigrants, many of them Puritans, arrive on the shores of Massachusetts Bay under John Winthrop, establishing the Massachusetts Bay Colony. The rigid orthodoxy of the Puritan rule was not to everyone's liking. Roger Williams objected to the colony's seizure of Indian lands and its relations with the Church of England. Williams urges a humane policy toward the Indians. He is banished from Massachusetts Bay and sets up a new American colony in 1636, in present-day Rhode Island.

1631

WARS. The Lenni Lenape (or Delaware) Indians attack the Dutch settlement of Swanendael (the site of present-day Lewes, Delaware), destroying the town and killing 32 settlers. The Dutch West India Company chooses to negotiate with the Indians instead of retaliate against them, offering them increased trade and gifts.

1632

TRAD. The Pequot Indians attack a Dutch trading post called House of Hope, established at present-day Hartford, Connecticut, where Indians from other tribes are gathered to trade. The Pequot are angered that the Dutch are trading with other tribes in the area, bypassing Pequot middlemen. The Dutch retaliate against the Pequot, killing their leader Tatotem.

1633

MIGR. The first white venture is made to Lake Michigan and the Wisconsin region by French explorer Jean Nicolet. Brought to Canada by Champlain in 1618, Nicolet has lived among the Huron of the upper Ottawa River, and now travels west in search of furs and a Northwest Passage. He lands at present day Green Bay, where the Menominees have a settlement. Most of the indigenous tribes are being pushed westward by the Ottawa, Huron, and other eastern tribes.

RELI. In 1629, the Spanish sent four priests and some soldiers to convert the Zuni of New Mexico. After four years, the Zuni rebel against the foreigners in their country and kill the soldiers and two of the missionaries.

1633–1635

HEAL. A widespread epidemic of smallpox spreads among Indians throughout New England, New France, and New Netherland, the area now known as the northeastern United States and southeastern Canada, killing huge numbers. The Huron tribe alone loses more than 10,000 members.

1634

TREA. The Pequot have been suffering from a smallpox epidemic, and agree to sign a treaty with the colonists of Massachusetts. The colonists offer to help the Pequot fight the Narragansett, and in return the Pequot must pay the British a large tribute of wampum. The treaty will be broken by the colonists in 1636.

1636

SETT. Roger Williams purchases land from the Narragansett Indians and establishes an American colony in what is now Providence, Rhode Island, with complete separation of church and state. Williams was expelled from the colony of Massachusetts for advocating separation of church and state. He also believes in negotiating fairly with tribes for all lands the English want from them.

WARS. On August 25, the Massachusetts colony troops attack the Pequot of Block Island. This leads to an attempt by the Pequot to organize other tribes to drive the whites out of their lands. When this attempt at a pan-Indian alliance fails, the Pequot battle the English alone. The English come to regard the Pequot as their greatest Indian enemy.

1636–1638

WARS. The Pequot War in New England is a turning point in Indian-white relations. Over 200 well-armed white colonists, along with about 100 Indians (mostly Mohegan and Narragansett warriors), kill between 600 and 1,000 Pequot in a surprise attack on their main village near the Mystic River on May 25, 1636. The Pequot village is burned, and women and children are brutally killed along with the men. The English hunt down the Pequot who have escaped, killing many and taking others captive. About 50 captives are made into slaves to serve the colonists. Some of the more hostile Pequot are sold into slavery in the West Indies in exchange for Africans, who become the first black slaves in New England. This massacre unites the Massachusetts colonists against the Indians and puts fear in other area tribes that resistance to the English is futile. The *Treaty of Hartford* in 1638 ends hostilities between the Massachusetts colonists and the Pequot, who are now powerless and offered nothing in the treaty.

1638

SETT. In March, Swedish colonists purchase land around the Delaware Bay (at the site of present-day Wilmington, Delaware) from the Indians of the region. They maintain a trading outpost here, becoming important trading partners with the Susquehannock, Lenni Lenape (Delaware), and Mingo until the colony is disbanded in 1655.

LAND. On November 14, the English establish the first Indian reservation, compelling the Wappinger Indians of present-day Connecticut to cede most of their territory and to live on just 1,200 acres. The Indians are forbidden to leave this land or to sell it, and their activities are to be monitored by an English agent.

C. 1640

ANIM. Beavers and otters are nearly exterminated by this time in Iroquois country. To expand their territory, the Iroquois launch "Beaver Wars" against Huron and other tribes that go on for about 10 years. In 1650, 300 Huron survivors will settle at Lorette under French protection.

1641

WARS. Bounties of from four to eight dollars are offered by the Dutch in New Netherland (later New York) for enemy Indian scalps. After two Dutch farmers are killed by Hackensack Indians because the farmers' cattle trampled the Indians' corn fields, the Dutch demand the tribe give up the killers. When the Indians refuse, the New Netherland governor, Willem Kieft, offers bounties for Hackensack scalps.

1642

SETT. The French found Montreal.

1643

POLI. The New England Federation is formed to protect the colonists against the Indians and to settle boundary disputes. The four English colonies of the New England Confederation are Massachusetts, Plymouth, Connecticut, and New Haven.

PUBL. Roger Williams, the founder of Providence, publishes *A Key into the Language of America,* one of the earliest books on Indian language by a non-Indian. Williams is a student of Narragansett language and culture.

TREA. The Dutch negotiate a treaty of alliance with the Iroquois Confederacy tribes, in which the Dutch exchange guns for furs. This arrangement will spell doom for many of the enemy tribes of the Iroquois in the next decade.

WARS. On February 26, the Dutch massacre about 100 Wecquaesgeek Indians seeking refuge from the Mohawk at the Dutch settlement of Pavonia (in present-day New Jersey). The Dutch soldiers kill men, women, and children, bringing about 30 Indian prisoners back to New Amsterdam where they are publicly tortured to death. This brutal action, intended to frighten other tribes into submission, backfires by motivating tribes to seek revenge against Dutch settlers in a series of bloody attacks.

The Swedish settlers of Maryland aid the Susquehannock with guns and ammunition, which they use to force other settlers off their territory in Maryland.

1643–1645

WARS. In a war with the Dutch, the Wappinger Indians of eastern New York lose 1,500 people out of a population of 5,000.

1644

WARS. A combined force of Dutch and English kill over 500 Tankiteke, Wiwanoy, and Wappinger Indians in their settlements in present-day New York and Connecticut.

The second Powhatan Confederacy war under Opechancanough takes place against the English colony of Jamestown on April 18. About 500 colonists are killed in the surprise attack. Opechancanough had led an earlier uprising against the Virginia colony in 1622. The Virginia colonists move to retaliate, and the fighting continues for two years. Opechancanough will be captured in the attack and taken to Jamestown, where he is shot and killed in 1646.

1645

TREA. The Narragansett reluctantly agree to a treaty with the colonists of New England on August 28, whereby they cede land, must pay a tribute for every Pequot living among them, and give up several members of their tribe to the English as a guarantee they will obey the colonists in the future.

1646

TRAD. The Huron trading empire is the most powerful in North America. In September, a fleet of 80 Huron Indian canoes loaded with furs beaches at Montreal in New France to trade with the French.

TREA. The Powhatan, exhausted after two years of fighting and dealing with the loss of their leader, Opechancanough, agree to a peace treaty with the Virginia colonists.

1648–1650

WARS. The Iroquois Confederacy launches successive invasions of Huron territory in New France (in present-day Canada), resulting in thousands of Huron fleeing their villages, dying

"When it was day, the soldiers returned to the fort, having massacred or murdered eighty Indians, and considering they had done a deed of Roman valor, in murdering so many in their sleep; where infants were torn from their mother's breasts, and hacked to pieces in the presence of their parents, and the pieces thrown into the fire and in the water, and other sucklings were bound to small boards, and then cut, stuck, and pierced, and miserably massacred in a manner to move a heart to stone." Dutchman Willem DeVries on the Pavonia Massacre (Jennings 1975, 164).

of starvation, and seeking refuge with other tribes to the west.

1650–1651

WARS. Having conquered and destroyed the Huron Indian Confederacy, the Iroquois Confederacy moves to conquer the Neutral Indian Confederacy, which had tried to remain neutral in the Huron-Iroquois wars. Most of the conquered Neutrals will be assimilated into the Seneca tribe of the Iroquois Confederacy.

1653

PUBL. The first book to be printed in an Indian language in New England is *Catechism in the Indian Language,* written in Algonquian by John Eliot, the New England "Apostle to the Indians."

1654

EXPL. French fur traders Radisson and Groseilliers explore the southwest area of Lake Superior and discover the Mississippi River.

MIGR Ottawa, Fox, Sauk, Mascouten, and Kickapoo Indians flee the present-day Michigan region to present-day Wisconsin to avoid war with the Iroquois Confederacy.

1655

RELI. Spanish priest Salvador de Guerra performs a grisly murder on Juan Cuna, a Hopi man, for idolatry, when the priest finds Cuna with a kachina doll. After publicly whipping Cuna almost to death, the priest carries him inside the church and pours turpentine over him, setting him on fire. When Cuna rushes outside the church in flames, the priest mounts a horse, knocks Cuna over and tramples him to death.

WARS. The Timucua of what is now northern Florida are devastated by smallpox, and are subjugated by the Spanish. However, they make one more attempt to rise up against their oppressors. Joined by Apalachee Indians in a revolt against the Spanish, they kill several Spaniards at the San Pedro mission near St. Augustine, Florida. After several months, the Indian rebels are captured and are hanged or sold into slavery by the Spanish. Some Timucua escape and join the Seminole

tribe. The Timucua are destroyed as a tribe and soon disappear.

1655

WARS. The Peach War begins between bands of Lenni Lenape (Delaware) and Wappinger Indians and the Dutch, and will continue until 1664.

1658–1660

EXPL. French fur trader Pierre Esprit Radisson, 22, explores the western end of Lake Superior as far as Chequamegon Bay and trades with *les sauvages*. Radisson came from France in 1651, was captured and adopted by the Iroquois, and escaped in 1654.

1659

ANIM. The Navajo launch raids on horseback in the New Mexico region. The Governor of Santa Fe reports of attacks by Navajo on horseback, the first documented Native American use of the horse. Horses are traded northward from tribe to tribe, reaching the region of Montana by about 1690.

1660

WARS. The Dutch, under Governor Peter Stuyvesant, take Indian children as hostages, holding them in settlements in the present-day New York area to force the Indians to comply with their demands. Many tribes are weakened by warfare and offer children as hostages. The Esopus Indians (Catskill, Mamekoting, Wawarsink, and Waranawonkong), who have a deep hatred and distrust of the Dutch since their leaders were murdered at a peace council by Dutch soldiers in 1659, refuse to give up their children. The Dutch take several of their women and children captives and sell them as slaves in the West Indies.

1660–1680

HEAL. The Pueblo Indians of present-day New Mexico experience a severe drought and famine and an epidemic in 1671 that kills many people and most of their cattle. They also have frequent raids from the Apaches, Navajos, and sometimes Comanches.

1661

RELI. Sacred kivas of the Pueblos in the Southwest are raided by the Spanish in an effort to suppress native religion. Around 1,600 kachina masks and many other ceremonial materials are destroyed.

1662

CONT. The Plymouth Court at Massachusetts summons Wampanoag leader Wamsutta (the son of Massasoit, who had worked hard to maintain peaceful relations with the English) to Plymouth after suspecting a planned Indian attack. He is taken at gunpoint, held for intensive questioning, and soon after gets sick and dies. His younger brother and successor, Metacom, believes Wamsutta was poisoned while in Plymouth. This greatly angers the Wampanoag, and along with other negative events and bad relations with the Plymouth colonists, leads up to King Philip's War (1675).

1664

POLI. England gains control of New Netherland from the Dutch and becomes allies and trade partners with the Iroquois. The colony of New Netherland and the city of New Amsterdam are both renamed New York by the British.

1670

POPU. By this time, the Indians of New England are outnumbered by the white settlers (10,000 to 75,000). War and disease have taken their toll and the Indians' land holdings have been reduced by half.

TRAD. The Hudson's Bay Company is chartered in London by King Charles II to promote British trade. The Company soon builds trading posts along water routes used by Indian traders and hunters.

1672

ECON. Colonial postal officials employ Indian couriers to carry mail between New York City and Albany because winter weather is too severe for the white couriers.

1673

EXPL. French fur trader Louis Jolliet and explorer and Jesuit missionary Father Jacques Marquette explore the western Great Lakes and Mississippi River. The French explorers travel down the upper portion of the Mississippi to below the Arkansas River, where de Soto had been in 1541. They stop for a few days in a village of the Quapaw Indians before returning northward upstream, recording their observations of the village life. Marquette also visits the principal village of the Kaskaskia Indians on the Illinois River, near present-day Peoria. The Kaskaskia are a part of the Illinois confederacy of tribes and this village is an important gathering place for the confederacy. Later explorers in 1680 and 1692 estimate the population of the town to be 8,000–9,000.

C. 1675

ARTS. The use of European glass beads spreads among eastern Indians and begins to replace porcupine quillwork.

1675

RELI. The Spanish authorities are frustrated in their inability to convert the Pueblo Indians to Christianity. Spanish leaders in Santa Fe order the arrest of 47 pueblo leaders who are charged with sorcery, resulting in four being hanged. The rest are whipped, including Popé who will lead the Pueblo revolt in 1680.

1675–1676

WARS. King Philip's War in New England begins in late June, 1675, with Wampanoag warriors attacking the town of Swansea, Massachusetts. The war between Wampanoag, Narraganset, and Nipmuc Indians and the New England Confederation of Colonies is one of the bloodiest and most costly wars in American history and is the bloodiest conflict between Indians and settlers in the seventeenth century. The colonists' hunger for land and the ill treatment of the Wampanoag and other tribes by government officials lead to this disastrous war. The Wampanoag leader Metacom (known to the English as King Philip), leads the Indians from New Hampshire to Connecticut in an attack against the British colonists. Not all Indians side with Philip, however. Most of the Christianized Indians side with the English, or remain neutral. The war ends in August, 1676, with the killing of Chief Metacom (King Philip) in battle on August 12, and the breaking up of his confederacy. The final surrender of the Indians takes place on August 28, 1676. The soldiers take the head of King Philip to Plymouth where it will be put on exhibit for the next 20 years. Of New England's 90 towns, 52 are attacked, around 600 settlers are killed, at least 12 towns are completely destroyed, and about 1,800 houses are burned to the ground. In the two years of the war, the Wampanoag, Narraganset, and other tribes are nearly exterminated. The conflict costs approximately 3,000 Indian lives, amounting to 40 percent of the Indian population of southern New England. It will take many years for Plymouth and the other colonies to recover. King Philip's widow and children are sold as slaves in the West Indies, and militiamen hunt down other survivors of the war to sell into slavery. Five hundred Wampanoag Indians are shipped out of Plymouth alone. Many Indian women and children are forced to become servants locally. This war changes Indian relations with New England colonists forever, marking the end of organized resistance to the white colonists by the southern New England tribes.

1676

WARS. During King Philip's War, Mary Rowlandson is captured by Wampanoag and Narragansett warriors in an attack on the small settlement of Lancaster, Massachusetts, on February 10. Rowlandson, the wife of a Puritan minister, is held captive for 12 weeks before being turned over in exchange for a ransom. Her account of her captivity will become one of America's bestsellers when it is published in 1682 as *The Sovereignty & Goodness of God, Together with the Faithfulness of His Promises Displayed; Being a Narrative of the Captivity and Restoration of Mrs. Mary Rowlandson and Related Documents*. After the Bible, it becomes the most popular book in colonial America and establishes the conventions of a new publishing genre, the captivity narrative.

1678–1679

EXPL. Frenchman Duluth (Daniel Greysolon, Sieur du Luth) explores the Lake Superior region in search of a water route to the Pacific. He establishes relations with the Ojibwe (Chippewa) Indians near Sault Ste. Marie, the Sioux Indians of northern Minnesota, and the Assiniboine of Canada. He negotiates treaties between the warring Ojibwe and the Sioux.

1680

ANIM. Western Indians begin to acquire the "Big Dog" (horses) from the Spanish.

HUNT. The French missionary Father Hennepin visits the Miami Indians of the Great Lakes region and witnesses how the Indians hunt buffalo (bison). The Indians set fire to the grass surrounding a buffalo herd, leaving an open passage where they wait with bows and arrows to shoot the buffalo as they run by.

WARS. The Pueblo Revolt takes place in New Mexico. The Pueblo Indians organize a rebellion against Spanish rule in present-day New Mexico from August 10–21. Led by Popé, a Tewa medicine man, the Pueblo Indians stage a well-planned revolt against the Spanish occupiers in their lands. The Pueblo Indians tell the Spanish to leave, and allow settlers to escape voluntarily with their lives. The northern Pueblo attack Santa Fe, and the Hopi, Acoma, and Zuni attack the settlers and missionaries near their villages. About 400 Spanish are killed during the conflict, and their churches and houses are burned and destroyed. The remaining 3,000 Spanish survivors of the revolt flee southward to El Paso del Norte and Mexico. This is the most successful Indian uprising ever staged. The Pueblo Indians acquire horses from the Spanish, further spreading horses northward to the Plains tribes. In 1689, the Spanish will return to reconquer the Pueblos.

1680–1683

WARS. The English of South Carolina wage war on the Westo band (probably Yuchi and Eire Indians) for the slave trade.

1682

EXPL. René-Robert Cavelier de la Salle claims the entire Mississippi Valley for France, naming the area Louisiana.

PUBL. Captivity narratives by whites become a new literary genre. One of the first and most famous published is *The Sovereignty & Goodness of God, Together with the Faithfulness of His Promises Displayed; Being a Narrative of the Captivity and Restoration of Mrs. Mary Rowlandson and Related Documents* (1682), which tells of her experiences of being captured and held for ransom by the Narragansett Indians during King Philip's War in 1676.

TREA. William Penn, the English Quaker and founder and governor of the Pennsylvania colony, makes a treaty with the Lenni Lenape (Delaware) Indians, beginning a 60-year period of friendly relations between the Quakers and the Delaware. In agreements with Chief Tamanend (Tammany), the Delaware grant Penn and his followers land in southeastern Pennsylvania in exchange for a wide array of trade goods. Penn's treaty reflects the Quaker's respect for Indian land and the belief that it should never be taken from them without their consent and proper compensation. The Quakers trade wampum, blankets, clothing, knives, and guns with the Indians for lands along the Delaware River. This exchange with the Delaware Indians becomes a popular metaphor for peace in American art, with famous romanticized paintings by American painters Benjamin West in 1771–72 and Edward Hicks in 1848.

1683

RELI. Catholic missionary Father Louis Hennepin returns to France after exploring Minnesota and being held captive by the Dakota.

1684

TREA. A peace treaty is signed between the English at Albany, New York, and the Oneida, Cayuga, and Onondaga Indians, ending hostilities between the Indians and the Virginia and Maryland colonies. After exchanging wampum belts and gifts, a hole is dug in the ground and

William Penn's treaty with the Lenni Lenape (Delaware) Indians, which brought about 60 years of good relations between the Lenni Lenape and the Quakers. Courtesy of Library of Congress.

five axes—one for each of the three tribes and the two colonies—are buried, symbolizing the end of warfare between them.

1688

WARS. The Iroquois Confederacy is angered by the poor treatment of Indians by the French. They attack Montreal in New France on July 26, killing around 1,000 colonists and burning their plantations. The Abenaki War against the New England colonists begins (part of the French and Indian Wars) and will last until 1724.

The Pueblo Indian town of Sia (now Zia) is attacked and destroyed by the Spanish under the governor of New Mexico, Domingo Petris de Crusate, who attempts to reconquer the Pueblos after their revolt of 1680. Hundreds of Indians die in the battle, many choosing to die in their burning homes rather than face a life of slavery.

1689

EXPL. Nicolas Perrot formally claims the upper Mississippi region for France.

1689

WARS. King William's War breaks out in 1689, the first in a series of French and Indian Wars, pitting the English colonists against France and their Indian allies. King William's War is the first European conflict to spread to North America. These colonial wars will continue to 1763. During these wars, the Iroquois League Indians generally side with the English, and the Algonquian tribes side with the French. The Indians are used by both sides—the British and the French—but realize too late that they are engaged in exterminating each other with the white men being the ultimate winners.

1691

LAWS. Virginia outlaws interracial marriage. The Virginia legislature bans from the colony any English person who marries someone of Indian or African descent. This comes 87 years after Pocahontas and John Rolfe wed in 1614. Similar laws will soon be passed in Massachusetts, Maryland,

Delaware, Pennsylvania, Georgia, North Carolina, and South Carolina.

1692–1694

WARS. The Pueblos are reconquered by the Spanish under New Mexico Governor Diego de Vargas. The Pueblo Indians have been weakened by drought, famine, internal dissension, and attacks by bands of Apaches and Navajo. Some warfare ensues in Pueblo towns and villages, but by 1694 most of the region is again under Spanish control. Uprisings against the Spanish will still occur, however, in the northern area with the Indians of Picuris, Taos, and Jemez in 1696. The Spanish offer the Pueblos protection from their Indian enemies, and are also more tolerant now of Indian religious practices than before the Pueblo Revolt of 1680.

1695

WARS. The first Pima (Akimel O'odham) Uprising occurs against Spanish authorities in present-day Arizona. The second uprising will occur 56 years later in 1751.

1697

WARS. Hannah Duston is captured by the Abenaki during a raid on her town of Haverhill, Massachusetts, on March 15. With her are her nurse and her infant child, whom the Indians later murder. Duston and another captive, 10-year-old Samuel Lennardson, attack their captors while they are sleeping on the night of March 30, using hatchets. They kill and scalp 10 Indians, including several children, and then flee back to Haverhill. Her story will be told in Cotton Mather's *Humiliations Followed with Deliverances* (1697), and retold in the nineteenth century by Nathaniel Hawthorne in articles published in *The American Magazine of Useful and Entertaining Knowledge* in 1836, and by Henry David Thoreau in *Week on the Concord and Merrimack Rivers* (1849). These versions of Duston's capture have been compiled and reprinted in *Captivity Narrative of Hannah Duston* (1987) by Richard Bosman (text by Cotton Mather, John Greenleaf

Whittier, Nathaniel Hawthorne, and Henry David Thoreau).

1699

SETT. In the lower Mississippi region, an Indian population center of about 30,000 is encountered by French-Canadian Pierre Le Moyne after he establishes the permanent French settlement in Louisiana at Ft. Maurepas (on the site of today's Biloxi, Mississippi). The Indians are mainly from the Choctaw, Chickasaw, and Natchez tribes.

LATE 1600S

WARS. Navajos, Apaches, and Comanches begin raids against the Pueblo Indians.

18TH CENTURY

1700

EDUC. The College of William and Mary (established in Williamsburg, Virginia, in 1693), begins admitting Indian students.

RELI. Jesuit missionary Eusebio Kino establishes the San Xavier del Bac mission in present-day Tucson, Arizona, for the conversion of the Pima (Akimel O'odham) Indians. Kino will convert up to 4,500 Indians to Christianity, and will explore and chart much of the region, expanding the boundaries of New Spain.

The Sun Dance originates with the Plains Algonquians. This religious movement will diffuse throughout the Plains tribes, and by the early 1800s will develop into the most magnificent aboriginal ceremony of this culture area. The Sun Dance, known under many names in many Indian languages, will become the best known and most dramatic of North American Indian ceremonies.

WARS. The Hopi destroy one of their own villages, Awatovi. Hopi from other villages attack and slaughter the Hopi men of Awatovi who they believe have agreed to allow the Spanish to settle on their lands and who have fallen under the Spanish missionary influence. After killing the men, the women and children are sent to live in other Hopi villages. This reflects the intense hatred the Hopi have for the Spanish.

1701

SETT. Detroit is founded as a French fur trading post.

1702–1713

WARS. Queen Anne's War (or the War of Spanish Succession, 1701–1714) breaks out in Europe, with England and France united against Spain. The conflict soon extends to North America, drawing many Indian tribes to be allied with the European powers in their battles. This is the second of the French and Indian Wars, between England and France in the Northeast, and between England and Spain in the Southeast, and their various Indian allies. The English and the Creek Indians, for example, launch military campaigns against Franciscan missions in Spanish Florida during 1703–1704.

1703

WARS. Massachusetts is paying 12 pounds sterling for an Indian scalp, an equivalent to about $500 today. In 1722, the bounty rises to 100 pounds, over $4,000 today.

1704

WARS. In March, Caughnawaga, Mohawk, and Abenaki Indians aid the French in a raid on Deerfield, Massachusetts, in which about 50 colonists are killed and another 100 are captured.

1708

POPU. A census in South Carolina records that there are around 1,400 Indian slaves and about twice as many black slaves there.

1710

MIGR. The Tuscarora Indians petition the provincial government of Pennsylvania for permission

In the Sun Dance many tribes pierce the chests or backs of the participants, and insert skewers with thongs or ropes attached to the center pole of the arena. "During the whole of this operation the young buck never quailed, nor did his eye, which bore a perfectly stolid expression, reveal the slightest trace of suffering. The initiates danced while attached to the center pole, continuing to pull on the ropes until by degrees the wooden pegs were torn out of the chest. . .this after forty-eight hours of fasting, and with no sleep." From a white man's observations of a Sun Dance (Lane 1887, 25).

to move to Pennsylvania from their homes in North Carolina. They are losing their lands to white settlers, who are also kidnapping their young and selling the children into slavery. However, the petition was denied.

POLI. A delegation of Iroquois Confederacy Indian chiefs (three Mohawk chiefs and one Mahican chief) are received in Queen Anne's court in London, England, as "The Four Kings of the New World." The Indian leaders are there to request increased military protection from the French.

1711–1712

WARS. The Tuscarora War on the North Carolina frontier is fought between the British settlers and the Tuscarora Indians. The Tuscarora are angered by the kidnapping and enslavement of several Indians and the invasion of their lands by white settlers. Aided by the Coree, Pamlico, Machapunga, and other tribes, the Tuscarora attack a white settlement on the Pamlico River, killing up to 200 colonists. Carolina officials counter the attack by sending troops who surround and destroy Tuscarora villages in retaliation. The Tuscarora have lost as many as 1,000 in battles, with several hundred others captured and sold as slaves. Remnants of this Iroquoian tribe migrate north to New York. In 1722, the Tuscarora will become the sixth tribe of the Iroquois Confederacy.

1712

EDUC. The Mohawk Indians of New York establish their own schools.

1712–1718

WARS. War between the Fox Indians and the French in the Great Lakes area rages on and off during this period.

1713

TREA. With the *Treaty of Ultrecht,* Queen Anne's War ends, and the French acknowledge that members of the Iroquois Confederacy are British subjects. In this treaty, France cedes to England its claims to what is now Nova Scotia and the Hudson Bay region. Peace between the English and the French established by this treaty will last for more than 30 years.

WARS. An advertisement in the *Boston News Letter* offers Tuscarora Indians for sale who were captured by Col. John Barnwell, British commander of the South Carolina forces, who fought against the Indians in the first Tuscarora War, 1711–12.

1714

EXPL. French trader, St. Denis, reaches the Rio Grande River.

1715

POLI. The Chickasaw and Cherokee form an alliance to drive the Shawnee out of the Cumberland Valley of Maryland and Pennsylvania and into the Kentucky-Tennessee area.

1715–1716

WARS. The Yamasee War takes place in South Carolina, between the English and Yamasee

Indians. The Yamasee Indians of South Carolina organize an anti-British uprising among the coastal tribes. Angered by the cheating of fur traders and by the stealing of their lands by white settlers, the Indians kill more than 200 settlers and traders before the uprising is suppressed by troops from the surrounding colonies. After fighting the English who are joined by the Cherokee, the Yamasee are forced to flee to Florida in 1717 where they settle among the Spanish around St. Augustine. The Yamasee are so reduced in numbers they are nearly extinct as a tribe. Yet, they continue to stage small raids on Carolina settlements, and aid the Spanish, for more than a decade.

1719

TRAD. The Wichita Indians of the Canadian River area of Oklahoma establish trade relations with the French. The population of the Wichita is around 6,000 at this time, but will be reduced to less than 600 by 1868, due to smallpox and forced removal from their lands.

1720

WARS. The Pawnee and Otoe Indians defeat the Spanish army on the Platte River in Nebraska, stopping Spanish advancement onto the Great Plains. Pedro de Villasur and an army of 42 Spanish soldiers and 70 Pueblo warriors travel to the southern Plains in an effort to prevent the French from establishing trade with the tribes there. They are attacked by a force of Pawnee and Kaw (Kansas) Indians with French guns, who kill 45 of Villasur's forces and drive the others back to the Spanish capital of Santa Fe. French traders are established among the Pawnees of the Upper Platte.

1720–1724

WARS. Fighting continues between the Chickasaw and the French and their Choctaw allies in the Mississippi Valley in the southeast. The Chickasaw are allied with the English with whom they trade goods. The French and the Choctaw want to end the Chickasaw relationship with the English and therefore attack their lands. The Fox Indians engage in warfare resistance against the French in Great Lakes country. This fighting will continue into the 1730s.

1721

LAWS. Spain abolishes the *encomienda* system that was implemented in 1512. The system gave conquistadors land grants in the Spanish colonies as rewards for service, and the Indians were forced into brutal servitude by their Spanish owners. Spain became fearful that the *encomienda* owners were becoming too independent of the Crown.

POLI. The English Board of Trade suggests to the British Crown that intermarriage be encouraged between colonists and Indians as a means of securing peace between the English and their Indian allies.

TREA. Iroquois tribes sign a treaty with the Virginia Governor Alexander Spotswood, agreeing not to cross the Potomac River or the Blue Ridge Mountains without the governor's permission.

1722

POLI. The Tuscarora Indians join the Iroquois Confederacy, making six tribes in the group. The Tuscarora had been living among the Iroquois since their exodus from North Carolina around 1713, and they share cultural traits with the Iroquois tribes. The British officially recognize the confederacy now as the Six Nations.

1722–1727

WARS. The Abenaki Indians of New England develop friendly relations with the French. This leads to violent conflicts between the British colonists and the Abenaki. In June, 1722, a group of Eastern Abenaki attack English settlements near present-day Brunswick, Maine, burning houses and taking several of the English as captives. Troops are called in by the acting governor of Massachusetts. The fighting goes on until 1727, when the Abenaki receive little support from the French. After the Abenaki settlement at Norridgewock is destroyed in a British raid and a French missionary who lives among the tribe is killed, the Abenaki are dispersed, and a large number migrate to the St. Francis River region of eastern Canada.

1723

EDUC. The first permanent school for Indians in the British colonies of North America is opened in a part of the College of William and Mary in Williamsburg, Virginia.

1727

WARS. A Yamasee Indian town near the Spanish settlement at St. Augustine, Florida, is destroyed and the residents killed in a raid by the British and their Indian allies.

1727–1737

WARS. The Fox Indians and the French continue their war, with both sides recruiting various Indian tribes as allies. The Fox gain the support of the Abenaki, Sioux, and some of the Iroquois, while the French gain the support of the Ojibwe (Chippewa), Potawatomi, and Menominee. Between 1728 and 1730, the French group kills almost 1,200 Fox, destroying many of their villages. The Fox who survive the wars eventually leave the Michigan area, and the fur trade there, and return to their former homes near Green Bay, Wisconsin.

1729

WARS. The Natchez Revolt takes place against the French along the lower Mississippi River. Fort Rosalie, a French fort on the Mississippi River, is destroyed by the Natchez Indians of Louisiana on November 28. The attack is precipitated by the French governor of Louisiana, who, wanting the site of the principal Natchez village (White Apple) for a plantation, orders the Natchez Indians to vacate their capital (and their sacred burial ground). The Natchez in the Louisiana colony attack settlers and soldiers at Fort Rosalie, killing over 200 and taking several hundred women, children, and black slaves as prisoners. In retaliation, the French, joined by their Choctaw allies, destroy several Natchez villages, scattering the tribe into several groups. The Natchez had previously fought the French in 1716 and in 1722. One group of about 450 Natchez will be captured by the French in 1731 and sold into slavery on the island of Santo Domingo.

1730

POLI. Seven Cherokee chiefs visit London and form an alliance, the *Articles of Agreement,* with King George II. In an effort to gain Cherokee support for the British against the French, Sir Alexander Cuming crowns Cherokee chief Moytoy Emperor of the Cherokee at the Cherokee village of Tellico in present-day Tennessee. Afterwards, Moytoy and six other Cherokee chiefs are taken to England and are received with great ceremony by George II. The Cherokee leaders sign the *Articles of Agreement,* which defines the terms of the Cherokee alliance with the British.

WARS. French troops attack a large group of Fox Indians who are traveling east to seek protection in Seneca lands. A massacre of around 400 Fox, with another 500 sold into slavery, ends decades of warfare between the two groups. The Fox survivors scatter with some joining nearby tribes such as the Chickasaw, Creek, and Cherokee.

1731–1743

EXPL. French fur trader Pierre Gaultier de La Vérendrye and his sons explore the Great Plains.

1736

PUBL. Benjamin Franklin begins printing and publishing Indian treaties in small booklets in Philadelphia.

1733

SETT. The site of Savannah, Georgia, is chosen by British general and philanthropist James Oglethorpe. The site is currently the Creek Indian town called Yamacraw under Chief Tomochichi. The Creek Indians are friendly and helpful to the new colony. The following year Tomochichi and a contingent of Creeks accompany Oglethorpe to England.

1735

RELI. The British Society for the Propagation of the Gospel launches an aggressive campaign to Christianize the Iroquois nations Indians. By the

1760s, many of the Mohawk, Oneida, and Cayuga will be converted and baptized.

1736–1739

WARS. The Chickasaw Indians continue their resistance against the French and Choctaw in the Southeast.

1737

TREA. The "Walking Purchase" treaty is completed by the colonists with the Lenni Lenape (Delaware) Indians of Pennsylvania. This is one of many such "walking treaties" in which the land to be purchased or ceded was described in terms of the distance a man could walk in a day or a given number of days. William Penn, an English Quaker and founder of Pennsylvania, concluded the original treaty for this area with the Delaware Indians in 1686 when he was granted the 40 miles he walked in a day and a half. When the purchase is renegotiated here in 1737, professional "walkers" are hired who cover a distance of almost 67 miles in one and a half days. The walkers actually run the entire distance, ignoring the rules, and Pennsylvania claims 1,200 square miles of Lenni Lenape (Delaware) territory. The land dispute resulting from the fraudulent run will be mediated in 1742 at a conference in Philadelphia by the Iroquois, who will support the Pennsylvanian officials. The Lenni Lenape (Delaware) are ordered off the land.

1738

HEAL. Smallpox spreads to the Cherokee Indians in North Carolina from white settlements in South Carolina. The disease spreads in the Southeast, killing almost half the Cherokee population, and also reaching tribes in western Canada.

1739–1741

EXPL. French fur traders Paul and Pierre Mallet explore the Missouri, Platte, and Canadian Rivers.

1740

WARS. James Oglethorpe, the governor of Georgia, leads an Indian force of Creek, Chickasaw, and Cherokee warriors in an invasion of Spanish Florida. This is part of a larger conflict called the War of Jenkins's Ear (1740–1743) involving disagreements between England and Spain over treaties. The Indians are not able to capture St. Augustine and retreat back to Georgia.

1741

CONT. Vitus Bering, a Danish navigator in service to Russia, reaches Alaska with an exploration party. These are the first non-Indians to encounter the indigenous peoples of Alaska and the Aleutian Islands. The Russians soon begin trading with the natives for sea otter pelts, which will become a sensation back in Russia. In the years ahead, the Aleutians will suffer greatly in the sea otter trade, as the Russian tradesmen take hostages and rape and murder Aleutians.

1744–1748

WARS. King George's War takes place, the third of the French and Indian Wars between France and England and their respective Indian allies.

1745

TRAD. Russian explorer Mikhail Nerodchikov visits the Aleutian Islands in September. Soon thereafter, Russian traders flock into the area, overwhelming the Aleuts with war and disease, and greatly reducing their population. Russian traders kidnap women and children from an Aleut village of the island of Attu and force the Aleut men to hunt for their ransom. When the number of sea otters is not enough to satisfy the Russians, the traders murder 15 of the hunters as a warning to other Aleuts to meet the Russians' demands.

1746

HEAL. A typhoid fever epidemic breaks out among the Micmac of Nova Scotia.

TRAD. Rivalries between the Choctaw over trading with either the French or the English lead to a civil war in the tribe. Peace is restored in 1750, with three divisions in the tribe—a southern and western division which support the French, and a northeastern district which sides with the British.

1750

EDUC. Moor's Indian Charity School is founded in Connecticut. It will move to New Hampshire in 1769 and become Dartmouth College, which encourages enrollment of Indians.

WARS. Ojibwe (Chippewa) Indians defeat Sioux tribesmen at the Battle of Kathio and gain undisputed possession of wild rice stands in the lakes of northern Minnesota.

1751

LAWS. A regulation to curb the abuses of whiskey trading among the Indians is passed by the British.

MIGR. Lenni Lenape (Delaware) Indians, under pressure by both white settlers and the Iroquois Confederacy, leave their homelands in Pennsylvania to live among the Huron Indians in Ohio.

POLI. Benjamin Franklin cites the Iroquois League as the model for his Albany Plan of Union, later an influence on the formation of the U.S. Constitution.

WARS. The second Pima Uprising occurs in the Southwest against the Spanish authorities. The Pima (Akimel O'odham) kill over 100 Spaniards and burn their churches before they are subdued and punished.

1752

TREA. Ohio tribes agree to the *Treaty of Logstown,* which turns over lands on the Ohio River for a large amount of trade goods. Leaders of the Lenni Lenape (Delaware), Mingo, Shawnee, and other Ohio Valley tribes meet with British officials and representatives of the Ohio Company of Virginia at a Mingo village at Logstown in Pennsylvania for the exchange.

1753

WARS. The French are building forts in the Ohio River Valley, and George Washington,

a 21-year-old Virginia surveyor at the time, is sent to negotiate with the French and demand that they abandon their forts. When the French refuse, Washington recommends that the Virginiamilitia be sent in to remove them. The militia attacks on July 4, 1754, and this attack initiates the French and Indian War.

1754

POLI. The Albany Congress of English Colonies assembles representatives of New York, Pennsylvania, Maryland, and the New England colonies in a meeting with chiefs of the Iroquois Confederacy (Six Nations) in order to organize a united military offensive by Iroquois and British colonial forces against the advances of the French. The plan of union is drawn up by Benjamin Franklin and modeled after the Iroquois Confederacy, but it is not adopted. The Iroquois are unimpressed with the divisiveness and disorganization of the British.

WARS. War with the Ute Indians causes the Navajo to abandon Dinétaa, the old Navajo country of northwestern Colorado, and move southward into the Pueblo Indian region. During this time, the Spanish of New Mexico try to convert the Navajo to Catholicism, but without success.

1754–1755

EXPL. Anthony Henday, sponsored by the Hudson's Bay Company, explores the Canadian Plains.

1754–1763

WARS. The French and Indian War (fourth of the French and Indian Wars) is fought by the British and their Indian allies against the French and their Indian allies. The Iroquois Six-Nation Confederacy allies itself with the British, while many of the Algonquian tribes side with the French. The Cherokee initially become British allies until 1758. Ohio River tribes become British allies in 1758. Indians participate in major battles such as Fort Duquesne (1755), German Flats (1757), Fort William Henry (1757), and Lake George (1757). The 1763 *Treaty of Paris* ends the war, with the British in control of Canada. France cedes New France to England, and Louisiana to Spain.

1755

PUBL. In July, Shawnee Indians attack a community of settlers in western Virginia and capture Mary Ingles, her two sons, and her sister-in-law. The story of their captivity and remarkable journey into western Ohio and back home over several months and 800 miles is recounted in the popular novel *Follow the River* by James Alexander Thom.

WARS. A British force of 1,500 from Virginia is defeated on July 9 by French and Indian forces on the Monongahela River, seven miles from Fort Duquesne. Nearly 1,000 British colonists are killed or wounded, and General Braddock sustains mortal wounds.

Massachusetts offers 40 pounds for the scalp of a hostile male Indian over 12 years of age, 25 pounds for the scalp of a hostile female Indian over 12, and 20 pounds for the scalp of any hostile Indians less than 12 years of age. This offer is made for the scalps of Indians allied with the French during the heat of war between the French and British.

1755–1756

POLI. The Iroquois League is persuaded to break its neutrality and side with England against France.

1757

WARS. Fort William Henry, on Lake George in what is now New York state, is attacked and captured by a force of 6,000 French soldiers and 2,000 Indian warriors during the French and Indian War (1754–1763).

1758

LAND. The Brotherton Reservation is one of the first Indian reservations in North America, established by the New Jersey colonial assembly in Burlington County. First called Edge Pillock, the 3,000-acre tract is settled by about 100 Indians, mostly of the Unami tribe. With American

independence, it will become the first state Indian reservation. (In 1638, the English had established the first Indian reservation, compelling the Wappinger Indians of present-day Connecticut to cede most of their territory and to live on just 1,200 acres.)

WARS. The Spanish and Apache mission of San Saba in Texas is attacked by 2,000 Comanches and other Indians. The following year the Spanish make a retaliatory raid but are turned back by a force of 6,000 Plains Indians.

C. 1760

ANIM. The Cheyenne and other Plains Indian tribes obtain horses. This enables them to live as nomadic hunters who follow buffalo and other wild game.

1760

WARS. On September 9, Montreal is overtaken by the British, forcing the French to surrender. This effectively ends the French and Indian War, although the official peace will not be concluded until 1763.

1760–1761

WARS. The Cherokee War on the Carolina frontier flares up over continuing treaty violations by English colonists. In August, the Cherokee destroy the British Fort Loudoun on the Little Tennessee River after a dispute with the governor of South Carolina. The British retaliate by sending a force of 2,600 soldiers to burn and destroy Cherokee towns. After a peace agreement is signed in 1763, white settlers will pour into Cherokee lands in Kentucky and Tennessee.

1761–1766

WARS. Aleut people revolt against Russian abuses in Alaska. On the Aleutian island of Umnak, Aleuts attack a group of Russian traders in 1761 who have tried to force Aleut men to hunt for them by taking their Aleut women and children as hostages. This cruel practice by the Russian traders is met with force by the Aleut men, who continue a series of raids and attacks on traders and their ships for the next five years.

1762

RELI. The Delaware Prophet, a religious leader named Neolin of the Lenni Lenape, begins preaching a rejection of the white man's ways and culture and a return to traditional Indian ways. As the movement spreads through the Ohio Valley and eastern Great Lakes area, the Ottawa chief Pontiac uses its force to advance his efforts to drive the white man from the region.

1763

HEAL. In June, British soldiers at Fort Pitt (present-day Pittsburgh) give Indians blankets that had belonged to smallpox victims, spreading smallpox through the Lenni Lenape (Delaware) and Shawnee village, killing much of their population. This idea of biological warfare is the work of Sir Jeffery Amherst, the command-in-chief of the British colonies, who suggested the idea in a letter to an officer at the fort.

LAWS. King George III signs a proclamation banning settlements west of the Appalachians and establishing a protected Indian Country there. The proclamation is highly unpopular with the American colonists and most settlers ignore the boundary line. Britain's attempt to enforce the proclamation contributes to the American Revolution.

MIGR. Around 350 Calusa Indians who had resisted British encroachments into Florida are forced to migrate to Cuba when the British gain control of the area.

TREA. The French and Indian War ends with a British victory after nine years with the signing of the *Treaty of Paris* on February 10. In the agreement, France cedes New France to England, and Spain receives the Louisiana Territory. Great Britain wins claim to all lands from Canada to Florida and from the Atlantic Ocean to the Mississippi River. Most of the Indians in the Northeast and Midwest had sided with the French, whose policies were much more accommodating to Indians than those of the British.

WARS. Pontiac's War (or Pontiac's Rebellion) threatens British control of the Great Lakes region

and the Ohio River Valley. Pontiac, chief of the Ottawa, forges an alliance of Indian tribes including the Lenni Lenape (Delaware), Ottawa, Wyandot, Potawatomi, Ojibwe (Chippewa), and Seneca. On May 9, they attack and capture all the British forts west of Fort Niagara and the Appalachian Mountains, with the exception of Fort Detroit and Fort Pitt (Pittsburgh). Pontiac's warriors besiege Detroit for six months but lift the siege when the Indians learn that their French allies have already capitulated to the British. During August 4–5, British troops defeat Pontiac's forces near Fort Pitt in the Battle of Bushy Run. On September 14, Pontiac's warriors ambush an English wagon train delivering supplies for Fort Niagara. This conflict becomes known as the Battle of Devil's Hole Road and is the greatest Indian victory of Pontiac's War. Pontiac sees support for his Indian confederacy running out and will sign a peace accord with the British at Detroit on August 17, 1765. Pontiac will be killed in 1769 by a Kaskaskia Indian in Illinois.

A notorious event of Pontiac's War occurs when Ojibwe (Chippewa) Indians stage a surprise attack during a lacrosse game outside Ft. Michilimackinac, Michigan on June 4, 1763, between two large teams of Indians. One account states that British garrison troops gathered outside the fort to watch the game, and the Indians suddenly attacked them and burned the fort to the ground. Another account states that during the lacrosse game, a player tossed the ball into the fort, and several Indians rushed in to ostensibly retrieve the ball, but instead pulled guns on the British, killing the commander and taking several soldiers hostage.

The Paxton Riots in western Pennsylvania come in response to Indian raids. A group of 57 frontier vigilantes known as the Paxton Boys attack and kill six peaceful Conestoga (Susquehannock) Mission Indians on December 27 near Lancaster, Pennsylvania, in retaliation for the Indian raids in Pennsylvania. The last 14 of the Conestoga Indians are placed in the Lancaster jail for protective custody, but they are also attacked two weeks later by the Paxton Boys and killed. These were the last of the Conestoga tribe, which had numbered more than 3,000 until their numbers were reduced in the seventeenth century by war with the Iroquois Confederacy.

1764

WARS. Bounties are offered for enemy Indian scalps by various white colonies. The Pennsylvania Assembly offers a bounty for every enemy Indian above 10 years of age.

1765

POLI. The Reserve system in Canada begins with the provision of a tract of land for the Maliseet tribe.

WARS. Pontiac's War officially ends on July 23, ending organized Indian resistance to British settlement in the Ohio River valley.

1766

POLI. Catherine the Great of Russia declares that the Aleutian Island peoples and natives of Alaska are Russian subjects who can be taxed by the Russian government. She decrees that the indigenous peoples, as Russian subjects, should also be treated well.

WARS. Russian traders launch assaults against Aleut villages. The Aleuts had fought back against the traders by attacking their ships. Russian mercenaries shell the Aleut homes with cannons from ships and execute or enslave all they can capture, greatly reducing the Aleut population.

1767–1775

EXPL. Daniel Boone explores the wilderness areas of Tennessee and Kentucky, including the Cumberland Gap in the Appalachians.

1768

TREA. Cherokee Indian claims to land west of a line running through the Blue Ridge Mountains of Virginia to a point on the Ohio River are recognized by the *Treaty of Hard Labor* signed on October 13 in the colony of South Carolina concluded between the British and the Indians. When the colony of Virginia points out that white settlers are already occupying Cherokee lands west of the boundary, the line is moved six miles west by the *Treaty of Lochaber* in 1770.

The *Treaty of Fort Stanwix,* signed on November 5, confirms the cession of Iroquois lands between the Ohio and Tennessee rivers to the British Crown. The British compel the Iroquois to grant them this first major cession of land west of the Appalachians since the *Proclamation of 1763,* which reserved the land in this region exclusively for Indians. The second *Treaty of Fort Stanwix* will be signed in 1784.

1769

EDUC. Dartmouth College is founded in Hanover, New Hampshire, as a school for Indians. However, the emphasis will soon change to teaching English students. Only nine Indians will graduate from the college over the next 200 years.

RELI. The first California mission is established in San Diego. Gaspar de Portolá, 46, governor of Baja California, leads a party north from New Spain (Mexico) to California, claiming California for Spain and establishing the mission system under Father Junipero Serra, 56, a Franciscan priest. Mission San Diego de Alcalá is the first of 21 California Franciscan missions. Portola's group then travels on to Monterey to establish the second mission. The missions will change the tribes of California forever with this clash of cultures. The use of Indians by the Franciscans in a form of enslavement, forced religious conversions, and the introduction of European diseases devastates the traditional social structures and lifestyles of California tribes.

WARS. The Ottawa chief Pontiac is murdered on April 20 by another Indian in the village of Cahokia, Illinois. Rumors are that the British had him killed to prevent any repetition of the 1763–1766 rebellion.

1770

ARTS. The first "cigar store Indian" is displayed in North America. A large sculpture in a tobacco shop in Pennsylvania is used to advertise cigars. These become popular in Europe depicting stereotypical chiefs or squaws.

Regarding the fate of the Mission Indians in California by 1874: "Generally throughout the country they gain a precarious living by wandering about in search of employment; they pick grapes, herd and wash sheep, chop wood, and do ordinary menial service. In the vicinity of towns the women give themselves up to prostitution. . .which is soon ended by disease and drunkenness. . .they have become outcasts. . .they lost their traditional and customary rights, and had become trespassers in the land, vagrants, and troublesome neighbors to the whites" (Wetmore 1875, 5).

POPU. The Creek Indian Confederacy of the present-day southeastern United States reaches the peak of its power. Numbering around 20,000 people in about 60 towns and villages, they are courted at various times by the Spanish, French, British, and American governments.

WARS. Crispus Attucks, a leader among the Boston patriots, and four others are killed by the British in Boston on March 5 during a protest against taxation. They are the first casualties in the American struggle for independence. Attucks had a Massachuset Indian mother and a black father.

The Beothuk and Micmac Indians of the region of Newfoundland, Canada, fight each other until the Beothuk are gradually exterminated by the Micmac who have a greater population. The Micmac also receive a reward from the French for every Beothuk killed.

1770–1804

TRAD. Grand Portage, Minnesota, develops into the western fur-trading capital of the British Empire in North America. Fur trading continues to be the main source of commerce in Minnesota through the early nineteenth century.

1771

EXPL. Captain James Cook (British) completes his first voyage around the world.

1773

POLI. The Boston Tea Party takes place. Colonists in Boston protest British taxes and manipulation of the tea market in the American colonies by dressing as Mohawk Indians and dumping 10,000 pounds worth of tea into the harbor.

1774

CONT. Juan Francisco la Bodega y Quadra (Spanish) anchors his ship near today's Point Greenville, Washington, on July 14. He sends a party ashore to obtain fresh water and firewood when around 300 Indians attack and kill the Spanish party. Bodega then sails north into Alaskan waters, discovering Bucareli Sound and claiming the coast for Spain.

EDUC. The education of Indian youth at Dartmouth College, New Hampshire, is supported by a $500 appropriation of the American Continental Congress on July 12. The amount will be raised to $5,000 later. Dartmouth was an outgrowth of Moor's Indian Charity School founded in Connecticut in 1754 for the purpose of providing a free school where Indian and white children could be educated together.

EXPL. Daniel Boone leads a party of settlers into Kentucky. Boone leads a party of 30 westward from North Carolina and blazes the 300-mile Wilderness Road across the Appalachians, through the Cumberland Gap, and into Cherokee lands. Boone is employed by the Transylvania Land Company of North Carolina and negotiates a sale of land from the Cherokee that covers all the land between the Kentucky River and the Cumberland Valley, including the Cumberland Gap, a total of about 20 million acres. In the *Treaty of Sycamore Shoals* the company pays the Cherokee 10,000 pounds of merchandise on March 17. Many Cherokees are unhappy about the sale and attempt in vain to regain their lands when the American Revolution breaks out the following year. Over the next 15 years about 100,000 white settlers will travel along the Wilderness Road and settle in this region in defiance of the *Proclamation of 1763*.

POLI. The first American Continental Congress establishes the position of commissioner of Indian affairs and allocates funds to deal with negotiations with tribes.

WARS. Lord Dunmore's War is fought in Virginia between settlers and Shawnees and Mingo (a band of Iroquois). The Virginia governor (the earl of Dunmore) takes Shawnee and Ottawa land in western Pennsylvania as part of his colony, which precipitates the war. The area was protected for the Shawnee by the *Treaty of Fort* Stanwix and the *Proclamation of 1763,* which prohibited white settlement west of the Appalachian Mountains. Tensions between Indians and squatters on the land leads to violence when a group of settlers kill five Mingo Indians on April 30, leading to revenge. On October 9, the Battle of Point Pleasant occurs between Lord Dunmore's army at the Shawnee villages near present-day Chillicothe, Ohio. On October 10, the Indians are defeated by Virginia troops and forced to give up their hunting rights in Kentucky, and also to grant the colonists access to the navigation rights on the Ohio River.

1775

POLI. The Second Continental Congress creates three departments of Indian affairs—northern, middle, and southern. It appoints 11 commissioners, including Benjamin Franklin and Patrick Henry, to staff these departments and preserve the peace.

The Tammany Society (or the Sons of King Tammany) is formed in Philadelphia with influential members such as Thomas Jefferson, James Madison, and Benjamin Franklin. The organization celebrates American culture as the blending of the best of Indian and European societies. The society is named after Tamanend, a Delaware Indian chief who established friendly relations with William Penn.

As the American Revolution approaches, the Americans meet at German Flats, New York, in

August with the Six Nations Iroquois tribes to persuade them to remain neutral and not fight on the side of the English. In November, however, Joseph Brant, a Mohawk leader and secretary to Superintendent of Indian affairs Guy Johnson, travels to London and meets with King George III, who convinces Brant that the Iroquois should join the British in a victory over the Americans.

PUBL. The *History of the American Indians,* a book published by James Adair, will later become an important source for anthropologists on the tribes of the Southeast. Adair spent many years living among the Chickasaw, and in his book praises the character of the Indians and condemns colonial officials who have dealt incompetently with Indians.

TREA. Lord Dunmore's War formally ends with the *Treaty of Camp Charlotte*. The Shawnee promise to remain north of the Ohio River, giving up their hunting grounds in Kentucky. Soon, the Shawnee will violate this part of the treaty, and will ally themselves with the British in 1777.

1775–1783

WARS. The Indian tribes of eastern North America are drawn into the American Revolution, primarily on the side of the British. The Indians believe that an American victory will result in more settlers moving onto their lands. The Oneida Indians are the largest group to support the American cause.

1776

MIGR. A division occurs among the Hidatsa Indians living along the Missouri River in the Dakota region. One band migrates to the Rocky Mountain region where they will become known as the Crow Indians.

RELI. The Spanish, under Juan Bautista de Anza, establish a mission at San Francisco, California.

WARS. The American Revolution begins. One of the offenses of King George III, as noted in the American Declaration of Independence of July 4th, is the British stirring up the Indians against the American colonists. Initially, the colonists and the British sought guarantees of neutrality from Indian tribes, not trusting armed warriors to attack only the enemy. But, with the prospect of thousands of Indians fighting on their side, Indian tribes are pressured by the American colonists and by the British to join their ranks. Tribes try to determine on whose side to fight based on their sense of which group poses the lesser threat to them. Most of the Iroquois side with the English, but the Oneida and Tuscarora become allies of the colonists. In August, 1777, the Mohawk will join the British in a battle at Fort Stanwix, near present-day Rome, New York, against the Americans and the Tuscarora and Oneida, fellow Iroquois Confederacy tribes. At the end of the war, all tribes will be treated as defeated enemies and their lands will be viewed as rewards for victory.

Cherokee leader Dragging Canoe attacks settlers on his tribe's lands.

1777

POLI. The *Articles of Confederation* establish the first national government of the United States. The document defines federal and state relationships, and assumes that Indian tribes are sovereign nations. It is accepted in principle that the central government, and not the states, should regulate Indian affairs and trade. The *Articles* will be ratified by Congress in 1781.

1778

EXPL. British navigator James Cook arrives in the Pacific Northwest in search of a Northwest Passage, a presumed water route between the Atlantic and Pacific Oceans. He anchors off Vancouver Island, and trades for sea otter pelts in Nootka Sound. On the basis of this exploration, England will claim lands in what is today Oregon, Washington, Idaho, and parts of Montana and Wyoming.

Fur trader Peter Pond explores the Canadian Plains and Rocky Mountains country.

FOOD. When George Washington's troops are suffering through the bitter winter at Valley Forge, Pennsylvania, at the American Army's headquarters, Oneida leader Skenandoah brings relief to

the troops by delivering 300 bushels of corn. Washington later shows his appreciation by naming Virginia's Shenandoah Valley after him.

TREA. The Delaware Treaty, signed on September 17, is the first Indian treaty made by the United States. It is negotiated at Fort Pitt (Pittsburgh) between the United States and the Lenni Lenape (Delaware) Indians, and includes the possibility of the formation of an Indian state with representation in Congress. In return for the Delaware's allegiance during the American Revolution, the treaty holds open the provision that Lenni Lenape territory could enter the Union as the fourteenth state (but it does not materialize). There will be 370 treaties signed with Indian nations between 1778 and 1871, when treaty-making will end.

WARS. In spring, a series of Indian attacks drive settlers out of most of Kentucky. In one attack, Daniel Boone is captured and taken to the Shawnee village of Chillicothe. After three months, he escapes and rushes to the fort at Boonesboro to warn the settlers that the Shawnee are coming to attack and assists in the defense of the settlement.

In April, the Cherokee settlements along the Chickamauga Creek, in present-day Tennessee, are attacked by 600 troops and destroyed.

Iroquois Indians and British forces under Mohawk Joseph Brant attack and massacre American settlers on the western New York and Pennsylvania frontiers (Wyoming Valley and Cherry Valley massacres).

1779

ARCH. The remains of the ancient Indian city of Cahokia are discovered near the confluence of the Missouri and Mississippi Rivers. Cahokia had a population of around 20,000, making it the largest urban center north of Mexico before the Europeans arrived. The city had more than 100 mounds, including the large Monks Mound, a monumental structure whose base is larger than that of the Great Pyramid of Egypt.

HEAL. A smallpox epidemic decimates the Cree and Chipewyan Indian tribes in the Lake Athabasca region of Canada.

WARS. The Americans launch a counteroffensive to the 1778 Iroquois and British attacks on American settlers in New York and Pennsylvania. Under Gen. John Sullivan of the Continental Army, about 4,000 American troops attack the Tories and their Iroquois allies in New York's Genesee Valley, laying waste to Indian towns and crops and breaking the power of the Iroquois League. The Iroquois Confederacy never recovers from the blow. The Americans go on to defeat the British in the Battle of Newtown.

On July 10, American troops attack and burn Chillicothe, one of the Shawnee's most significant villages. In the following year, another attack by American troops destroys what is left of the village.

Captain James Cook (British) is killed by Hawaiian natives, cutting short his search for a Northwest Passage.

C. 1780

ARTS. Great Lakes Indians develop a ribbonwork style of dress, using European materials. The craft spreads southward and westward.

1780

CONT. The British visit the Nez Percé village west of the Bitterroots.

1780–1782

HEAL. Smallpox spreads north from Mexico to the Great Plains, wiping out thousands of Cree, Assiniboine, Chipewyan, Gros Ventre, and Shoshone.

1780–1800

HEAL. Smallpox and measles spreads among the Indians in Texas and New Mexico, decimating tribes.

1781

WARS. The Yuma Uprising breaks out under Palma. The Quechan Indians (or Yuma Indians) of present-day southwestern Arizona and southeastern California, rebel against the domineering Spanish, killing about 75 soldiers, settlers, and priests and destroying two missions. This revolt greatly hinders Spanish colonization along the lower Colorado River, cutting off the primary land route between Alta California and Mexico.

1782

WARS. About 90 unarmed Christian Lenni Lenape (Moravian/Delaware) Indians are massacred in March by a group of Kentucky frontiersmen at Gnadenhutten, Ohio. When Mohawk war leader Joseph Brant fails to persuade the Indians to assist his forces in raiding white settlements in western Pennsylvania, they are advised to leave the area. After they decide to stay, they are attacked by American troops who execute the Indian women and men by striking them in the head with mallets. This becomes known as the Gnadenhutten Massacre.

The Kentucky militia suffers one of their worst defeats in Kentucky on August 19 when they are ambushed at Blue Licks Springs, losing approximately 100 soldiers.

A Lenni Lenape (Delaware) chief spoke to David Heckewelder, a Moravian missionary, on the Gnadenhutten Massacre of 1782: "White men would be always telling us of their great Book which God had given them. They would persuade us that every man was bad who did not believe in it. They told us a great many things which they said was written in the Book; and wanted us to believe it. We would likely have done so, if we had seen them practice what they pretended to believe—and acted according to the good words which they told us. But no! While they hold the Big Book in one hand, in the other they held murderous weapons—guns and swords—wherewith to kill us poor Indians. Ah! And they did too. They killed those who believed in their Book as well as those who did not. They made no distinctions" (MacLeod 1928, 516).

1782–1783

HEAL. A smallpox epidemic hits the Sanpoil Indians of Washington and other Plateau tribes.

1783

LAND. The Mohawk Indian chief Joseph Brant (Thayendanegea), who had fought on the side of the British during the American War of Independence, leads a group of his people to Ontario, Canada, where they are given a tract of land to settle that is six miles wide on each side of the Grand River. Brant and his followers will found the present-day town of Brantford, with more than 2,000 Indians moving to the Grand River settlement.

LAWS. The Continental Congress issues a proclamation warning against white squatters on Indian lands. Also, the purchase or receipt of any gift or cession of land from the Indians by a private person without the permission of the U.S. Congress is prohibited. This ends such transactions as the 1775 purchase of Cherokee land by the Transylvania Land Company of North Carolina.

TREA. The *Treaty of Paris* ends the American Revolution. England cedes its lands from the Appalachian Mountains to the Mississippi River to the United States. The United States will now ignore the British *Proclamation of 1763* which prohibited white settlement in the area, and will open the ceded region to the many land-hungry settlers.

1784

POLI. Congress orders the War Office to provide militia troops to assist commissioners in their negotiations with Indians. In 1786, the Secretary of War will be made responsible for Indian Affairs. In 1789, Congress will establish a Department of War and formally grant the Secretary of War authority over Indian affairs.

SETT. A Russian settlement is established at Kodiak off the southern coast of Alaska. The settlement of Three Saints is the first permanent non-Indian settlement in Alaska. Aleut hunters begin offering furs to Russian traders and the Russians will dominate the fur trade in the region, brutally exploiting the indigenous population.

TRAD. The North West Company is chartered in Montreal to compete with its greatest competitor, the Hudson's Bay Company. The North West Company joins English, Scottish, and American merchants who will explore uncharted areas in western Canada and establish trade with Indians in that region. The two companies will merge in 1821.

TREA. In June, the Creek Indians sign the *Treaty of Pensacola* with the Spanish, in which the Spanish agree to protect Creek lands in Florida and to allow the Indians to import guns and other goods.

Representatives from the Iroquois Confederacy (Six Nations) meet with U.S. government officials at Fort Stanwix, near present-day Rome, New York. They are informed that as former British subjects and sympathizers they lose their land with the treaty that ended the American Revolution. The Iroquois are forced to sign the *Treaty of Fort Stanwix* (the second treaty with this name), which cedes their lands west of Pennsylvania and New York in exchange for peace with the United States. The Iroquois are only granted the New York lands they are occupying, which angers many Iroquois.

1785

LAND. On May 20, the *Land Ordinance* is passed by the Confederation Congress which provides a means of distributing public domain land in the Old Northwest. Land will be divided into townships and lots and sold by auction for a minimum of one dollar per acre, accelerating the settlement of whites in the present states of Ohio, Indiana, Illinois, Michigan, and Wisconsin. In 1787, the Confederation Congress will pass the *Northwest Ordinance* for governing the Old Northwest.

LAWS. The Assembly of Virginia defines any person with one-quarter African-American ancestry as a mulatto, and Indians with this mixture are no longer legally considered to be Indians and are

Cornplanter, the Seneca, spoke before President George Washington in 1790, six years after the Treaty of Fort Stanwix. Once more, he feared the prospect of having to cede land: "When your army entered the country of the Six Nations, we called you *Caunotau-carius,* the Town Destroyer; and to this day when that name is heard, our women look behind them and turn pale, and our children cling to the knees of their mothers. Our councilors and warriors are men and cannot be afraid; but their hearts are grieved with the fears of their women and children, and desire that it may be buried so deep as to be heard no more. When you have us peace, we called you father, because you promised to secure us in possession of our lands. Do this, and so long as the lands shall remain, the beloved name will remain in the heart of every Seneca" (Beauchamp 1913, 137).

denied all rights and privileges accorded Indian status.

RELI. The Christian Indian settlement known as Brothertown is established on Oneida land in central New York by Samson Occom, a Mohegan, who conceives of a haven where Christian Indians can retreat from the corruption of white settlers.

TREA. Under the *Treaty of Hopewell,* concluded on November 28 at Hopewell, South Carolina, the Cherokee are placed under the protection of the United States. The treaty promises to order American settlers out of the tribe's lands and to permit the Cherokee to send a deputy of their choice to the U.S. Congress. However, little will be done to limit the rush of whites settling in Cherokee lands.

WARS. An Indian uprising occurs at the San Gabriel Mission, near present-day Los Angeles, California, under the leadership of Toypurina, a Gabrieleño medicine woman. Six villages of Indians organize an attack against Spanish priests and soldiers, but the Indians are stopped and arrested.

1786

POLI. The Secretary of War is given responsibility for Indian affairs, with a northern and a southern department. In 1789, Congress will create the Department of War, formalizing the Secretary of War's responsibilities regarding Indians.

New Mexico governor Juan Bautista de Anza makes peace with the Comanches.

TREA. As a result of the *Treaty of Hopewell,* official relations are established between Choctaw and Chickasaw Nations and the United States, and boundaries are set for each tribe.

1787

LAND. The *Northwest Ordinance* plan is laid out by the U.S. Congress for the settlement of the Northwest Territory (or Old Northwest) and its division into states (Ohio, Indiana, Michigan, Wisconsin, and Illinois). Indian tribes of the Northwest had been concerned for several years with treaties ceding most of their Ohio lands. The *Northwest Ordinance* sets guidelines for the development of the Old Northwest which will lead to increased white settlement. But, it also calls for Indian rights, the establishment of reservations, and the sanctity of tribal lands. This reinforces the British *Proclamation of 1763*.

1788

HEAL. A smallpox epidemic virtually wipes out Pecos Pueblo in New Mexico, with survivors relocating to Jemez Pueblo.

LAWS. The new *U.S. Constitution* is ratified, superseding the *Articles of Confederation*. This is the blueprint for the government of the United States, which gives the federal government, and not the states, sole power to regulate commerce with Indian tribes and foreign nations. This will lead to a series of Indian Trade and Intercourse Acts in the next several years. In the following year, George Washington will argue that the Senate should have to ratify all Indian treaties.

1789

POLI. The first U.S. Congress establishes a Department of War and grants the Secretary of War authority over Indian affairs. Congress appropriates $20,000 for negotiating and making treaties with Indian tribes. A separate bureau for the administration of Indian affairs will be established within the War Department 35 years later, in 1824.

WARS. The French Revolution begins.

1789–1793

EXPL. Alexander Mackenzie (British, sponsored by the North West Company), while seeking a northern river route to the Pacific Ocean, discovers the river now bearing his name during his journey in western Canada and Alaska. He meets with Kutchin Indians along the way. On a second expedition, he completes the first overland journey across North America north of Mexico, making contact with many tribes.

1790

LAWS. The *Indian Nonintercourse Act* passed by Congress forbids taking of lands from Indian tribes without congressional approval beginning in 1791. However, certain states such as Maine and Massachusetts will continue to take Indian lands without such approval. The act also intends to help maintain peace between Indians and traders and regulates the fur trade.

TREA. Spain signs the *Nootka Convention,* ceding the Pacific Northwest to England and the United States, and granting England the right to trade along the coast of the Pacific Northwest.

Creek leaders sign the *Treaty of New York,* ceding about 3 million acres of hunting territory to the United States. The U.S. government promises in return to protect the Creek from white settlements and invasion.

1790–1794

WARS. Little Turtle's War takes place during these years, involving the Miami, Shawnee, Potawatomi, Lenni Lenape, Ottawa, Wyandot, and Ojibwe (Chippewa) Indians living north of the Ohio River who continue to resist American settlement on their lands. In 1795, the Old Northwest tribes will sign the *Treaty of Fort Greenville,* ceding lands in Ohio.

1790–1799

LAWS. Four *Trade and Intercourse Acts* are passed regulating Indian commerce and creating the "factory system" of government trading houses. Under the system, all trading houses are government-owned, all agents are appointed by the President, and the agents' accounts are audited by the Secretary of the Treasury. The purpose of this system is to ensure that the Indians are supplied with necessary goods at a fair price and are given a fair price for their furs. The system will be abolished in 1822. An informal Indian Department within the War Department is responsible for enforcing these regulations. In 1802, a new *Trade and Intercourse Act,* a continuation of the four earlier acts, will become federal law.

1791

WARS. Little Turtle's War continues in the Old Northwest. On November 4, in the Battle of the Wabash, near the Miami River in Ohio, a combined force of Miami, Shawnee, Delaware, Ojibwe (Chippewa), Potawatomi, and Ottawa tribes, led by Chief Little Turtle (Michikinikwa), defeats Gen. Arthur St. Clair's American troops who lose around 630 men, with another 300 wounded in a three-hour battle. The Indians lose 23 warriors. This is the one of the worst defeats of American troops by Indians in U.S. history.

1791–1812

EXPL. David Thompson (1770–1857), Canadian geographer, explorer, and fur trader, ranks as the premiere surveyor of North America. Working for the Hudson's Bay Company (and later the North West Company), he explores and maps much of the Canadian and American West, encountering Piegan, Blackfoot, Assiniboine,

Mandan and other tribes. He marries a Métis woman, Charlotte Small, and has 13 children.

1792

EXPL. Robert Gray and William Broughton (U.S.) sail up the Columbia River.

1792–1795

EXPL. English explorer George Vancouver explores the Pacific Northwest.

1793

EXPL. Alexander Mackenzie, a Scottish fur trader, explorer, and employee of the North West Company, leads an overland journey that reaches the Pacific Ocean at Bella Coola. Mackenzie and his men are the first Europeans to cross the continent of North America and the first to have contact with many western tribes. This exploration will speed the fur trade in the West.

1793–1795

WARS. The Chickasaw and Creek Indians fight a war in the lower Mississippi Valley.

1794

EDUC. The first treaty to include education as a provision is made by the United States. with the Oneida, Tuscarora, and Stockbridge (Christian Mohegan Indians) of New York on December 2. The United States wants to show appreciation of the tribes' support during the American Revolution and offers compensation for property destroyed during the war, and also offers to build a gristmill and sawmill for their use. The United States agrees to hire one or two people for three years to instruct the Indians in the arts of the miller and the sawyer.

TREA. The *Jay Treaty* between Britain and the United States establishes a neutral commission to settle border disputes between the United States and Canada. The British agree to abandon trade and military posts on U.S. land between the Great Lakes and the Ohio River. The treaty restores trade between the United States and the British colonies of Canada, and guarantees

Mohawks and other Indians the right to travel freely between the United States and Canada. Also, normal goods such as furs that are transported by the Indians will not be subject to duty levied by either side.

WARS. In the Battle of Fallen Timbers in the Ohio River Valley on August 20, the Ottawa, Shawnee, and other Indians led by chiefs Blue Jacket and Tecumseh are defeated by approximately 4,000 U.S. Army troops. Hundreds of Indians are killed, destroying Little Turtle's confederacy and ending organized Indian resistance to whites north of the Ohio River. In the following year, the Indians must cede territory to the United States lost in this war.

The Arikara Indians engage in war with the Sioux and are driven from their villages on the Missouri River in the Nebraska area into the South Dakota region. They will return to an extensive agricultural economy.

1795

TREA. Ohio tribes sign the *Treaty of Geenville* at Fort Greenville, in present-day Ohio on August 3. Due to the Indians' losing in the Battle of Fallen Timbers in 1794, and the end of Little Turtle's War, the Shawnee, Lenni Lenape (Delaware), Ottawa, Wyandot, Ojibwe (Chippewa), Kickapoo, Potawatomi, Miami, Kaskakia, Eel River, Piankeshaw, and Wea tribes cede more than 25,000 square miles of land in eastern and southern Ohio and southeastern Indiana to the United States in exchange for $25,000 in goods and a $9,500 annuity. More than 1,000 Indians gather for the treaty, including Little Turtle. The Indians are allowed to keep a large territory of land along with a guarantee that the United States will prohibit white settlers on Indian land. However, the United States also gains title to 16 areas throughout these lands for the establishment of a chain of strategic forts, including Fort Dearborn (Chicago).

Under the *Pinckney Treaty,* Spain and the United States agree to keep their Indian allies along the Florida border from warring with each other, and agree not to make treaties of alliance with Indian tribes living within the territory of the other.

1796

LAND. The *Land Act* is passed by Congress allowing Americans to buy tracts of public domain land in the Northwest Territory for a minimum of two cents per acre. This encourages white settlement in the area that is now Ohio, Indiana, Illinois, Michigan, Wisconsin, and parts of Minnesota, displacing the Indians native to the region.

1797

HEAL. A smallpox epidemic spreads among the Indians of Mexico.

1797–1811

EXPL. David Thompson (formerly of the Hudson's Bay Company, and now with the North West Company) explores the Canadian and American West, traveling to Mandan villages and charting the headwaters of the Mississippi River.

1799

RELI. Handsome Lake, a Seneca Indian, founds the Longhouse Religion. After Handsome Lake wakes up from unconsciousness, he claims to have seen three visions which include instructions that will become known as the Code of Handsome Lake. His Code combines the traditional Iroquois religion with certain white values. He encourages his followers to work hard as farmers, value marriage and children, educate their children, build permanent homes, and shun alcohol and drunkenness as well as witchcraft, gambling, sexual promiscuity, selfishness, and vanity. Indians are also instructed to perform the Great Feather Dance, the Drum Dance, and other rituals of thanksgiving. The Code of Handsome Lake spreads throughout the Iroquois nations of Canada and the United States and into the late twentieth century. Handsome Lake will die in 1815, after 15 years of preaching his code.

TRAD. The Russian American Company is chartered, launching an aggressive policy of fur trading in the Aleutians and on the Northwest Coast.

19TH CENTURY

C. 1800

ARTS. Silverwork becomes widespread among the Indians of the Northeast, eventually reaching the Indians of the Southwest.

1800

ANIM. By this time most of the Indian tribes of the Columbia Basin region of the northwestern United States have acquired horses and begun to adapt their lifestyles around them.

LAND. France acquires Louisiana Territory from Spain.

LAWS. Congress passes the *Peace Preservation Act* to stop European settlers from inciting Indian attacks on the western frontier.

SOCI. At the beginning of the nineteenth century, the Cherokee Indians are the most unified of Indian groups in the southeastern United States, occupying 75 towns and villages in Georgia, Alabama, and Tennessee.

1802

EDUC. Congress appropriates funds to "civilize and educate" the Indians. The sum of money is not to exceed $15,000 a year.

LAND. Georgia cedes to the United States its claims to lands west of the present-day state boundary. In exchange, the federal government promises to relocate all Indians living within the state's borders. This agreement will lead to the Cherokee Trail of Tears in 1838, 36 years later.

LAWS. Federal law prohibits the sale of liquor to Indians. The law will remain in effect for nearly 150 years, but will not discourage traders from offering alcohol to Indians.

TRAD. A second *Trade and Intercourse Act* is passed by Congress to regulate Indian commerce and government trading houses. The first of these acts was passed in 1790.

WARS. Tlingits resist Russian incursions into their territory. The Tlingit Indians rise up against the Russian trading post and fort at Sitka, in southern Alaska, killing about 20 Russians and 130 Aleut working for them, and driving the others away. Two years later, the Russians will retake the fort and make Sitka the capital of Russian America.

1803

LAND. The Louisiana Purchase is completed by the United States from France under President Thomas Jefferson, extending U.S. control west of the Mississippi River. The purchase from France doubles the size of the United States, encompassing around 828,000 square miles bordered on the east by the Mississippi River, on the west by the Rocky Mountains, on the north by Canada, and on the south by the Gulf of Mexico. The land adds a large Indian population to the country. Jefferson views this region as a place where eastern Indians can be relocated, and white settlers can move onto the Indians' former lands. The *Louisiana Territory Act* will be passed next year, showing the intent of the United States to move eastern tribes west of the Mississippi River.

WARS. The Nez Percé and Shoshone Indians in Idaho begin fighting against each other. Soon, the Nez Percé will decisively defeat the Shoshone in battle due to their use of newly obtained guns against the bows and arrows of the Shoshone.

1803–1839

TRAD. The Blackfeet Indians resist fur traders along the upper Missouri River.

1804

LAND. A small group of Sac and Fox Indians without authority sign the *Treaty of St. Louis* with the United States, relinquishing sections of western Illinois, southern Wisconsin, and eastern Missouri for $2,000 in trade goods and a $1,000 annuity. The lands are rich in minerals and agricultural wealth. The Indians who signed the treaty believe this allows whites to hunt in their territory, and not that it cedes 50 million acres of land to the United States. Many Sac and Fox leaders who had no representatives at the conference, including Black Hawk, will denounce the treaty.

LAWS. The *Louisiana Territory Act* shows the intent of the United States to resettle eastern tribes west of the Mississippi.

1804–1806

EXPL. The Lewis and Clark expedition begins on May 14, 1804, down the Missouri River. The goal of the expedition is to determine whether the Gulf of Mexico and the Pacific Ocean are linked by a river system. In the absence of any such water connection they pioneer an overland route across the Rocky Mountains to the Pacific Ocean in present-day Oregon. The expedition also should strengthen American claims to the Oregon Territory, and gather information about Indian tribes living between the Mississippi River and the Pacific Ocean. The 35-man expedition is funded by Congress and headed by Capt. Meriwether Lewis, 29, and William Clark, 33. When Lewis and Clark spend the winter near the Hidatsa villages on the Knife River, in present-day North Dakota, they meet Sacagawea, a young Lemhi Shoshone Indian woman and her French-Canadian

husband. The couple, with Sacagawea carrying her infant baby, join the expedition in April 1805, to serve as interpreters. She helps guide the group up the Missouri River and through the Rocky Mountain passes of Montana and Wyoming to the land of the Shoshone people from whom she was taken at age 13.

Sacagawea (1786–1812?) was born into a Shoshone tribe in present-day Idaho. She was captured as a young girl by a group of rival Indians, the Hidatsa, and forced into slavery. The Hidatsa eventually sold her to Toussaint Charbonneau, a French Canadian fur trader, and she became one of his several Indian wives. She gave birth to a child, Jean Baptiste, and the family stayed for a time at Fort Mandan in North Dakota where Charbonneau and Sacagawea met Lewis and Clark who were preparing for their expedition. In April 1805, the couple agreed to accompany the expedition and serve as negotiators with tribes, with Charbonneau speaking French and Hidatsa, and Sacagawea speaking Hidatsa and Shoshone. Sacagawea was the only woman on the grueling journey, and she carried her infant son and gathered edible plants, berries, and roots. Her presence with her child sent a message to Indians that the expedition was a peaceful one. In August of 1805, the expedition encountered a large group of Shoshone Indians, and Sacagawea recognized their leader, Cameahwait, as her long-lost brother. After an emotional reunion, her brother supplied the group with several horses that were badly needed to assist the expedition across the Continental Divide. The Lewis and Clark expedition reached the Pacific in November 1805 when they located the point where the Columbia River empties into the Pacific Ocean, near present-day Astoria, Oregon. Sacagawea assisted the expedition on the way back with her knowledge of trails and landmarks. The group made it back to Fort Mandan in August 1806, where Sacagawea and her husband left the group. She gave birth six years later to a daughter named Lisette. There is controversy over what happened to Sacagawea after that. She may have died in 1812, or may have returned to her Shoshone people and lived a long life. William Clark legally adopted her two children and provided an education for Jean Baptiste in St. Louis. When Jean

Baptiste was around 18 years of age, he was sent to Europe with a German prince. Lisette, her daughter, may have died in childhood.

1805

EDUC. The Choctaw Indians of Mississippi establish a school which they pay for with annuity funds.

RELI. Tenskwatawa, a Shawnee Indian known as the Prophet (and brother of the great chief Tecumseh) comes out of the Ohio area preaching a return to the Indian way of life and religion and denouncing the white man's customs, dress, and use of alcohol. The Prophet attracts followers from many tribes who believe his promise of a return to a time when only the Indians will inhabit the land. News of the Shawnee Prophet spreads quickly and is used by Tecumseh as a focal point for gathering support for the establishment of an Indian nation of which he dreams. The spiritual attraction of the Prophet's doctrines and the statesmanship of Tecumseh will bring together the Indian tribes of the region in a stand against the white man, although an unsuccessful one, during 1809–1811.

A Lenni Lenape (Delaware) woman known as the Munsee Prophetess has a vision that the Lenni Lenape's Big House Religion must be reformed. This religious movement encourages their traditional ways and resists the adoption of non-Indian customs and Christianity.

1805–1807

EXPL. Zebulon Pike (sponsored by the United States) leads expeditions to the source of the Mississippi River and through the Rocky Mountains.

1805–1808

EXPL. Simon Fraser (Canada), sponsored by the North West Company, explores the river now bearing his name, and he becomes the first white man to visit the Carrier tribe.

1806

EXPL. On September 23, the Lewis and Clark Expedition returns to its original starting point at St. Louis, after nearly 28 months of exploration. The public, who believed the party was lost and had died, widely celebrate the event. The successful expedition encourages traders and trappers to move into this territory for the large beaver population.

TRAD. The Office of Indian Trade is established within the War Department to regulate the fur trade and oversee the federal employees of the government-run Indian trading houses.

The Russian-American Fur Company collects otter pelts in the area from Alaska down to Spanish California.

1807

EXPL. John Colter becomes the first explorer to enter the boundary of present-day Yellowstone National Park. Colter, part of the returning Lewis and Clark Expedition, met two trappers. The trappers persuaded the 35-year-old John Colter to join them in trapping on the Yellowstone River. Colter explored the surrounding area, discovering the area known today as Yellowstone National Park. Three years later, John Colter and John Potts will be captured by several hundred Blackfeet Indians. Potts will be killed while Colter will be stripped and told to run for his life (Colter's Run). His escape is a legendary epic of survival.

TRAD. The American Fur Company is chartered by John Astor to compete with the Canadian fur trade, establishing trading posts along the Lewis and Clark route. During 1811–1812, the Astorian overland western expedition, guided by Ioway Indian Marie Dorion, will establish trade relations with Indians. His company will become the most successful fur-trading operation in the country, and his traders will be the first white men to encounter many Indian groups in the West. By the time Astor dies in 1848, he will be the richest man in the United States.

1807–1808

TRAD. Manuel Lisa carries out the first American fur-trading expedition to the upper Missouri River.

1808

ARTS. On April 6, the first American theatre play about an Indian subject premiers in Philadelphia. James Nelson Barker's *The Indian Princess; or, La Belle Sauvage,* relates the story of Pocahontas as presented in John Smith's *General History of Virginia* (published in London in 1624).

RELI. Prophet's Town is established in western Ohio by the Shawnee brothers Tenskawatawa and Tecumseh. Thousands of Indians from the Ohio River valley and the Great Lakes region move here, drawn by the teachings of the Prophet, Tenskawatawa, and by the efforts of Tecumseh to form a confederacy of tribes to stop the sale of Indian land and resist further settlement of whites in the Indian lands.

TREA. A treaty signed on November 10 at Ft. Clark, Kansas, compels the Osage tribe to give up a large part of Missouri and northern Arkansas. Most the tribe's remaining lands, which include parts of Oklahoma, will be given up by treaties in 1825, 1839, and 1865.

1809

LANG. Sequoyah (1776–1843), a part-Cherokee Indian, begins work on the creation of a Cherokee alphabet. He will complete the task in 1821.

TRAD. The Missouri Fur Company (or the St. Louis Missouri Fur Company) is chartered by the Chouteau family and others.

TREA. The *Treaty of Fort Wayne,* negotiated on September 30 with the Lenni Lenape (Delaware), Potawatomi, Miami, Kickapoo, Wea, and Eel River tribes, cedes over 2 million acres of Indian land in Ohio and Indiana. Land along the Wabash River in present-day Indiana and Illinois will be sold to white settlers for about $10,000, or about two cents per acre. Part of the land belonged to the Shawnee, and their chief, Tecumseh, declares the transaction to be illegal and unethical. Tecumseh travels to the territorial capital where he confronts the Indiana governor, William Henry Harrison, who negotiated the treaty, and tells him that the Shawnee will not abide by the fraudulent treaty. In the summer of 1811, Tecumseh will seek the support of other tribes to oppose the whites.

1809–1811

WARS. Tecumseh's Rebellion attempts to unite tribes against the United States. The Shawnee chief Tecumseh, and his brother Tenskawatawa, the Prophet, endeavor to unite tribes of the Great Lakes, Ohio Valley, Mississippi Valley, and the Southeast against the United States. On November 7, 1811, a combined force of the Shawnee, Ojibwe (Chippewa), Miami, Kickapoo, Ottawa, Potawatomi, Sauk, and Fox Indians are defeated under the leadership of the Prophet (Tenskawatawa), at the Battle of Tippecanoe on the Wabash River in what is now Indiana, by a force of 1,000 soldiers and militiamen led by Indiana Territory governor William Henry Harrison. Chief Tecumseh was away at the time gathering support among the southern tribes for an Indian confederacy. Prophet's Town is destroyed, and Tenskawatawa is discredited by many of his followers. The defeat weakens Tecumseh's confederacy, and severely discourages his hopes of preventing the further westward flood of white settlers. However, on December 5, one of the most powerful earthquakes to ever occur in North America strikes in what is now southeastern Missouri. Many of the Creek Indians believe this was caused by Tecumseh, who had told them during the previous month that he would stomp the ground when he was safely home in Prophet's Town. This event convinces many Creek to become true believers in Tecumseh and his confederacy.

1810

LAND. The Supreme Court case of *Fletcher v. Peck* determines that a state can legally sell land occupied by Indians, whether or not the Indians approve of the sale.

TOOL. With the introduction of firearms to the Indians, the Sauk and Fox begin mining lead in southwestern Wisconsin. Shortly thereafter, white miners move into the mining area, driving the Indians out.

The Battle of Tippecanoe. Courtesy of Library of Congress.

1812

ENVI. An earthquake destroys the San Juan Capistrano mission in southern California, killing 40–50 Indians while they are attending Mass.

WARS. The Potawatomi Indians destroy the American-held Fort Dearborn on the Chicago River by Lake Michigan. The inhabitants and troops of the fort, including 12 children, are massacred on August 15 by the Indians while the whites are retreating to Fort Wayne.

1812–1813

WARS. A Georgia militia invades Spanish Florida after Seminole Indians offer to protect runaway slaves. At this time, Florida is still held by the Spanish, although there is a general feeling in the southern states that Florida should belong to the United States. Allegations of slave raiding and cattle rustling by the Seminoles instigates a unit of the Georgia militia to invade Seminole Indian territory in Florida. However, the Georgia unit is nearly annihilated. The following year, Tennessee volunteers raid and burn their way through Seminole villages in northern Florida for three weeks.

1812–1814

WARS. The War of 1812 takes place between the United States and Great Britain. The Shawnee, Dakota, Winnebago, and Ojibwe serve as allies of the British in the war. Tecumseh, the great Shawnee chief, serves as Brigadier General for the British, and his followers will fight alongside British in a series of battles hoping to stop the westward flood of American settlers. Tecumseh will be killed on October 5, 1813, in the Battle of the Thames near Chatman, Ontario.

1812–1841

TRAD. Russian traders maintain Fort Ross, near present-day Bodega Bay in northwestern California. The Pomo are native to this area and are treated brutally by the Russians during this time.

1813–1814

WARS. The Creek War (also called the Red Stick War) in the Southeast begins on July 27, 1813, when the Red Sticks (Upper Creek Indians) are attacked by militia troops at Burnt Corn Creek, a tributary of the Alabama River. Then, on August

30, 1813, Creek warriors attack Fort Mims, north of Mobile, Alabama, killing around 500 white inhabitants. This leads to the intervention of Gen. Andrew Jackson and his Tennessee militia and the outbreak of the Creek War. In the decisive Battle of Horseshoe Bend (Alabama) on March 27, 1814, Jackson's force of 5,000, including around 600 Cherokees, overwhelm nearly 1,000 Creek warriors, killing all but about 70. The surviving Creeks retreat to the villages of their Seminole relatives in Spanish Florida. The war ends in the *Treaty of Fort Jackson,* under Andrew Jackson, signed on August 9, 1814, which strips the Creek (Muskogee) Indians of about 2.3 million acres of their land in present-day Alabama and Georgia.

1814

TREA. The *Treaty of Ghent* ends the War of 1812. In the peace negotiations with the United States after the War of 1812, Britain attempts to have a buffer state created between the Great Lakes and the Ohio River for Indians to be free to inhabit. This proposal is vetoed by the United States, but the U.S. government does agree to a clause requiring that a separate peace treaty be signed with each tribe that was allied with Britain, and that those tribes will not be punished for their participation in the war. In 1815, the United States will make treaties with 19 Indian tribes of the Missouri River region as partial fulfillment of the articles of peace signed with the *Treaty of Ghent.*

1815

MIGR. A group of about 700 Lenni Lenape (Delaware) Indians leave the main group and move to the Brazos Valley of Texas where they live among the Caddo and Wichita Indians. In 1859, the three tribes will move to Indian Territory, near present-day Anadarko, Oklahoma.

RELI. Handsome Lake, the Seneca Indian religious leader, dies after 15 years of preaching his code.

TREA. A peace treaty is negotiated between the U.S. government and the Dakota Indian nation.

1815–1824

WARS. Pomo Indians in northern California resist the Spanish and Mexicans.

1815–1825

TREA. A series of treaties with tribes north of the Ohio River starts the removal of Indians west of the Mississippi.

1816

WARS. The Métis in the Red River Valley of Canada kill 19 Scottish settlers in a battle at Seven Oaks over farmland.

American troops under Andrew Jackson attack the Seminole settlement at Prospect Bluff in Spanish Florida. The attack will instigate a series of Seminole retaliatory raids on American settlements, leading to the First Seminole War.

1817

MIGR. Thousands of "Old Settler" Cherokee cede their lands in Georgia in exchange for lands west of the Mississippi River. These are the first Cherokee to leave their homeland due to pressures and harassment by white settlers.

WARS. The Patwin Indians resist the Spanish in California.

1817–1818

WARS. The First Seminole War is fought in the Southeast. Gen. Andrew Jackson invades Florida in a punitive expedition against the Seminole Indians. This results in the destruction of the Seminole villages and farms of northern Florida, and leads to the cession of Florida to the United States by Spain. The Second Seminole War will take place during 1835–1842, and the Third Seminole War will occur in 1855–1858.

1818

LAND. The state of Massachusetts buys land from the Penobscot Indians.

MIGR. Beginning this year, Chief Philip Bowles (also known as Bowl, Diwal'li, or Duwali;

1756–1839) leads Cherokees into present-day east Texas from their homelands in North Carolina. Bowles was born in North Carolina from a Scottish father and a full-blooded Cherokee mother. As the leader of a village at Little Hiwassee in western North Carolina, he led his band across the Mississippi River in early 1810 to the St. Francis River Valley near New Madrid, Missouri. In 1812–1813, his people moved into northwestern Arkansas, and in 1819 they will move to Nacogdoches, Texas. In Texas, Chief Bowles will become the civil chief or peace chief of a council that unites several Cherokee villages. In 1836, Sam Houston will negotiate a treaty with the east Texas Cherokee, guaranteeing the tribe possession of the lands they occupy. However, after the Texas Revolution, the treaty will be invalidated by the Senate of the Republic of Texas. This is when Bowles will ally himself with agents soliciting a Mexican reinvasion of Texas. As a result, Texas President Mirabeau B. Lamar will order Bowles and the Cherokees to leave Texas. In 1839, the Texas Rangers will go to war with the Texas Cherokees, nearly wiping out the tribe.

WARS. The Yokuts Uprising takes place under Chalpinich in central California against the Spanish.

1819

CONT. Col. Josiah Snelling begins construction of Fort St. Anthony on land purchased from the Dakota Indians for $2,000.

EDUC. Congress allocates money for the "civilization fund." Whites will be employed to teach Indians to farm and to establish schools for Indians to learn to read and write in English. Mainly used to finance schools set up by missionaries to convert Indians, the fund will contribute to 32 schools for Indian children during the next five years. The "civilization fund" will be repealed by Congress in 1873 for violating the separation of church and state.

LAND. Spain cedes Florida to the United States under fears that the region (present-day Florida and portions of Alabama and Georgia) will be under increasing attacks by U.S. forces. The Indians in Florida will be subject to removal by the U.S. government to lands in the West.

The Ojibwe (Chippewa) Indians cede a large part of their lands in the United States by the *Treaty of Saginaw*. The Ojibwe (Chippewa) lands will be further reduced by treaties in 1820, 1821, 1825, 1837, 1854, 1855, and 1863.

1819–1824

MIGR. Kickapoo bands in Illinois country under Kennekuk resist removal to lands in the West, defying the treaties of Edwardsville and Fort Harrison which call for their relocation.

1820

LAND. On October 18, the *Treaty of Doak's Stand* is signed between the Choctaw Nation and the United States. This requires the Choctaw to cede more than 5 million acres, much of the tribe's southeastern homeland, establishing new boundaries for the tribe. In 1830, the Choctaw will be forced to give up this land and move to a new reservation west of the Mississippi River.

1821

LANG. Sequoyah finishes the creation of a Cherokee syllabic alphabet with 85 letters. After 12 years of work, this alphabet enables the Cherokee people to have a written language. Sequoyah has taken the name George Guess from a U.S. trader he believes to be his father. He is probably the only person in human history to single-handedly invent an entire written language. Based on a combination of the Roman alphabet and other symbols, the letters represent all the vowel and consonant sounds in the Cherokee language. Sequoyah's "talking leaf" will be avidly learned and used by thousands of Cherokee people in a short time and make the Cherokee the first literate tribe. In 1824 and 1828, parts of the Bible will be printed in Cherokee, and in 1828, a weekly newspaper, *The Cherokee Phoenix,* will begin publication in Cherokee and English, becoming the first Native American newspaper. The Cherokee's use of a written language is at least partly responsible for their being viewed as the most "civilized" of eastern tribes.

POLI. Mexico wins its independence from Spain. In 1824, Mexico will adopt a constitution and

A portrait of Sequoyah, creator of the Cherokee syllabic alphabet, c. 1836. Courtesy of Library of Congress.

become a federal republic. Indians are granted citizenship rights.

TRAD. The Santa Fe Trail opens to international trade.

The Hudson's Bay Company and the North West Company, the two largest trading companies in North America, merge after 40 years of competing for furs and trade with Indians. The company continues with the Hudson's Bay name.

1822

EDUC. Henry Rowe Schoolcraft is appointed Indian agent and begins his ethnological research of Indians of the western Great Lakes region.

TRAD. The Office of Indian Trade and the Indian trading houses (the "factory system"), which was established in 1792, is abolished by Congress as a result of pressure from the fur trading companies and the inability of the trading houses to accommodate the growing demands for furs.

1823

LAND. The Seminole Indians give up their claim to the whole territory of Florida. Under the terms of the *Treaty of Moultrie Creek,* signed with the United States on September 18, the Seminoles will get a reservation of about 4 million acres as well as supplies, food, and other payments and annuities. The Indians have to agree not to welcome runaway slaves on the reservation. The reservation boundaries are set at least 20 miles from the coast in order to cut the Indians off from trade with Cuba, their source of ammunition and arms. In 1832, the *Treaty of Payne's Landing* will coerce the Seminoles into giving up these remaining Florida lands.

1824

POLI. Mexico is established as a federal republic.

The U.S. Bureau of Indian Affairs (BIA) is created within the War Department by Secretary of War John C. Calhoun. Thomas L. McKenney is appointed as the bureau's first head, charged with managing funds allocated for Indians, regulating Indian trade, and overseeing Indian schools. In 1832, the BIA will be formally recognized by a Congressional law.

PUBL. A widely-read Indian captivity story, *The Life of Mary Jemison,* is published in the United States. It tells of Mary Jemison's life among the Seneca for nearly 70 years after being taken captive in southwestern Pennsylvania during the French and Indian War. She was adopted into the tribe, had two Indian husbands, and chose not to return to white society when she later had the chance.

WARS. The Chumash Indian Uprising takes place against Mexicans in southern California under Pacomio.

1824–1825

EXPL. Expeditions backed by William Henry Ashley of the Rocky Mountain Fur Company explore the Missouri, Platte, and Green Rivers and develop the American fur trade.

1824–1834

RELI. During this time, most of the Aleuts of the Aleutian Islands and the northern part of the Alaska Peninsula are converted to Christianity by the Russian missionary Bishop Veniaminov.

1825

EDUC. The Choctaw Academy, a boarding school for Choctaw boys, is founded in Kentucky. This is the first school for Indians to learn farming and shop work as well as academic and religious instruction.

LAND. The *Treaty of Prairie du Chien* attempts to settle land disputes between the Dakota and Ojibwe tribes. For over 100 years, these tribes have fought over control of lands to the west of the Great Plains, and the conflict will continue for another 30 years after this treaty is made until the tribes are confined on reservations.

SOCI. French nobleman Alexis de Tocqueville writes *Democracy in America* after a nine-month tour of the United States. His observations become a classic commentary on American behavior and values, and he notes the continual displacement of Indians from their homelands by western expansion.

TREA. The *Treaty of Indian Springs* is signed on February 12 by William McIntosh, a leader of the Lower Creek tribe, in which most of the Creek's remaining land in the Southeast is ceded to the United States. Believing that the tribe's removal is inevitable, McIntosh and 50 other Lower Creek agree to sell the territory to obtain money for the removal. On May 31, a force of 170 Creek men will capture McIntosh and hang him for signing the treaty.

1825–1830

EXPL. Peter Skene Ogden explores the American and Canadian West for Hudson's Bay Company.

1825–1860

ARTS. Plays about Indians are popular on the U.S. stage during this time with more than 50 produced.

1826

PUBL. *The Last of the Mohicans* (fiction) by James Fenimore Cooper is published and becomes a popular novel in the United States and Europe. Based on the Battle of Lake George in the French and Indian War, Cooper's Indian characters are usually portrayed as either vicious killers or noble savages, enduring stereotypes.

1827

EXPL. Jedidiah Smith, fur trapper and adventurer, leads the first white expedition from what is today southern California to southern Oregon, encountering several violent Indian groups. Along the Colorado River the Mojave attack Smith and his men, killing 10 of the group. The survivors travel north and are attacked along Oregon's Umpqua River after one of Smith's men rapes an Indian woman. Only Smith and three other whites escape with their lives.

POLI. The Cherokee adopt a constitution formalizing the organization of its government that is patterned on that of the U.S. Constitution. Later, however, it will be nullified by the Georgia legislature.

PUBL. David Cusick, Tuscarora artist and doctor, publishes *Sketches of Ancient History of the Six Nations*, concerning Iroquois history and mythology.

RELI. Kennekuk (or Kanakuk), a religious prophet among the Kickapoo Indians of Illinois, encourages the Kickapoo to resist in a peaceful way the efforts of the whites to remove them from their lands. Kennekuk preaches against drunkenness, quarrels, and superstitions. He and his group of Kickapoos eventually will exchange their Illinois homes for lands in Kansas by the terms of a treaty in 1832.

WARS. The Winnebago (Ho-Chunk) Uprising takes place under Red Bird in Wisconsin. Conflict and killing occurs between the Winnebago Indians and white settlers and miners in Wisconsin between June 26 and September 27. The U.S. government threatens an all-out war against the Winnebago, but the violence ends with the arrest of the respected Indian warrior Red Bird.

1828

ENVI. The first major gold discovery in the western United States is made in the Ortiz Mountains south of Santa Fe, New Mexico.

LAWS. The Georgia legislature passes laws holding that the Cherokee are under Georgia legal jurisdiction, abolishing the powers of the Cherokee tribal government, and banning Cherokee from testifying against whites in court.

POLI. John Ross is elected the principal chief of the Cherokee. He will serve as principal chief for over 40 years, attempting to maintain Cherokee sovereignty.

Andrew Jackson is elected to the presidency of the United States. He receives overwhelming support from the South, being known as a war hero and Indian fighter. He sets forth his Indian policy right away, calling for federal legislation to formalize the removal of eastern Indians to lands west of the Mississippi River. This policy will lead to the *Indian Removal Act of 1830.*

PUBL. *The Cherokee Phoenix,* a bilingual weekly newspaper, begins publication in February, 1828, in New Echota, Georgia, edited by Elias Boudinot, a young, educated Cherokee. Stories are printed in English and Cherokee, using Sequoyah's syllabary. The newspaper becomes a powerful tool for presenting the Cherokee's opposition to white encroachment on their lands. It continues until 1834 when it is suppressed by the state of Georgia. After the Cherokee are removed to Indian Territory, the newspaper is replaced by the *Cherokee Advocate,* which begins publication in 1844 at Tahlequah, in present-day Oklahoma.

WARS. Stanislaus leads a rebellion of Mission Indians at the Santa Clara and San Jose missions in central California. An Indian convert, Stanislaus (Estanislao) escapes from the San Jose Mission where he has lived since childhood. Along with Cipriano, another disgruntled recent Christian convert, he organizes a revolt against the Spanish priests at the two missions. It takes three attempts by the Mexican army to subdue the revolt the following year. Later, Stanislaus is given sanctuary back at the San Jose Mission and is pardoned by Spanish authorities.

1829

DEAT. The last Beothuk Indian, Nancy Shawanahdit, dies in present-day Newfoundland, and the tribe becomes extinct.

ENVI. Gold is discovered in Cherokee territory and thousands of miners rush in. President Andrew Jackson removes all federal troops from the region, violating U.S. treaties to protect Cherokee lands from white encroachment.

PUBL. William Apess publishes *A Son of the Forest,* the first autobiography written by an Indian.

1830

LAWS. The *Indian Removal Act* is passed by Congress and is signed by President Andrew Jackson on May 28. The act provides for the general removal of Indian tribes in the east to lands west of the Mississippi River in Indian Territory. This act formalizes the removal policy of the federal government. The act is supported by government officials who want to open eastern Indian lands for white settlement, and by some reformers who believe the only way to protect Indians from whites is to resettle them away from homesteaders. Cherokees contest the act in court, and in 1832, the Supreme Court decides in their favor, but Andrew Jackson ignores the decision.

TREA. The *Treaty of Dancing Rabbit Creek,* signed September 15, cedes Choctaw lands east of the Mississippi to the United States in this first removal treaty negotiated by the U.S. government. The United States had earlier agreements with the Choctaw that the tribe would not be forced to leave its ancestral homes. Most Choctaw refuse to negotiate this treaty, but some do so, giving up more than 10 million acres of land in Alabama and Mississippi to the United States. As a tribe, the Choctaw had never warred

"The consequences of a speedy removal will be important to the United States. . .[it] will perhaps cause [the Indians] gradually. . .to cast off their savage habits and become an interesting, civilized, and Christian community." Andrew Jackson defending the removal policy in his first annual message to Congress (Jackson 1830).

against the United States and had even aided Gen. Andrew Jackson in his war against the Creeks. The Choctaw are given a reservation in the southeastern part of present-day Oklahoma, but they are not compensated for livestock, farm buildings, school houses, and other items they give up in their homeland. The move to Indian Territory takes nearly three years, and hundreds of the Choctaw die along the way.

1830–1833

HEAL. There are outbreaks of European diseases among tribes in California, Oregon, and British Columbia.

1831

LAWS. On March 18, the Supreme Court rules in *Cherokee Nation v. United States* that an Indian tribe may not sue in federal courts because the tribes are not foreign nations. Chief Justice John Marshall (1755–1835) holds that the Cherokees have no standing at court to appeal the state of Georgia's seizure of their lands. The Cherokee were attempting to stop the state of Georgia from applying its laws to tribal members. The suit was prompted by a series of abuses by the state including the case in 1830 *(Georgia v. Tassel)* where the state of Georgia executed a Cherokee convicted of murder before his case could be appealed.

WARS. Chief Black Hawk agrees to withdraw his tribe to lands west of the Mississippi after the Illinois militia is sent in June to destroy the Sac Indian village of Saukenuk, near present-day Rock Island, Illinois. The followers of Sac leader Black Hawk had refused to leave their village, defying the 1804 *Treaty of St. Louis,* in which some of the Sac and Fox relinquished their claims to all lands east of the Mississippi.

1832

ARTS. Self-taught American artist George Catlin (1796–1872) begins traveling west to paint Indians in their native lands. Over the next seven years Catlin will travel more than 1,800 miles and visit many tribes along the Missouri River, in the Great Lakes region, and on the southern Plains. He will produce hundreds of paintings and thousands of sketches and document ceremonies and customs of many of the Indians. His most enduring work, *The Manners, Customs, and Conditions of the North American Indians,* will be published in 1841. Much of our present-day knowledge about the habits and customs of American Indians comes from Catlin's journals and paintings.

EXPL. Henry Schoolcraft travels with his Ojibwe guide Ozawindib to find the source of the Mississippi River at Lake Itasca, Minnesota.

HEAL. Congress appropriates funds for vaccination of the Indians against smallpox.

LAND. The *Treaty of Payne's Landing* between the United States and the Seminole Indians, signed on May 9, provides for the removal of the Seminoles from Florida to Creek Indian lands in the West. This is subject to the approval of a delegation of 15 Seminole chiefs who will inspect the new lands. Plus, a payment of two cents per acre is to be paid for the 4 million acres given up. Controversy over the treaty erupts with some chiefs claiming they never signed it and others saying that they were forced to sign the treaty. This leads to the second Seminole War (1835–1842).

On March 24, the Creek Indians sign a treaty ceding their lands east of the Mississippi to the United States.

> "The tract of country over which we passed. . .is stocked, not only with buffaloes, but with numerous bands of wild horses. . . There is no other animal on the prairies so wild and so sagacious as the horse. . . We saw all the colours. . .Some were milk white, some jet black—others were sorrel, and bay, and cream colour—many were of an iron grey; and others were pied, containing a variety of colours on the same animal. Their manes were very profuse and hanging in the wildest confusion over their necks and faces—and their long tails swept the ground. . .The wild horse of these regions is small, but a very powerful animal. . .and undoubtedly, have sprung from a stock introduced by the Spaniards, at the time of the invasion of Mexico; which having strayed off upon the prairies, have run wild, and stocked the plains from this to Lake Winnepeg, two thousand miles to the North" (Catlin 1841, 57).

On October 14, the Chickasaw cede the last of their lands east of the Mississippi to the United States in the *Treaty of Pontotoc.*

LAWS. The U.S. Supreme Court rules on March 3 in the case of *Worcester v. Georgia* in favor of the Cherokees, stating that the Cherokee Nation constitutes a sovereign nation within the state of Georgia subject only to federal law. Chief Justice John Marshall writes that native nations have a degree of sovereignty that denies the state of Georgia the right to compel an oath of loyalty. This ruling establishes the basis for American Indian tribal sovereignty. Marshall defined Indian nations as "domestic dependent nations," and the laws of Georgia are contrary to the Constitution, laws, and treaties of the United States. The U.S. government has exclusive authority over tribal Indians and their lands within any state.

POLI. The Cherokee legal challenge to the *Indian Removal Act* (passed by Congress in 1830), requiring them to be relocated to lands west of the Mississippi, results in the Supreme Court ruling in favor of the Cherokees, but Andrew Jackson ignores the decision.

Ralph Waldo Emerson, the American poet and essayist, writes an emotional appeal to U.S. President Andrew Jackson against the removal of the Cherokee Nation of Georgia to lands west of the Mississippi.

The office of U.S. Commissioner of Indian Affairs is created by the U.S. Congress within the Department of War. Elbert Herring is appointed by President Andrew Jackson as the first Commissioner.

WARS. The Black Hawk War breaks out in Illinois during April to August. Black Hawk, the chief of the Sac and Fox Indians, engages in warfare with the Illinois militia. When the Sac and Fox returned from their winter hunt in 1831, they found their village on the Rock River in Illinois occupied by white squatters. The Indians moved across the Mississippi River to Iowa. In the spring of 1832, they return to Illinois, and the Illinois militia is called out to oppose the band of about 1,000 Indians, consisting primarily of women and children. Black Hawk and his group of Sac and Fox are pursued in the 4-month campaign through Illinois and Wisconsin by 8,000 militiamen and 150 regular army troops. Atrocities are committed on both sides, but the Indians are finally nearly annihilated on August 2, 1832, during the Battle of Bad Axe, near the Bad Axe River in Wisconsin Territory, where about 140 Indians are killed. Black Hawk takes refuge with the Winnebago at the village of Prairie du Chien to the north, but is soon captured. The survivors of the band return to Iowa where they are forced to cede 6 million acres in what is now the eastern portion of Iowa as punishment for the fighting.

1832–1842

MIGR. During this period, the Cherokee, Chickasaw, Choctaw, Creek, and Seminole, who

"Some of our chiefs make the claim that the land belongs to us. It is not what the Great Spirit told me. He told me that the land belongs to Him, that no people owns the land; that I was not to forget to tell this to the white people when I met them in council" (Radin 1927, 367). Kennekuk, addressing Gen. William Clark in 1827 at St. Louis, where he was called to calm down the Kickapoo who resented losing lands in south central Illinois.

will later become known as the Five Civilized Tribes, are forced to move from the Southeast to Indian Territory (present-day Oklahoma).

1833

EXPL. An expedition led by Alexander Philipp Maximilian begins exploring the American interior. This German prince and amateur anthropologist leads a two-year expedition up the Missouri River, taking along Karl Bodmer, a Swiss artist hired to document the exploration. Bodmer's detailed drawings and paintings reveal the life of western Indians before extended contact with non-Indians.

PUBL. Black Hawk, the Sac Indian leader, has his autobiography published, one of the first Indians to provide one through an interpreter.

RELI. The Kickapoo band, under spiritual leader Kennekuk (the Kickapoo Prophet), move from Illinois to present-day Kansas after years of resisting removal. Kennekuk will instruct his tribe in a new religious movement that teaches them to live peacefully with non-Indians while refusing to give up more of their lands.

WARS. A war party of Osage Indians attacks and destroys a Kiowa village in Oklahoma on Rainy Mountain Creek, north of the Wichita Mountains.

1834

LAWS. Congress passes the *Indian Country Crimes Act* which gives federal courts the responsibility of trying Indians accused of most criminal acts.

Congress passes the *Intercourse Act of 1834*, another law intended to protect Indians from ruthless traders. It gives Indian agents more power in determining who can trade with tribes, and also prohibits the use of alcohol in trade negotiations.

MIGR. Florida Seminoles are ordered to move west beginning on October 28 in accordance with a treaty signed on May 9, 1832.

POLI. Congress reorganizes the Indian Offices, creating the U.S. Department of Indian Affairs (still within the War Department) on June 30. The Department defines Indian Territory as lands west of the Mississippi River. The *Trade and Intercourse Act* redefines Indian Territory and the Permanent Indian Frontier, and gives the army the right to quarantine Indians.

RELI. Mexico secularizes the California missions. This ends the Mission Period in California with priests replaced by civil authorities as administrators of the missions. Indians are free to leave the missions, but are denied legal equality or legal title to lands.

WARS. The Mashpee Indians revolt against white interference in their colony on Cape Cod. Led by William Apess, a Pequot minister and writer, the tribe convinces the Massachusetts governor to recognize the tribe's right to control their own land.

1835

LAND. A small, unauthorized contingent of Cherokee men sign the *Cherokee Removal Treaty* (or the *Treaty of New Echota*), ceding all remaining lands east of the Mississippi River for $5 million, as well as 8 million acres of land in the West. Most of the Cherokee people protest the treaty, with Chief John Ross collecting more than 15,000 signatures on a petition requesting the U.S. Senate to withhold ratification. However, the petition fails to stop the treaty. The majority of the Cherokees are outraged by the treaty and vow to stay in their lands in the Southeast. The Cherokee leaders under Major Ridge who signed the treaty believed that removal was inevitable and further resistance was futile.

The Caddo Indians cede their lands in northwestern Louisiana for $80,000 in a treaty with the United States. They move to the Brazos River area of Texas where they become farmers and ranchers, building houses and sending their children to school. In 1859, however, white settlers will drive them out of Texas to Indian Territory (present-day Oklahoma), where they are provided a reservation in 1872.

POLI. Texas declares itself a republic independent from Mexico.

PUBL. The second Indian newspaper begins publication. The *Shawnee Sun,* a monthly newspaper printed in Shawnee using the English alphabet, is printed in present-day Kansas by the Shawnee Indians.

WARS. The Texas Rangers are organized to campaign against the Comanches.

1835–1843

WARS. The second Seminole War in Florida Territory is brought on by the pending relocation of the Seminoles to Indian Territory by the 1832 *Treaty of Payne's Landing* and other attempts to remove the Seminole from Florida. Led by Chiefs Osceola, Wild Cat, Alligator, and Aripeka, the Seminole fight a guerrilla war which costs the lives of around 1,500 U.S. troops and more than $20 million. It begins against the whites following the arrest and imprisonment of Osceola, 31, who thrusts his knife through the 1832 treaty that ceded Seminole lands to the United States. Osceola escapes, and with his braves kills a chief who signed the 1832 treaty and the U.S. Indian agent at Fort King. This begins years of guerrilla warfare against the U.S. forces while Seminole

women and children hide deep in the Everglades. In one engagement, Seminoles and their black slaves ambush and kill 101 men in a U.S. Army force of 102 men led by Major Francis Dade on December 28, 1835. In 1837, Osceola, the Seminole leader of the resistance, is captured and dies in prison in 1838. After five more years of swamp fighting and destruction of Indian villages the war finally ends, and most of the 5,000 Seminoles are removed to the west.

1836

CONT. Cynthia Ann Parker is captured by the Comanche during a raid by several hundred Comanche, Caddo, and Kiowa Indians on Fort Parker, in present-day Texas. This nine-year-old will stay in captivity for six years, after which the Comanches say she has adopted them and wants to stay with the tribe. She becomes known as Preloch and marries Peco Nocoma, a respected Comanche warrior who participated in the raid on Fort Parker. One of their three children will become Quanah Parker, the most important Comanche leader of the reservation era.

HEAL. A smallpox epidemic wipes out about 4,000 Assiniboine Indians in the Saskatchewan River region of Canada.

LEGE. The *Walam Olum* (called the Red Record), the sacred tribal chronology of the Lenni Lenape (Delaware) Indians, is first published by a French botanist, Constantine Samuel Rafinesque. The original is a remarkable pictographic record of the history of the world from creation to the coming of the white man as carved and painted on wood over many years. Spanning 100 generations, the story tells of the Lenni Lenape ancestors coming from a far-off land, encountering other Indians in the new land, enduring the Great Flood, and migrating to a great body of water. Some scholars today discount the authenticity of the *Walam Olum,* believing it is a hoax.

1836–1840

HEAL. An epidemic of smallpox sweeps through the southern coastal region of Alaska, killing hundreds of Indians.

1837

HEAL. A smallpox epidemic occurs along the upper Missouri River killing 15,000 Indians and nearly wiping out the Arikara, Hidatsa, and Mandan. In the Mandan tribe in Dakota, all but about 125 out of a total of 1,600 are decimated by smallpox. Between 1837 and 1870, four major smallpox epidemics will ravage western tribes.

LAND. Land-cession treaties are negotiated with the Dakota and the Ojibwe (Chippewa) Indians for U.S. rights to a portion of land between the Mississippi and St. Croix Rivers (current day eastern Minnesota). This new land stimulates the lumber industry in Minnesota.

1838

MIGR. The "Trail of Tears" takes place for the Cherokees. The *Treaty of New Echota* in 1835 stipulated that the Cherokee relocate to Indian Territory within two years. Up to 17,000 Cherokees are forcibly removed from their tribal lands in the states of Georgia, Tennessee, Alabama, and North Carolina to land west of the Red River, in Indian Territory. The Cherokees are forcibly rounded up beginning in May. In October, the main group begins its trek westward escorted with their horses and oxen by 7,000 federal troops under the command of Gen. Winfield Scott. They travel by wagon and keelboat along the 1,200-mile route. Over 4,000 Cherokees die along the way from disease, starvation, and cold weather. Most of those who die are infants, children, and old people who develop measles, whooping cough, pneumonia, pleurisy, tuberculosis, or pellagra, and can't survive the hardships of the journey and the bitter winter weather. The last group reaches their destination in Indian Territory (in what is now northeastern Oklahoma) in March, 1839.

1838

LAND. The Seneca reservations in western New York State are taken by the *Treaty of Buffalo Creek*. The reservations of Allegany, Buffalo Creek, Cattaraugus, and Tonawanda are sold to the Ogden Land Company, and the Seneca are sent to Kansas. Protests over the treaty will lead to the resto-ration of the Allegany and Cattaraugus Reservations in 1842.

WARS. Seminole chief Osceola is taken captive along with 80 Seminole warriors and dies of malaria while in prison at Fort Moultrie near Charlestown, South Carolina.

1839

WARS. The Texas Cherokees, led by Chief Philip Bowles, are attacked by the Texas Rangers. Around 500 Texas Rangers march on the Cherokee villages of East Texas, killing the Indians and burning their houses and possessions. On July 16, 1839, Chief Bowles is killed in the fighting. The few surviving Cherokees head north into Arkansas and some eventually join the Cherokees in Indian Territory.

On June 22, three Cherokee leaders are assassinated by rival Cherokee. The leaders of the Cherokee's Treaty faction, John Ridge, his father, Major Ridge, and his cousin, Elias Boudinot, are brutally murdered by members of the Cherokee National party who had opposed the *Treaty of New Echota*.

C. 1840

TRAD. The fur trade begins to decline when beaver hats go out of style in Europe.

1840

POLI. The Cheyenne, Kiowa, Arapaho, and Comanche form a four-nation alliance on the western Plains.

1841

PUBL. Painter George Catlin publishes *The Manners, Customs, and Conditions of the North American Indians* which chronicles his eight-year journey through Indian country through stories and engravings.

1842

WARS. The Second Seminole War ends after almost seven years of fighting. Almost 4,000 Seminoles are convinced to move to western lands, while another 500 hide out in the swamps of southern Florida and stay in the region.

1842–1853

EXPL. John C. Fremont (sponsored by the United States) explores the Far West. His Paiute guide, Truckee, guides Fremont to California in 1845–1846.

1843

MIGR. The first of 300,000 American settlers follow the Oregon Trail west.

RELI. The Russian Orthodox Church founds its first mission school for Inuits (Eskimos) in Alaska.

WARS. A band of 15 Texas Rangers attack a group of 300 Comanches. The Rangers kill half the Indians and intimidate the rest with Colt revolvers that can fire six shots without reloading.

1844

PUBL. The first issues of the *Cherokee Advocate* newspaper are published in Oklahoma by the Cherokee Tribal Council. This is the first Indian newspaper to be published in Indian Territory. It will continue publication until 1911.

1845

POLI. Texas becomes part of the United States and assumes dominion over its Indian peoples.

PUBL. Journalist John O'Sullivan writes of the concept of "manifest destiny" in *The United States Magazine and Democratic Review*. The term becomes the ideological basis for further westward expansion—to express the belief that it is God's will for the United States to settle the West, to take Indian lands, and for the country to extend from the Atlantic Ocean to the Pacific Ocean.

1846

EXPL. Paul Kane travels among and paints Indians of southern Canada and the American Northwest.

LAND. Great Britain and the United States settle the long-disputed boundary of Oregon Territory. Oregon Country becomes part of the United States, assuming responsibility over its Indian peoples.

TREA. After the annexation of Texas by the United States in 1845, a general peace treaty is signed at Council Springs, Texas, under which the Wichita, Comanche, Lipan, Kichai, and Caddo Indians recognize the jurisdiction of the U.S. government.

1846–1848

WARS. The Mexican-American War is the first war driven by the idea of "Manifest Destiny." After winning its independence from Mexico in 1836, the Republic of Texas was annexed by the United States in 1845. The southern and western borders of Texas remained disputed, however, which led to border clashes and eventually, invasions. With the *Treaty of Guadalupe Hidalgo* in 1848, the Spanish Southwest and its many Indian tribes became part of the United States.

1847

MIGR. The "Mormon Battalion" opens a wagon road from Santa Fe, New Mexico, to San Diego, California. Arriving at the San Diego Mission on January 29, it has taken 100 days to make the trip from Santa Fe. Lt. Col. Philip St. George Cooke and his 400 men dug wells along the way to establish the Santa Fe Trail which will be followed by thousands of immigrants to California.

RELI. Mormon settlers reach the site of present-day Salt Lake City.

"Our manifest destiny [is] to overspread and to possess the whole of the continent which Providence has given us for the development of the great experiment of liberty and federated self-government entrusted to us" (O'Sullivan 1845, 7).

TRAD. The U.S. *Trade and Intercourse Act* attempts to regulate commerce with Indian tribes and maintain peace on the frontier.

WARS. The Taos Pueblo Indians are angered by the United States in the Mexican War, and they kill the U.S. governor of New Mexico and about 10 other Americans. The U.S. military troops retaliate by attacking Taos and killing around 150 of the Taos Indians, and executing 15 others.

Fur trader Charles Bent, 47, assumes his new post as governor of New Mexico Territory. But, on January 19, Pueblo Indians and Mexicans attack him at home in Taos, killing him and 12 other whites. A punitive expedition goes after the Pueblo Indians using howitzers and hand grenades against them as they are holed up in a church on August 19, killing 150 and wounding 300.

1847

WARS. The Cayuse War under Tiloukaikt takes place against missionaries in Oregon. An outbreak of measles occurs among the Cayuse Indians at the Presbyterian mission school in the village of Waiilatpu in Oregon Territory. Cayuse Indians attack the mission and kill Marcus Whitman, the founder of the missionary school, and 11 of the missionary family members. Fighting between the Cayuse and militia forces will continue throughout the next two years. In 1850, five Cayuse will be tried and executed for the murders.

1847–1852

ARTS. Swiss artist Rudolph Kurz paints Prairie Indians.

1848

LAND. The Menominee Indians cede most of their land in Wisconsin by the *Treaty of Lake Pow-aw-hay-kon-nay*. In return, they are granted some lands that were ceded by the Ojibwe (Chippewa) Indians which they will be forced to relinquish in 1854. Then, they will retire to a small reservation on the Wolf River in Wisconsin.

The Qualla Cherokee of North Carolina receive a settlement from the U.S. government. These Cherokee did not move west on the Trail of Tears. They owned their land outside of tribal territory near Quallatown, North Carolina. Due to the work of William H. Thomas, a white man who was adopted as a boy by a Qualla chief, the state of North Carolina convinces the United States to give every Qualla the $53.33 it appropriated to remove each Cherokee. This money is used to purchase the mountain land that will later become the reservation of the Eastern Band of Cherokee Indians.

TRAD. Commercial whalers first arrive in Alaska.

TREA. The Mexican American War that began in 1846 ends with the *Treaty of Guadalupe Hidalgo* on February 2. Mexico loses 35 percent of its territory, giving up claims to lands north of the Rio Grande River and ceding vast territories, including California, in return for $15 million and the assumption by Washington of U.S. claims against Mexico. More than 100,000 Indians are added to the U.S. population with the annexation of Texas, the settlement of the Oregon boundary dispute, and the *Treaty of Guadalupe Hidalgo* with Mexico. The treaty contains provisions that the United States will honor the treaties and agreements made by Mexico with the Indians.

1848–1849

ENVI. The California Gold Rush begins soon after gold is discovered on the American River in northern California, on January 24, 1848. James Marshall and about 20 men are working to free the wheel in the millrace for a sawmill they are building for John (Johann) Sutter. Sutter's Fort and ranch is located near the village of Culloma in the lands of the Nisenan Indians. Sutter tries to keep the discovery a secret, but the news soon spreads, and by the end of the year there are around 6,000 men working in the goldfields. By mid-1849, however, the gold is running low and the work is more difficult for the little rewards left. But, news of last year's gold discovery at Sutter's

Mill brings a rush of 7,000 "Forty-Niners" to California. The population of gold miners in California will jump in the next seven years from 15,000 to nearly 300,000 as the gold fields yield $450 million. There is a collision of cultures with miners rushing into California from all over the world as well as from all over the United States. This is the beginning of the end for many California tribes. Many thrive from the Gold Rush, but not Native Americans. The influx of miners brings about an upheaval in the whole socioeconomic survival of Native Americans. Some historians estimate the native population of the region is radically reduced from about 300,000 to about 50,000 because of the Gold Rush. In the 1850s, many California tribes will be coerced into signing treaties that cede half the state to the United States. However, the U.S. Senate does not ratify the treaties, which are hidden away in files and discovered in 1905. In the meantime, the California tribes had given up their lands, while the 8 million acres promised to them in perpetuity were sold to whites. The total Indian population of California subsequently dwindles from 120,000 in 1850 to less than 20,000 in 1880.

1849

HEAL. A cholera epidemic spread by gold-rush emigrants crossing the Texas Panhandle wipe out the leadership of the Comanche tribe, but the Indians continue to resist settlement of their lands.

POLI. The Bureau of Indian Affairs (BIA) is transferred from the War Department to the Department of the Interior. Many object to this move by the U.S. government, and instead want a new, separate department devoted solely to Indian matters. The Interior Department at this time has been concerned with "civilizing" Indians and containing them on reservations, and taking away Indian lands and resources and turning them over to private individuals and corporations. In the 1850s, the population of Indians in the United States will double with the organization of the territories of Texas, Oregon, New Mexico, Arizona, and California, increasing the responsibilities of the BIA.

WARS. The Courthouse Rebellion takes place in Canada, involving the Métis of the Red River.

Quechan Indians attack a party of westward-bound whites at Yuma Crossing in August. When members of the Duval party attempt to cross the Colorado River they are attacked and several members of the party are killed, with their animals, baggage, and food stolen. This prompts the U.S. Army to build a fort at Yuma Crossing the following year to ensure safe passage for whites.

1850

LAND. Treaties are concluded with the Dakota Indians at Traverse de Sioux and Mendota, Minnesota, whereby the Dakota cede their lands east of the Red River, Lake Traverse, and the Big Dakota River, and south of a boundary line between the Dakota and Ojibwe (Chippewa). In return the Dakota receive $1,665,000. Of this amount, $1,360,000 was put into a trust fund of which the interest would be distributed to chiefs partly in cash, partly in supplies, and partly in education and civilization funds. However, the vast majority will end up being used to pay off Indian debts to white traders.

On September 29, Congress passes the *Donation Land Act,* a year after Oregon is organized as a territory. This law offers free land to the settlers flooding into the region, even though the land has not been ceded to the U.S. government by the Indian peoples who occupy it.

LAWS. California passes the *Act for the Government and Protection of Indians,* which allows whites to indenture Indians to forcibly work for whites. By the time the act is repealed in 1863, around 10,000 California Indians will have been indentured or sold into slavery.

POLI. New Mexico (which at this time includes present-day Arizona, southern Colorado, southern Utah, and southern Nevada) is designated a territory of the United States but denied statehood.

RELI. Smohalla, a Wanapam shaman from present-day Washington state, creates the Dreamer Religion which teaches a message of passive resistance to white encroachment and influence. He and his followers form a new village near what is now Vernita, Washington.

TREA. The first of a series of treaties between Canada and Canadian tribes are enacted. This policy of treaty making will continue until 1923.

WARS. The Mariposa Indian War breaks out in California between white miners and Miwoks and Yokuts under Tenaya. These Indians in the San Joaquin Valley attack prospectors, who then clash with state militia forces throughout the next year.

After a group of Pomo Indians kill two white ranchers in northern California who have been abusing them, a force of army troops and volunteers attack a Pomo camp on Clear Lake and kill around 60 people. The soldiers then attack a nearby Pomo village on the Russian River, killing another 70 Pomo.

1850–1860

HEAL. A cholera epidemic sweeps through the Indians of the Great Basin and southern Plains.

1851

PUBL. Henry Rowe Schoolcraft publishes the first volume of his six-volume ethnological work titled *Historical and Statistical Information Respecting the History, Condition, and Prospects of the Indian Tribes of the United States*. The six volumes will be completed in 1857.

Lewis Henry Morgan publishes his detailed study of the Iroquois titled *League of the Ho-de-no-sau-nee, or Iroquois*. Working with an Indian informant, this is the first book concerning the culture and beliefs of a tribe as told in the Indians' own terms.

The Oatman family is attacked by Yavapai Indians about 80 miles west of Fort Yuma in present-day Arizona. As Royce and Mary Ann Oatman and their seven children travel by covered wagon from Illinois to California, they are set upon by Yavapai who kill the parents and four children. Their son, Lorenzo, is left for dead but survives. Two girls, Olive and Mary Ann, are taken captive. The Yavapai sell the girls to the Mojave Indians as slaves, and Mary Ann soon

dies. Olive Oatman will remain a captive with the Mohave for five years before she is rescued and reunited with her brother Lorenzo. Her ordeal will be published in 1857 as *Life among the Indians* and will become the most popular captivity narrative since Mary Rowlandson's capture by the Wampanoag in 1672 (published in 1682).

SETT. The Russian settlement at Nulato on the lower Yukon River of western Alaska is destroyed in an uprising by the Koyukon Indians.

TREA. The *Treaty of Fort Laramie* marks a turning point in U.S.-Indian relations on the northern Plains of Wyoming, Montana, and the Dakotas for a 40-year period. Around 10,000 Indians of the Sioux, Cheyenne, Arapaho, Crow, Arikara, Assiniboine, and other western tribes meet with U.S. officials at Horse Creek near Fort Laramie in Wyoming Territory. With this treaty, the Indians agree to allow free access to wagon trains on the Oregon Trail, the building of roads, and the establishment of a chain of U.S. forts in their lands. However, the treaty does not stop the increase of whites arriving in the Plains and their threat to Indian lands and ways.

Eighteen treaties are negotiated with California tribes by a three-person commission formed by Congress. As the commission travels throughout California, they begin negotiating treaties with many Indian bands and groups, calling for the cession of Indians' lands in exchange for around 8 million acres of reserved areas for California tribes. However, unknown to the California tribes, these treaties fail to be ratified by the U.S. Senate in 1852, and will become known as the "lost treaties." For 50 years they will be stored in the Senate archives, not being discovered until 1905.

The *Treaty of Traverse des Sioux* provides the Dakota Sioux with two reservations along the Upper Missouri River in exchange for the surrender of 24 million acres of contested land.

WARS. In California, Cupeño Indian leader Antonio Garra leads an Indian uprising to expel all non-Indians from their lands in present-day northern San Diego County. Although only a few people are killed, the news of the uprising spreads through California, creating a panic and anti-Indian feelings throughout the white population.

1852–1853

HEAL. Smallpox strikes the Kansas Indian reservation at Council Grove, Kansas, with over 400 Indians dying in one winter.

1853

ARTS. Delgadito, a Navajo, begins the tradition of silverwork among his people.

HEAL. The last Chumash Indian is found on San Nicolas Island, off the California coast. The woman has lived alone on the island for 18 years since the rest of her tribe, the San Nicolas Chumash, were moved to the mainland by mission priests. All of those Chumash have already died of diseases by the time the woman is discovered by hunters on the island. She is taken to Santa Barbara, where she is baptized and dies of disease seven weeks later. Her story will be recounted in several publications, including the young-adult novel *Island of the Blue Dolphins* by Scott O'Dell, which will win the 1960 Newbery Award.

LAND. The United States negotiates land cessions from many tribes in northern Indian Territory to clear land for the transcontinental railroad to be built through the Great Plains. The liquidation of the northern portion of the Indian Territory during 1853–1854 will create the Kansas and Nebraska Territories.

On December 30, the Gadsden Purchase transfers Mexican lands in southern New Mexico and Arizona to U.S. ownership. This extends the boundary of the United States into Mexican territory for 45,535 square miles (nearly 30,000,000 acres), settling boundary disputes unresolved by the *Treaty of Guadalupe Hidalgo* in 1848. The purchase also provides the United States with lands needed to construct a railroad though the Southwest.

1853–1856

LAND. The U.S. government acquires 174 million acres of Indian lands during these years through 52 treaties. All these treaties are eventually ignored by white settlers and broken by the government.

1854

HUNT. Puget Sound tribes, such as the Quixiault, Lummi, Nisqually, and Puyallup, that have ceded their lands in the Northwest receive treaty rights to fish for salmon in the rivers of that region.

LAND. In a treaty with the United States on March 16, the Omaha Indians of Nebraska cede over 43 million acres of land, retaining only about 300,000 acres for their own use.

The *Kansas-Nebraska Act* signed into law by President Pierce on May 30 reduces Indian Territory, opening to white settlement western lands that have been reserved by sacred treaty for the Indians in the northern portion of Indian Territory. The act creates the Kansas and Nebraska territories which will be inhabited by more than 100,000 white settlers during the next decade.

POLI. In Indian Territory, the Cherokee, Chickasaw, Choctaw, Creek, and Seminole Indian nations form a loose federation known as the Five Civilized Tribes. The federation will end in 1907, when Oklahoma will be admitted to the Union as the 46th state.

Regarding the land cessions negotiated with northern Indian Territory tribes to build the transcontinental railroad through their Indian lands, Commissioner of Indian Affairs, George W. Manypenny, notes that many of the Indian groups in the region "have been removed, step by step, from mountain to valley, and from river to plain, until they have been pushed halfway across the continent" (Manypenny 1972).

The Commissioner of Indian Affairs calls for an end to the U.S. government's Indian removal policy.

PUBL. In December, Chief Seattle delivers an eloquent and moving speech at the *Point Elliot Treaty* negotiations in Washington Territory. As the Suquamish chief speaks, poet Henry A. Smith takes notes in English. A version of Seattle's speech will appear 33 years later, written by Smith, for the *Seattle Sunday Star* newspaper. Although the speech will become one of the most famous examples of Indian oratory, there will be doubts about its accuracy in representing Seattle's actual words.

WARS. In the Grattan Affair in Wyoming, the peace is broken between the United States and the Lakota Sioux. In August, a party of Mormons traveling west along the Oregon Trail lose one of their cows as it wanders into the land of the Brulé band of the Lakota Sioux, and a Brulé kills the cow with an arrow. The Mormons tell army officers at Fort Laramie that the cow was stolen by the Indians. This leads to an attempt by the Army to arrest the Indian, and when he resists, the troops open fire on the Indians, killing an influential chief. The Brulé then attack the solders, killing all 30 of them.

The Spirit Lake Uprising of Santee Sioux (Dakota) takes place under Inkpaduta in Iowa.

1855

LAND. The Walla Walla Council in Washington Territory between white officials and tribes of the Columbia Plateau results in the Yakima, Walla Walla, Cayuse, Umatilla, Nez Percé, Flatheads, Kootenais, and Pend Oreille Indians ceding around 60,000 square miles of land in the Columbia Basin to the United States in exchange for two small reservations. During the tense negotiations there is mistrust and duress between the tribes and officials. White settlers are flooding into the Northwest and the government wants lands for construction of the northern route of the Pacific Railroad. Indians are paid about 3 cents per acre in return for some reservation lands. The treaty articles also guarantee the Indians fishing rights off their reservation lands in the ceded lands. This results in a century of conflict between Indians and territorial and state officials when the federal government does not protect the Indians' right to fish. Within days of the conference, much of the Indians' former lands are opened to white settlement, angering the Indians who were promised to be allowed two years before being displaced from their lands. This leads to the Yakama War in September.

The Salish and Kutenai (Kootenai) Indians sign the *Treaty of Hell Gate* in Montana on July 16, ceding their lands in Montana and Idaho to the United States.

In Indian Territory, the Chickasaw Indian lands are separated by treaty from those of the Choctaw. The Chickasaw were originally given the western section of the Choctaw Reservation.

PUBL. Henry Wordsworth Longfellow publishes his narrative poem *The Song of Hiawatha*, a romantic legend of an Ojibwe (Chippewa) chief.

WARS. Gold is discovered in the Pend Oreille River in northwestern Washington. Under Chief Kamiakin, the Yakima, Cayuse, Wallawalla, Paloos, and Spokane Indians resist the flood of miners on their lands for three years. In 1858, the Indians will finally be defeated by the U.S. cavalry and artillery units. Kamiakin refuses to surrender and crosses into Canada, escaping the fate of the 24 chiefs of the various tribes who are hanged or shot.

The Brulé Sioux are attacked by U.S. Army troops on September 2 on Blue Water Creek where they are camped near the North Platte River in present-day Nebraska. The Army is seeking retaliation for the Grattan Massacre from the previous year. Nearly 100 Indians are killed, and 76 women and children are taken as prisoners.

In October, the Rogue River War erupts. In southern Oregon, Indian camps are attacked by volunteer soldiers who kill 23 women, children, and elderly men. The Indian warriors retaliate by killing 27 white settlers. During the coming winter there will be ongoing fighting between volunteers and Indians camping in the mountains. The war will end in May, 1856, when the Indians lose in the Battle of Big Meadows.

In December, Chief Pu-Pu-Mox-Mox, a respected leader of the Walla Walla, is captured and killed by Oregon volunteers involved in the

Yakama War, during a peace council. The soldiers defile his body, outraging the Walla Walla, who raid white settlements with increased ferocity.

1855–1856

WARS. The Yakama War breaks out in September in Washington Territory under Kamiakin. Following the Walla Walla Council, tensions grow between whites and Indians as miners rush through the Indians' land en route to gold fields north of the Spokane River. When miners rape several Yakama women and steal horses from the tribe, a Yakama named Qualchin kills the criminals. Indian agent Andrew Bolon comes to investigate and is also killed by the Yakama. This sets into motion the Yakama War, involving the Yakama, Walla Walla, Umatilla, and Cayuse tribes, which goes on for 10 months.

The Rogue War takes place in Oregon, involving Takelma and Tututni Indians under Old John.

1855–1858

WARS. The Third Seminole War begins in November, 1855, in the Everglades of Florida. The Seminole chief Billy Bowlegs will surrender to U.S. troops in Florida on January 19, 1858, bringing an end to the guerilla warfare fought by the Seminoles. The surviving Seminoles withdraw further into the Everglades, seldom showing themselves to white men.

1856

WARS. The Nisqually Indians and their allies under Chief Leschi attack the city of Seattle in Washington Territory. Chief Leschi will be hanged in 1858 for this act, although some historians and descendants of Leschi today believe he was not involved in the attack at all.

1857

LAND. The Seneca are authorized to buy back their Tonawanda Reservation, which was sold under the terms of the *Treaty of Buffalo Creek* in 1838.

WARS. Dakota Sioux rise up against white settlers near Spirit Lake in northwestern Iowa on March 8 and 9, killing about 40 settlers.

The Battle of Solomon Fork in Kansas results as soldiers are sent to punish a group of Cheyenne in western Kansas for raiding mining camps. On August 29, about 300 soldiers meet around 300 Cheyenne warriors at a fork of the Solomon River, with the soldiers driving the Indians away by rushing them with sabers.

The Mountain Meadows Massacre in Utah Territory on September 11 kills 135 California-bound emigrants in a conniving scheme. Some 300 to 400 Pah-Ute braves, led by a few Mormons acting on orders from Brigham Young, ambush the Fancher wagon-train about 320 miles south of Salt Lake City. The wagon train is carrying around 150 settlers to California. Initially, the wagon train is able to fight back and hold off the attackers. After several days, John D. Lee, a young Mormon leader, persuades the settlers to lay down their weapons with the promise that the Ute will allow them to continue on their journey. Once the wagon train settlers piled their arms into a wagon, however, the Mormons and the Indians attack, slaughtering everyone except for 17 young children, whom the Mormons later adopted. Lee will be executed 20 years later for his part in the massacre.

The Yuma and Maricopa Indians of Arizona have been fighting an 80-year feud. In the last battle of this conflict, a war party of 93 Yuma Indians is wiped out by a combined force of Maricopa and Pima Indians.

1858

ENVI. Gold rushes take place to Washington and British Columbia.

WARS. The Coeur d'Alene War (or Spokane War) is waged in present-day Washington state, involving a coalition of the Coeur d'Alene, Spokane, Palouse, Yakima, and Northern Paiute tribes. On May 17, an enormous force of around 100,000 Indians drives a force of 158 troops led by Lt. Col. Edward J. Steptoe from the Colville Indian Reservation. In response to this humiliation, Army troops are sent back to the Colville Reservation and attack the Indians during September 1–5 in the Battle of Spokane Plains and the Battle of Four Lakes. The Army beats the Indians, whose arms cannot match the long-range rifles and howitzers of the Army troops.

Mojave Indians attack a wagon train of settlers crossing the Colorado River en route to California. The settlers turn around and head back to Albuquerque. In response to these attacks, troops from California establish an outpost at the crossing and later construct Fort Mohave in the area. The ongoing fighting between the troops and the Mojave will later be called the Mohave War.

The Third Seminole War ends in Florida on January 19. Many of the Seminole agree to move to Indian Territory, while others retreat to the Everglades and stay in Florida.

The Navajo (Dineh), led by Manuelito, attack U.S. Army troops at Fort Defiance. The Navajo and soldiers clash between July and October, and the animosity leads to an Indian attack on the fort in 1860.

1858–1859

ENVI. The Colorado Gold Rush (or Pike's Peak Gold Rush) takes place.

1858–1861

CONT. The stagecoach operates in the West.

1859

MIGR. A band of the Kickapoo Indians who migrated from Kansas to the northern Mexican state of Coahuila is given 17,290 acres by the Mexican government, which is called El Nacimiento Rancheria. In return, the Kickapoo are expected to protect Mexico from Apaches, Comanches, and Kiowas.

POLI. Conservative Cherokees in Indian Territory form the Keetoowah Society, which promotes social and political reform, including the ending of slavery and resisting assimilation into white society.

1860

POLI. The British government transfers control of Indian affairs to the Canadian provinces.

POPU. The Native American population in the United States and its territories is estimated to be 300,000, down from between 600,000 and 900,000 in 1607.

WARS. On February 26, a group of white vigilantes massacre Indians in villages along Humboldt Bay near the present-day town of Eureka, California. The whites believed these Indians were harboring members of mountain tribes suspected of killing the cattle of the white men. The vigilantes attack in the middle of the night, killing around 80 people, primarily women and children.

On April 30, a group of Navajo attack Fort Defiance, in New Mexico Territory. This attack prompts the U.S. Secretary of War to launch a full-scale military campaign against the Navajo tribe.

The Paiute War (also called the Pyramid Lake War) takes place in May in present-day Nevada under Numaga, pitting the Southern Paiutes against a group of volunteer army troops and miners. Fighting takes place near the Big Bend of the Truckee River where Paiutes kill 46 soldiers, and near Pinnacle Mountain where about 25 Paiutes are killed before the war ends.

In December, Cynthia Ann Parker is discovered by U.S. troops in a Comanche camp along the Pease River during an attack on the camp. Parker was taken captive in 1836 when she was nine years old, but adopted the Comanche people as her own and has a Comanche husband and children. She is not happy about being "rescued" and returned to her white relatives. One of her sons, Quanah, will later emerge as a great Comanche leader.

1860–1861

CONT. The Pony Express operates in the West.

1861

LAND. In the *Treaty of Fort Wise,* the Southern Cheyenne and Arapaho give up claim to nearly all their lands in Colorado Territory. On their small tract of land along the Arkansas River at Sand Creek, the Indians will have a difficult time surviving as farmers. Starving and suffering from an epidemic of smallpox, they will soon leave the reservation boundaries in Southern Colorado in search of buffalo herds to hunt.

TOOL. The first transcontinental telegraph line is completed on October 24. This will soon end the use of the Pony Express.

WARS. Chiricahua Apache chief Cochise, 49, appears at an army post in Arizona Territory to deny charges of raiding a white man's ranch and kidnapping one or more of his children. He is taken prisoner, escapes (by pulling out a knife and cutting a hole in the tent where the meeting is held), and takes hostages to be exchanged for other Chiricahuas held by the U.S. Army. The exchange does not take place, however, and the hostages are killed on both sides. Cochise joins with his father-in-law, Mangas Coloradas, of the Membreño Apache in raids that threaten to drive the whites from Arizona during 1861–1862.

1861–1865

WARS. The U.S. Civil War draws tribes to fight on both sides, with many tribes caught in the middle. In 1861, the Confederate government organizes a Bureau of Indian Affairs. Most tribes remain neutral in the war. The South makes promises to the Cherokee Indians and other tribes of the Five Civilized Tribes concerning the return of their tribal lands if they support the South in

Wounded Indian sharpshooters on Marye's Heights after the second Battle of Fredericksburg, 1864. Indians were recruited by both the North and the South to fight in the Civil War. Courtesy of Library of Congress.

the Civil War. The Confederacy makes treaties with the Choctaw, Chickasaw, Creek, Seminole, Quapaw, Seneca, Caddo, Wichita, Osage, Shawnee, and eventually with the Cherokee, promising to protect the Indians' land from invasions by Union troops in return for an Indian defense of their territories. After the war, these tribes will be punished by the U.S. Congress for their support of the Confederacy by having to accept a treaty relinquishing the western half of Indian Territory to 20 tribes from Kansas and Nebraska. With the outbreak of the Civil War, soldiers in the West are recalled to help fight the Confederate rebels. Volunteer troops are recruited by state and territorial governments during 1860 and 1865, which clash with Indians on the Great Plains and in the Southwest. By the end of the war in 1865, as many as 10,000 Indians have been killed in Indian Territory who allied themselves with the Confederates.

1862

CONT. The Bozeman Trail opens to carry whites from the Oregon Trail to goldfields in present-day southwestern Montana. The trail runs straight through the Lakota Sioux hunting grounds, and the conflicts that result will lead to Red Cloud's War in 1866.

EDUC. Congress passes the *Morrill Act* which approves land grants for the establishment of agricultural colleges. The research at these colleges greatly improves agricultural techniques, enabling farmers to utilize previously unwanted lands. In coming years, the act will result in more settlers coming to the West.

HEAL. A smallpox epidemic sweeps through the Fort Victoria area and down the length of the Northwest Coast, killing an estimated 200,000 Indian people.

LAND. Congress passes the *Pacific Railroad Act,* which transfers 174 million acres of public land to transcontinental railroad companies. Nine major rail routes will result, transporting a flood of whites into

Indian territories and resulting in a rapid decline of the buffalo herds.

Congress passes the *Homestead Act,* which opens up Indian land in what is today Kansas and Nebraska to white homesteaders who are deeded 160-acre parcels after inhabiting the land for five years. This act will be extended to qualified Indians in the *Indian Homestead Act* of 1875.

RELI. Anglican missionary William Duncan establishes the village of Metlakatla on the Northwest Coast with 50 Tsimshian followers, who adopt the Christian faith and European lifestyles. By 1880 more than 1,000 converts will live there.

WARS. An uprising by the Santee Sioux begins in Minnesota on August 17 under the guidance of Chief Little Crow. Attacks by the Indians are motivated by hungry Dakota enraged by the failure of the government to deliver promised supplies and unfair fiscal practices of local traders. Around 486 white settlers are killed during the conflict. In 1863, the fighting spreads to North Dakota and involves the Teton Sioux as well. The insurrection is eventually subdued, and 306 braves are sentenced, with 38 hanged on December 26, 1863, at Mankato. This is the largest mass execution in the history of the United States. The Sioux are then forced to give up their Minnesota lands and to move into the Dakotas, although some flee to Canada.

Navajo raiders in New Mexico, in this one year alone, steal about 100,000 sheep. The U.S. Army will launch a war against the Navajo in 1863.

1863

LAND. The Nez Percé in the Northwest are forced to sign a treaty agreeing to vacate lands desired by the whites.

The *Ruby Valley Treaty,* signed with the Shoshone, Washoe, and other tribes in the Nevada Territory, gives more than 23 million acres to the tribes, with most of it being desert. The whites receive rights to build railroads across Indian lands, which account for 86 percent of the territory.

POLI. The Cherokee Indian Nation, severing its connection with the Confederacy (the 11 Southern States that seceded from the United States in 1860–1861), also abolishes slavery. Several of the southern Indian tribes in the United States had owned black slaves before the Civil War.

WARS. The Shoshone War (also called the Bear River Campaign) takes place in today's Utah and Idaho. On January 27, around 224 Western Shoshone are killed, and 164 women and children are taken as captives at a Shoshone camp along the Bear River in Idaho.

Kit Carson, army scout and Indian fighter, and his troops battle the Mescalero Apache, who surrender in the springtime and agree to resettle at Bosque Redondo in what is now east-central New Mexico. This area has been reserved to confine renegade Apache and Navajo.

1863–1866

WARS. The Navajo War is fought in New Mexico and Arizona. Kit Carson leads a U.S. army force in a campaign against the Navajo Indians of the Southwest. He and his federal troops reach Fort Defiance in Arizona Territory on July 20, 1863, and are joined by a band of Ute braves. A peace treaty had been signed in 1849 at Canyon de Chelly (Arizona) in which the Navajo acknowledged the sovereignty of the United States. The Army kills all the Navajo sheep and burns their crops, forcing the tribe to surrender or face starvation. During February and March, 1864, about 8,000 Navajos are rounded up in northeastern Arizona and northwestern New Mexico and are herded over 300 miles on "The Long Walk" eastward to Ft. Sumner at Bosque Redondo, New Mexico. All captives who surrender voluntarily are to be taken to the reservation to become farmers. All males who resist will be shot and their livestock and food supplies destroyed. Many Navajos die along the way. By December, 1864, the camp holds 8,354 Navajos plus 405 Mescalero Apaches. During the next year, however, around 1,200 Indians will escape. The Navajos endure the camp for four years, with hundreds dying of diseases and starvation. Carson is relieved of his command in the fall of 1866, and the Navajos will be eventually allowed to return to a reduced homeland in 1868.

1864

LAWS. Under federal law, Indians are declared competent witnesses and allowed to testify in trials against whites.

WARS. Troops under Christopher "Kit" Carson campaign against Comanche and Kiowa Indians in Texas.

1864–1865

WARS. The Cheyenne-Arapaho War takes place in Colorado and Kansas. Cheyenne go on the warpath and are supported by Arapaho, Apache, Comanche, and Kiowa braves. Southern Cheyenne leader Black Kettle tries to secure the peace and meets with U.S. officials, but his camp is attacked on November 29, 1864, at Sand Creek in Colorado Territory. The Sand Creek Massacre takes place under the command of Col. John M. Chivington with 700 soldiers of the Third Colorado Cavalry who kill more than 300 Indians, mostly women and children. This brutal and bloody massacre will draw outrage by the public and by Congress, but no punishment of those responsible will be taken. During the early months of 1865, Plains Indians will try to take revenge on whites along the South Platte River for the Sand Creek Massacre.

1865

EDUC. The U.S. government gives contracts to Protestant missionary societies to operate Indian schools.

CONT. The Chisholm Trail is opened by Jesse Chisholm, a mixed-blood Cherokee. He drives a wagon from Texas to Kansas, creating a route that will become the primary path for Texas cattlemen to drive their herds to Kansas railroad terminals for shipment to eastern markets.

MIGR. The Winnebago Indians have been removed from their lands five times since 1840. The tribe lived in present-day Iowa, Minnesota, South Dakota, and Nebraska, and over 700 of them have died in the removal process. Now, the federal government establishes the Nebraska Winnebago Reservation by an act of Congress.

WARS. The Lumbee Indians in Robeson County, North Carolina, face conflicts with whites. In spring, a group of whites kill the father and brother of a Lumbee named Henry Berry Lowry. Lowry leads a group of relatives and friends in killing and looting to avenge their deaths. The fighting will continue for 10 years, with Lowry killing or driving out the murderers of his relatives. Lowry is never captured or killed by his pursuers and becomes a folk hero among the Lumbee.

The Bannock Indians are attacked by U.S. army troops in January while the Indians are camped at Battle Creek, Idaho. Around 224 Bannock are killed. The Bannock had been trying to turn back the white settlers entering their lands for several years by raiding settlements and wagon trains.

1865–1873

WARS. The Mexican Kickapoo Uprising in the Texas southwest goes on for almost 10 years. After many of the Kickapoo left present-day Kansas and relocated to Mexico in the early 1850s, they were attacked by Texas Rangers who crossed the international border. This infuriated the Kickapoo who launched a violent campaign against Texas ranches and settlements along the Rio Grande.

1866

LAND. The *Railroad Enabling Act* appropriates Indian lands as rights-of-way for construction of the transcontinental railroad.

MIGR. Twenty tribes from Kansas and Nebraska begin relocation to Indian Territory.

POLI. On January 1, U.S. officials define the status of freedmen in Indian Territory. Black slaves in Indian Territory are told they are now free and can be absorbed into Indian tribes. These freedmen are instructed that they can now sign up for Indian rations and can obtain 160 acres of Indian land to farm. Some tribes, such as the Creek and Seminole, largely comply with the federal government's directives, while other tribes, such as the Choctaw, refuse to give African-American freedmen citizenship in the tribe.

POPU. Whites in Arizona and New Mexico at this time own around 2,000 Indian slaves.

WARS. The War for the Bozeman Trail in Wyoming and Montana takes place involving Lakota Sioux, Cheyenne, and Arapaho forces under Chief Red Cloud against the U.S. Army. On December 21, 1866, Capt. William J. Fetterman leads 80 U.S. Army men into an ambush by Sioux Indians along the Bozeman Trail in Dakota Territory, becoming known to whites as the Fetterman Massacre and to Indians as the Battle of the Hundred Slain. This war will remain the only full-scale "Indian War" won by the Indians, a victory formalized in the *Fort Laramie Treaty* of 1868. The slaughter of the federal troops reveals the inability of the Army to police the Bozeman Trail when there is Indian resistance.

1866–1868

WARS. The Snake War occurs in Oregon and Idaho, involving the Northern Paiute bands of Yahuskin, and Walpapi bands of Northern Paiute (Numu) Indians. Around 800 Northern Paiute, known as the Snake Indians, will fight nearly 50 battles with troops under Gen. George Crook, with around 500 Snake Indians being killed during the two years of battle.

1867

LAND. The U.S. purchases Alaska from Imperial Russia on October 18 by the *Treaty of Cession*, adding approximately 29,000 Inuits (Eskimos), Aleuts, Tlingit, and Athabascan Indian groups, as well as 1,000 whites, to the U.S. population.

MIGR. The Lenni Lenape (Delaware) Indians move to Oklahoma from the eastern United States. The tribe had left their lands in New Jersey and Pennsylvania about 150 years earlier, making seven major moves under pressure from white settlers and from other Indian tribes, and losing most of their population in the migrations.

POLI. In January, 1867, the *Doolittle Report* from Congress challenges the wisdom of a military solution to Indian-white conflicts on the Plains. The report recommends that Indians be placed on reservations and taught farming and white customs.

In July 1867, the U.S. Peace Commission is formed by Congress to negotiate peace settlements with the Plains Indians. In 1868, the commission will report on corruption in Indian agencies.

The *British North America Act* establishes the Dominion of Canada on July 1. The Canadian constitution charges the federal government with responsibility for native affairs.

TREA. The *Medicine Lodge Peace Treaty* is signed in the largest gathering of Indians and whites in the history of the United States. Meeting near the Medicine River in Kansas Territory, Plains tribal leaders accept permanent lands within Indian Territory, which is declared to be the area south of the Kansas border.

The U.S. Peace Commission makes a survey of Indian affairs and recommends that the current treaty process be abolished. The treaty process will be formerly abolished in 1871 by Congress after the United States negotiates the last treaty with the Nez Percé Indians.

WARS. The Hancock Campaign takes place against the Cheyenne and Arapaho on the central Plains.

1868

POLI. The Fourteenth Amendment to the U.S. Constitution gives African American men the right to vote, but denies the vote to Indians.

TREA. Eager to end Red Cloud's War, the U.S. Peace Commission negotiates a treaty with Lakota Sioux leaders at Fort Laramie in present-day Wyoming on April 28. The Sioux Indians are guaranteed their sacred lands, the Black Hills of Dakota. (The United States will break the 1874 treaty by sending army troops under Gen. George A. Custer to prospect for gold in the Black Hills, the discovery of which will bring white prospectors pouring into the area. This will result in a war between the United States and the Sioux, after which, in February, 1877, the Sioux will be expelled from the Black Hills by an act of Congress.) Red Cloud refuses to speak with the U.S. negotiators until the Americans agree to abandon their three forts along the Bozeman Trail. On November 7, 1868, Red Cloud approves the *Treaty of Fort Laramie,* with the United States agreeing to abandon the forts on the Bozeman Trail, to prevent non-Indians from settling along the trail, and to establish the Great Sioux Reservation between the Missouri River and the Rocky Mountains.

The *U.S. Treaty with the Navajo, 1868,* brings peace between the U.S. government and the Navajo. The Navajo Indian Reservation, the largest in the United States, is created on June 1 by the *Treaty of Bosque Redondo* and signed by Navajo chiefs at Fort Sumner, New Mexico. The Navajo, with a population of around 9,000 at this time, agree to live on the reservation and cease opposition to whites. The treaty establishes a 3.5 million-acre reservation within the Navajo Nation's old domains (the Dinétah) in New Mexico, Arizona, and Utah. The main reservation will grow to include nearly 14.5 million acres (25,000 square miles) extending from the Four Corners area to northeastern Arizona, northwestern New Mexico, and southwestern Utah, most of it being desert and semidesert with only 68,000 acres of farmland.

The Nez Percé Indians sign the last treaty to be ratified by the U.S. Congress. In 1871, treaty making between Indian tribes and the U.S. government will officially end by Congress.

WARS. The Commissioner of Indian Affairs estimates that Indian Wars in the West are costing the federal government $1 million per Indian killed.

The Battle of Beecher Island (or Aricaree Fork) is fought from September 17–25 in Kansas. Around 600 Cheyenne, Lakota Sioux, and Arapaho under Chief Roman Nose are held off for eight days by a company of 52 U.S. army scouts until the unit is rescued.

In November, the Cheyenne camp of Chief Black Kettle on the Washita River in Oklahoma is attacked by the U.S. Seventh Cavalry under Lt. Col. George

A. Custer. A war party of young Cheyenne men had been raiding white settlements in Kansas. Custer erroneously blames Black Kettle's band. In the Washita River Massacre, Black Kettle and more than 100 Indians are killed. This is Custer's first major battle with the Indians. The Cheyenne will join the Sioux eight years later in their defeat of Custer at the Battle of Little Big Horn.

1868–1869

WARS. The Southern Plains War (or Sheridan Campaign) takes place, involving U.S. Gen. Philip Henry Sheridan and the Cheyenne, Lakota Sioux, Arapaho, Kiowa, and Comanche.

1869

ARTS. Amos Bad Heart Bull, an Oglala Dakota artist, is born in present-day Wyoming. He will draw battles of his tribe and record observations of the regalia, daily lives, religious rituals, and ceremonies of the Oglala. He will die in 1913.

CONT. The first transcontinental railroad is completed on May 10, joining the Union Pacific and Central Pacific lines at Promontory Point, Utah.

Red Cloud and Indians. Standing: Red Bear, Young Man Afraid of his Horse, Good Voice, Ring Thunder, Iron Crow, White Tail, Young Spotten Tail. Seated: Yellow Bear, Jack Red Cloud, Big Road, Little Wound, Black Crow. Courtesy of Library of Congress.

LAND. The Hudson's Bay Company sells its vast holdings of land (Rupert's Land) to the Dominion of Canada.

POLI. President Grant's "Peace Policy" is inaugurated and lasts until 1874. In 1870, Grant will transfer control of Indian agencies from army officers to Christian missionary groups.

Civil War general Philip H. Sheridan states while on a tour of the West "The only good Indians I ever saw were dead." This was said after the Comanche chief Tochoway (Turtle Dove) was introduced to Sheridan as a "good Indian." The quote became misconstrued to mean "The only good Indian is a dead Indian" (Roy 1992, 4).

The U.S. Board of Indian Commissioners is created by President Ulysses S. Grant, as part of his Peace Policy, to oversee the handling of Indian supplies and appropriations in an attempt to eliminate the corruption going on in Indian affairs. The board will last until 1933, when it will be disbanded by President Franklin D. Roosevelt.

Ely Sameul Parker (Donehogawa), a Seneca Indian chief, served as a Brigadier General in the Civil War under Grant. Now, he is appointed U.S. Commissioner of Indian Affairs, the first Indian to head the commission, and will serve until 1871.

WARS. The First Riel Rebellion in Canada is launched by the Red River Métis. Louis Riel, Jr., leads a group of Métis in the first Northwest Rebellion to establish an independent provisional government in Manitoba's Red River region.

1869–1870

HEAL. A smallpox epidemic strikes the Canadian Plains Indians including the Blackfeet, Piegan, and Blood.

1869–1872

EXPL. John Wesley Powell, geologist and ethnologist, explores the Colorado River and Grand Canyon.

1870

EDUC. The U.S. Congress appropriates $100,000 for federal administration of Indian education.

POLI. Red Cloud, the Lakota Sioux leader, visits Washington, D.C. and New York City. He negotiates with President Grant and other officials, claiming that the *Treaty of Fort Laramie* is invalid and "all lies."

The Cherokee Tobacco Case of 1870 (the Supreme Court case of *Boudinot v. United States*), rules that the Cherokees are not exempt from taxes on produce (as established in a 1868 treaty) and must pay taxes on tobacco produced in their factory in the Cherokee Nation. The Supreme Court establishes a "last-in-time" rule which states that the last law made overrides previous laws and treaties. This is devastating to Indian tribes because new laws may break treaty promises.

RELI. President Grant turns over control of Indian agencies from army officers to 12 different Christian missionary groups from various denominations. This happens after Congress passes a law prohibiting army officers from holding the position of Indian agent.

WARS. In Baker's Massacre, a village of Piegan Indians (a subtribe of the Blackfoot Indians) in what is now northern Montana is attacked on January 22 in bitter cold weather by U.S. cavalry troops under Col. E. M. Baker. Of the 174 Indians killed, 53 are women and children. Another 140 women and children are taken prisoners. Public outcry over the massacre leads to the defeat of a Congressional bill that would have transferred the Bureau of Indian Affairs back to the War Department.

C. 1870–1890

RELI. The use of peyote as a religious sacrament spreads from Mexican Indians to Comanches, Kiowas, and other Plains tribes.

1871

ANIM. White hunters begin the wholesale slaughter of buffalo on the southern Plains.

POLI. Gen. Sheridan issues orders forbidding western Indians to leave reservations without the permission of civilian agents.

TREA. The treaty-making period by the U.S. government formally ends as Congress passes the *Indian Appropriation Act* on March 3, and attaches a rider that stops the practice of treaty making. The Cherokee Tobacco Case of 1870, ruling that Cherokee are not exempt from taxes on produce (as established in an earlier treaty), sets the stage for this new law. This makes Indians wards of the federal government and discontinues the practice of according full treaty status to agreements made with tribal leaders. The act does not annul existing treaties, but it prevents recognition of Indian tribes as sovereign nations or independent powers. Indians are now subject to acts of Congress, executive orders, and executive agreements. Between 1778 and 1871, the U.S. Senate had approved 372 treaties with Indian tribes.

WARS. Gen. George Crook assumes command of the Army in Arizona Territory and uses Apaches as scouts. His men track down Chiricahua Apache chief Cochise and force him to surrender.

In Tucson, Arizona Territory, white vigilantes attack Eskiminzin's band of Apaches, killing around 100 of these peaceable Apaches near Camp Grant. Also, 29 Apache children are captured and will be sold as slaves.

Kiowa raids in Texas continue against white settlers and travelers. In May, Kiowas attack a wagon train in the Salt Creek Prairie, killing seven men and mutilating their corpses. Gen. William Tecumseh Sherman arrests Satanta and two other Kiowa leaders of the attack known as the Salt Creek Massacre.

1872

ARTS. Silver jewelry-making starts among the Zuni Indians.

POLI. In Arizona, Chiricahua Apache give up resisting whites on the promise of a reservation separate from that of the Mescalero Apache. Cochise, now 60, signs a treaty with the Indian commissioner Gen. Oliver O. Howard and retires to the new Arizona reservation where he will die in June 1874.

RELI. The Earth Lodge Religion is founded among northern California tribes.

1872–1873

WARS. The Modoc War in California and Oregon breaks out with the U.S. forces and the Modoc tribe, led by Chief Kintpuash (or Captain Jack). The Modoc had ceded their lands in northern California and southern Oregon in 1864 and been assigned to the Klamath reservation. The Klamath Indians refused to let the Modoc hunt or fish in the area, and in 1870 the Modoc returned to their old lands near Lost River. It takes more than 1,000 soldiers to bring the Modoc in from the lava beds of northern California on the shore of Lake Tule, where about 250 took refuge for about six months. Around 400 troops are killed in the fighting. Modoc Indian Captain Jack and three others are hanged in 1873, and the rest of the Modoc are sent to reservations in Oklahoma.

Gen. Crook's Tonto Basin Campaign occurs against Apache and Yavapai Indians under Delshay in the Southwest.

1873

ARTS. The first International Indian Fair is held in Oklahoma.

POLI. The "civilization fund" that was established by Congress in 1819 is repealed because of its violation of the separation of church and state. Money had been appropriated to finance Indian education at schools run by missionaries, but now the Bureau of Indian Affairs will establish government-operated schools for Indians.

WARS. The Fourth U.S. Cavalry under Col. Ranald Mackenzie crosses the border into Mexico and attacks the Kickapoo settlement at Nacimiento. These are the Kickapoo who fled Kansas eight years earlier in 1865 to escape confinement on the reservation. Most of the Indians killed in the attack by the Cavalry are women and children. As a result of the constant fighting with Texans, 317 of the Kickapoo agree to relocate to Indian Territory, while 200 more stay in Mexico.

1874

ENVI. Gold is discovered in the Black Hills of South Dakota, which are sacred to the Sioux.

Treaties protecting these Indian lands are ignored by white miners. In the summer, George Armstrong Custer leads soldiers through the Great Sioux Reservation, in violation of the *Treaty of Fort Laramie,* and the soldiers find gold in the Black Hills. Their discovery compels white miners to flock to the region.

WARS. The "Buffalo War" takes place in Oklahoma and Texas. This is a desperate attempt by the Cheyenne, Arapaho, Comanche, and Kiowa tribes to save the few remaining buffalo herds from destruction by white hunters. Chief Quanah Parker and his Comanche braves will give up their fight against the buffalo hunters and surrender at Ft. Sill in Indian Territory in 1875. By then, hunters will have killed so many buffalo on the southern Plains that the herds are nearly extinct. Between 1872 and 1874, whites slaughter an estimated 5 million buffalo. This destroys the traditional Plains Indian culture.

1874–1875

LAND. The *Indian Homestead Act* is enacted by Congress which extends the benefits of the *General Homestead Act* of 1862 to Indian heads of families over 21 years of age who have abandoned or will abandon their tribal relations. Qualified Indians can obtain 160 acres from the public domain if they will occupy the land for five years and make certain improvements to it. The act is intended to encourage Indians to leave the reservations and become farmers. Few will opt for the opportunity, though. The act will be superseded by the 1887 *Dawes Act,* under which Indians will be allotted reservation lands on an individual basis.

WARS. The Red River War takes place on the southern Plains, involving the Comanche,

Kiowa, and some Cheyenne, Arapaho, and Lakota Sioux, led by Quanah Parker, Satanta, and others. In 1875, Quanah Parker, the Comanche Chief, ends his resistance to white ranchers settling the Texas prairie. Col. R. S. Mackenzie of the U.S. Cavalry captures and destroys his herd of 1,400 horses during the previous fall season, and the chief now brings his warriors to a reservation created by the government. After surrendering to the U.S. Army, 72 Kiowa, Cheyenne, and Arapaho are sent to Fort Marion Prison in St. Augustine, Florida, where they will be kept for three years. In December, 1875 the commissioner of Indian Affairs announces that any Indians on the northern Plains who do not report to their reservation agencies by January 31, 1876, will be considered "hostiles" at war with the United States. When the Plains Indians refuse to return to their reservation in January, several battles will take place with Army troops.

1875

ARTS. Plains Indians who are being held at Fort Marion in Florida create ledger art.

1876

ANIM. White hunters begin slaughtering the northern Plains buffalo herds. During the early 1880s, over 5,000 white hunters and skinners will come to this region, because most of the buffalo of the southern Plains have been killed. By 1883, most of the buffalo will have disappeared.

MIGR. The U.S. government attempts to consolidate all Apaches in Arizona Territory on the San Carlos Reservation. Most Apaches agree to move to the desolate, hot area, a region with little game and food. Any one found off the reservation

"the Kansas Pacific Railroad . . .engage(ed) expert hunters to kill buffaloes. . .During my engagement as hunter for the company, which covered a period of eighteen months, I killed 4,280 buffaloes." William "Buffalo Bill" Cody on his career as a professional buffalo hunter (Sell 1955, 14).

By 1883, most of the buffalo in the Great Plains had disappeared, due to white hunters. Courtesy of Library of Congress.

is to be shot without being given a chance to surrender. However, about half of the Chiracahua Apaches under Geronimo (Goyathlay) move into Mexico, beginning a 10-year reign of terror against white settlers in the Southwest. During 1877–1880, there will be Apache resistance in the Southwest under Victorio.

POLI. The Homestead Mining Company is founded at Lead in the Black Hills of Dakota Territory. This will be the largest U.S. producer of gold.

The *Canadian Indian Act* is passed in Canada, defining Indian policy. This recognizes the Indian reserves established by treaty and creates a distinct legal status for Indians. The act also gives individual Indians the right to seek Canadian citizenship by renouncing their rights and privileges as Indians.

PUBL. Zitkala Sa (Red Bird, or Gertrude Simmons Bonnin; 1876–1938) is a Yankton Sioux born on the Pine Ridge Reservation in South Dakota. Her father is a white man and her mother is a full-blooded Sioux. She will be raised as a traditional Sioux until she leaves the reservation for a formal education in white men's schools. She will become one of the most educated and influential women Indian writers in a time when severe prejudice prevails toward American Indian culture and women.

1876–1877

WARS. The Sioux War for the Black Hills, involving the Sioux, Cheyenne, and Arapaho under Sitting Bull and Crazy Horse, goes on for two years. U.S. troops will be defeated at the Battle of Powder River, and meet strong opposition in the Battle of the Rosebud. On June 25, 1876, the Battle of the Little Big Horn ends in the massacre of the 264-man U.S. Seventh Cavalry under Lt. Col. George Armstrong Custer, 37. The Sioux were angered by the slaughter of buffalo in Montana Territory by the advancing whites in the Black Hills gold rush. Custer and

Crazy Horse, last of the Sioux war chiefs at large, finally was confined to a reservation in May 1877. He never adjusted to his new life. When he was ushered into the guardhouse at Fort Robinson, Nebraska, he resisted and was stabbed. His dying words were: "I was hostile to the white man. . .We preferred hunting to a life of idleness on our reservations. . .At times we did not get enough to eat and we were not allowed to hunt. All we wanted was peace and to be let alone. Soldiers came. . .in the winter. . .and destroyed our villages. Then Long Hair (Custer) came. . .They said we massacred him, but he would have done the same to us. . .Our first impulse was to escape. . .but we were so hemmed in we had to fight. After that I . . .lived in peace; but the government would not let me alone. . .I came back to the Red Cloud Agency. Yet I was not allowed to remain quiet. I was tired of fighting. . .They tried to confine me. . .and a soldier ran his bayonet into me. I have spoken" (Wheeler 1925, 199).

his men attack a large hunting camp of Sioux, Cheyenne, and Arapaho Indians on the Little Big Horn River in the territory of Montana. The Indians, led by chiefs Sitting Bull, Crazy Horse, and Gall, overwhelm Custer's troops. In the fall of 1876, the United States confiscates the Black Hills area of the Sioux reservation, violating the 1868 treaty. Sitting Bull and his followers seek refuge in Canada. During the first week of January, 1877, Cheyenne and Lakota Sioux forces fight against the U.S. Army in the Battle of Wolf Mountain. Later that year, Sitting Bull is killed while in custody. Crazy Horse and 900 Sioux, with more than 2,000 horses, surrender to U.S. forces on May 6, 1877, at Camp Robinson, Nebraska. On May 7, 1877, Lame Deer, the leader of the Minicounjou band of Lakota Sioux, is shot and killed in the Battle of Muddy Creek in Montana, as he tries to surrender to U.S. troops. Crazy Horse is killed while a prisoner on September 5, 1877. On September 9, Lakota Sioux war leader American Horse is killed in battle. On November 25, U.S. troops destroy Cheyenne leader Dull Knife's camp of 183 lodges along the Powder River in present-day Wyoming. By the end of 1877, the United States takes control of the Black Hills.

1877

LAND. Blackfeet tribes cede land to the Dominion of Canada.

WARS. The Nez Percé War breaks out on June 15, led by Chief Joseph. Nez Percé Indians in Oregon are ordered to leave their homeland or be forcibly removed after years of passive non-compliance with the treaty they signed in 1863. After some of the Nez Percé braves kill four white settlers in Idaho, U.S. troops are sent in but are nearly annihilated in the Battle of White Bird Canyon. After 18 subsequent engagements, the Nez Percé are weakened. Chief Joseph leads between 400 and 750 of his tribe, including 200 warriors, on a four-month, 1,400-mile retreat through the Rocky Mountain wilderness of Idaho, Wyoming, and Montana northward toward Canada, while being pursued by about 2,000 soldiers. But, on October 5, in the Bear Paw mountains of Montana, just 30–40 miles from the safety of the Canadian border, the tribe is surrounded by fresh army troops. Chief Joseph says "I will fight no more forever," and the Nez Percé surrender (Fee 1936, 263).

1877–1880

WARS. Apache resistance takes place in the Southwest under Victorio.

1878

EDUC. The Hampton Institute, a traditionally Black school in Hampton, Virginia, that was established as a school for freed African-American slaves, admits 17 Indian men students. These prisoners from Fort Marion in Florida become the first Indians to attend Hampton Institute.

Chief Joseph was never permitted to live again in his beloved hills. He was first taken to Fort Leavenworth, then to Indian Territory, then to Washington, D.C., twice, again to Indian Territory, and finally in 1885 to the Colville Reservation in the state of Washington, where he died in 1904. Chief Joseph pleaded "You might as well expect the rivers to run backward as that any man who was born a free man should be contented when penned up and denied liberty to go where he pleases. . .Let me be a free man—free to travel, free to stop, free to work, free to trade where I choose, free to choose my own teachers, free to follow the religion of my fathers, free to talk and think and act for myself—and I will obey every law, or submit to the penalty" (Fee 1936, 283).

HEAL. Around half of the Indian agencies now have a physician, and those physicians are now required by an act of Congress to be graduates of medical colleges.

HUNT. The first salmon cannery opens in southern Alaska, displacing the Native fishers.

POLI. Congress appropriates funds for an American Indian Police force. The Bureau of Indian Affairs hires Indian men to police reservations. The force is organized at all the Indian agencies and charged with preserving order, protecting property, preventing illegal liquor traffic, and returning truant students to school. However, many Indians resent following the orders of Indian policemen who they consider to be traitors to their people. In 1883, this policy will bring about the Court of Indian Offenses, which authorizes tribal units to administer justice in all but major crimes. In the *Major Crimes Act* of 1885, federal courts will be formally given jurisdiction over Indian cases involving major crimes on reservations.

TRAD. The Hubbell Trading Post opens on the Navajo Reservation. John Lorenzo Hubbell encourages Navajo women to weave rugs for sale to whites, helping to create a new industry for the Navajo. Hubbell's mail order catalog also creates a demand for Navajo wares among whites throughout the country.

WARS. The Bannock War in Idaho and Oregon involves the Bannock, Northern Paiute, and Cayuse tribes led by Buffalo Horn. The U.S. army fights separate campaigns on the western Plains against the Ute, Apache, Bannock, and Paiute Indians. The Indians are angered by continued threats to their food supplies by white ranchers. After the fighting is ended the Bannock are sent to live at the Yakima Reservation in western Washington. After five unhappy years there, the Bannock will be permitted to relocate to other reservations in present-day Oregon, Nevada, California, and Idaho.

1879

CONT. Frank Hamilton Cushing comes to live among the Zuni. At age 22, Cushing comes to the Southwest as part of the Bureau of Ethnology's first expedition, charged with learning as much as he can about Zuni culture. His willingness to learn the Zuni language and adopt their dress and customs impresses the Zuni governor who adopts Cushing into his family. After two months, the expedition leaves the Zuni pueblo, but Cushing stays behind for four years, accumulating knowledge for his later writings on Zuni mythology, beliefs, and culture.

EDUC. The Carlisle Industrial Indian Boarding School is established by Richard H. Pratt in Carlisle, Pennsylvania, as the first non-reservation school sponsored by the U.S. government. The philosophy of the school is to assimilate Indians into the dominant mainstream culture. The school teaches English (forbidding Indians to speak their own languages), provides a primary education, and instructs students in practical jobs such as mechanical skills and farming (for boys), and cooking, sewing, laundry, and housework (for girls). Pratt's slogan was "Kill the Indian and save the man" (Pratt 1892, 46). By 1905, the school will have an enrollment of 1,000, but it will close in 1918.

LAWS. The Federal Court at Omaha, Nebraska, responds to a habeas corpus trial brought by Standing Bear, a Ponca Indian, upholding the right of Indians to sue. The Ponca had been forcibly removed to Indian Territory in 1877 from their ancestral homelands in present-day Nebraska. Over one-fourth of the tribe died in the removal, including Standing Bear's children. When Standing Bear and a group of Ponca tried to return home to bury Standing Bear's son, they were stopped and held as prisoners by armed guards under Gen. George Crook. Several attorneys called for their release, but the U.S. attorney countered that habeas corpus could not apply to the Ponca because they were not legally considered human beings. In the case of *Standing Bear v. Crook,* Indians are declared in fact to be human beings under U.S. law.

PUBL. The Bureau of Ethnology (later renamed the Bureau of American Ethnology) is established by Congress to collect information about

Breakfast lesson in a home economics class of the Carlisle Industrial Indian Boarding School, c. 1900. Courtesy of Library of Congress.

The Sheepeater War (or Sheepeater Troubles) takes place from May to October in central Idaho. When five Chinese and two American prospectors are killed in present-day Idaho, the army accuses the Sheepeaters, a group of about 30 Bannock and Shoshone Indians in the area. It takes several months for troops to bring in the Indians. Although the Sheepeaters claim innocence, they are sent to a prison in Vancouver, Washington Territory, and then are relocated to the Fort Hall Reservation in Idaho.

The Ute War takes place in Colorado in September under Satanta and Lone Wolf. When the Ute are subdued, a treaty is negotiated by Ouray whereby the Ute cede their lands at White River and relocate to the Uintah Reservation in present-day Utah.

Indian tribes and cultures. As a unique organization within the Smithsonian Institution, it will sponsor and publish an enormous amount of ethnological and anthropological information about American Indians until it is disbanded in 1965.

WARS. Northern Cheyenne Indians, under chiefs Dull Knife, Wild Hog, and Little Wolf, surrender in Colorado to U.S. government forces. They are sent to Ft. Reno, Oklahoma, as prisoners. The prisoners make two escape attempts—first in Oklahoma and later from Ft. Robinson in Nebraska—to their homeland in Dakota Territory. Nearly half of the group of about 220 Indians are killed in their escapes and flights. Only seven of Dull Knife's followers manage to escape.

1879–1885

POLI. Many "Friends of the Indian" organizations are founded during this time, including the Indian Protection Committee, Indian Rights Association, Women's National Indian Association, and National Indian Defense Association.

C. 1880

RELI. The Drum Religion is founded among the Santee Dakota (Sioux), soon spreading to other western Great Lakes tribes.

Little Wolf and Dull Knife, Northern Cheyenne chiefs, were removed with their people from their lands in 1877 to malarial Indian Territory. In 1878, they protested, demanding to go home to their Powder River hunting ground. Little Wolf: "These people were raised far up in the north among the pines and the mountains. In that country we were always healthy. There was no sickness and very few of us died. Now, since we have been in this country, we are dying every day. This is not a good country for us, and we wish to return to our home in the mountains. . .We cannot stay another year; we want to go now. Before another year has passed, we may all be dead. . .I am going to leave here; I am going north to my own country. I do not want to see blood spilt about this agency" (Grinnell 1915, 386).

1880

WARS. Victorio, the renegade Apache leader, is killed in a battle with Mexican troops in Mexico's Chihuahua Desert. A force of 350 Mexicans and Tarahumara Indians kill 78 Apaches and capture 62 more in the Battle of Tres Castillos on October 15–16. Victorio and his Apaches had been raiding back and forth across the Mexican-U.S. border for two years.

1881

CONT. The second transcontinental railroad is completed, linking the Southern Pacific with the Atchison, Topeka & Santa Fe railroad.

PUBL. *A Century of Dishonor* is published by Helen Hunt Jackson, containing strong criticism of the treatment of Indians—including the history of broken treaties, denied Indian rights, and Indian removal from their lands over the past 100 years. The book becomes widely influential in intellectual circles, galvanizing the public on Indian rights.

RELI. The Indian Shaker Religion is born in the Pacific Northwest when John Slocum, a Coast Salish (Squaxon) laborer and Catholic convert, begins to preach a gospel of clean living and spiritual renewal.

WARS. Sitting Bull and his band of 187 followers surrender to U.S. officials at Fort Buford, North Dakota. The Lakota, facing starvation, return from their camp in Canada to the Lakota reservation where they can collect rations. They endure the humiliation of surrendering their weapons and horses and are sent to Fort Randall for two years of imprisonment.

1881–1886

WARS. Geronimo and his followers escape from the San Carlos Reservation in October, 1881, and join the remnants of the Apaches led by Victorio who had escaped to Mexico in 1877. Apache resistance will continue under Geronimo in the Southwest until Geronimo surrenders in 1886, marking the end of the Indian Wars.

1882

LAND. The Hopi Indian Reservation is established by executive order in the center of the tribe's ancestral homeland in present-day Arizona. When several Navajo families living within the new reservation's borders refuse to move, the conflict leads to the Hopi-Navajo land dispute that will continue for more than 100 years.

POLI. The Indian Rights Association (IRA) is organized in Philadelphia on December 15 for the purpose of securing citizenship, civil rights, and better education for American Indians. The non-Indian philanthropists who founded the IRA are concerned with protecting Indians from the avarice of land-hungry whites. The organization will become one of the most influential forces in U.S. Indian policy and will be instrumental in the passage of the *General Allotment Act* in 1887.

SETT. The Tlingit village of Angoon in southeast Alaska is destroyed by the U.S. Navy. After a dispute with the Northwest Trading Company over the deaths of two Tlingit men who were working

Sitting Bull abandoned his freezing sanctuary in Canada to return to the United States in 1881. "I do not come in anger toward the white soldiers. I am very sad. My daughter went this road Her I am seeking. I will fight no more. I do not love war. I never was the aggressor. I fought only to defend my women and children. Now all my people want to return to their native land. Therefore I submit. . .(later) My followers are weary of cold and hunger. They wish to see their brothers and their old home, therefore I bow my head" (Taylor 1932, 239).

for the trading firm, the Tlingit demand a payment of 200 blankets. The U.S. Navy, under Officer E. C. Merriman, instead threatens to shell the Tlingit village if they do not pay a fee of 400 blankets. When the Tlingit refuse, Merriman orders his men to demolish Angoon, which kills 26 children in the fires created by the ship's shells. It will take 10 years to rebuild the village.

1883

ARTS. *Buffalo Bill's Wild West Show* opens at Omaha, Nebraska, and will run for the next 20 years displaying sharpshooting, trick riding, and dramatic recreations of historical events such as famous battles between the U.S. Army and the Plains Indians. Promoter William Frederick Cody (Buffalo Bill) is the former buffalo hunter famous for the myth that he killed and scalped the Cheyenne leader Yellow Hand in a July 1876 duel. The show is a big hit with the public because of the actual Indians and cowboys Cody hires as performers. For one year, the show will include Sioux chief Sitting Bull.

CONT. The Northern Pacific Railroad is completed from St. Paul, Minnesota, to the Oregon coast.

POLI. The first Mohonk Conference is held at Lake Mohonk, New York. These conferences become a series of annual meetings of "friends of the Indians" in which the needs of American Indians are discussed and recommendations are made to improve things. The meetings, sponsored by Albert K. Smiley, a member of the U.S. Board of Indian Commissioners, brings various Indian experts together with key religious and humanitarian leaders; public-opinion makers, such as newspaper editors, legislators, and college presidents; and others who are interested in protecting Indians' rights, mainly through their assimilation into mainstream American culture. There will be 35 annual Mohonk Conferences (through 1916) which will have a great influence on U.S. Indian policy. Like the Indian Rights Association, formed in the previous year, this well-meaning group will help get the *General Allotment Act* passed in 1887.

In September, Lakota chief Sitting Bull is invited to Bismarck, North Dakota, to deliver a speech at a ceremony to dedicate the Northern Pacific Railroad. An interpreter is provided to translate his speech. Sitting Bull tells the crowd in part, "I hate all white people. You are thieves and liars. You have taken away our land and made us outcasts" (Glaspell 1941, 187). His startled translator ignores these words and reads from the prepared praiseworthy speech Sitting Bull was supposed to deliver. The speech receives a standing ovation from the audience.

PUBL. *Life Among the Piutes,* by Sarah Winnemucca, is the first published book written by an American Indian woman. It is a tribal history of the Northern Paiute combined with her autobiography.

RELI. The Sun Dance is declared illegal by the Commissioner of Indian Affairs. The U.S. Department of the Interior will ban the religious ceremony in 1904. The federal government will forbid the ceremony in 1910. The dramatic ceremony conducted among the buffalo-hunting tribal groups of the Great Plains originated around 1700.

1884

EDUC. The U.S. Industrial Training School opens in Lawrence, Kansas, on September 1. Operated by the Bureau of Indian Affairs, this Indian boarding school encourages assimilation of students into white society and abandonment of Indian ways and beliefs. The school will be renamed the Haskell Institute in 1894. It will become one of the largest Indian colleges by the late twentieth century and renamed Haskell Indian Nations University in 1993.

LAND. On May 17, Congress passes the *Organic Act,* acknowledging the rights of Inuit (Eskimos) to lands in the Territory of Alaska, which they use and occupy. However, future legislation will determine whether these peoples can be given legal title to their land.

LAWS. Indians are denied citizenship and the right to vote in the Supreme Court case of *Elk v. Wilkins.* In Nebraska, John Elk is an assimilated Indian who has chosen not to be a member of a tribe and does not live on tribal lands. The court finds that the Fourteenth Amendment to the Constitution does not apply to Indians, even those who renounce tribal membership.

PUBL. Helen Hunt Jackson publishes the novel *Ramona*. Jackson is the Indian reformer who published *A Century of Dishonor* in 1881. *Ramona* is a romantic, sentimental story of a beautiful half-Mexican, half-Indian woman in love with an Indian man whose tribe was dispossessed of its lands by settlers. The story is loosely based on the life of Ramona Lubo, a Cahuilla basketmaker. The novel becomes very popular and serves as a means of drawing attention to the injustices committed against California Indians.

RELI. Canada outlaws the Potlatch Ceremony among Northwest Coast tribes. In the traditional ceremony, a wealthy family hosts a great feast and distributes gifts to the guests. Missionaries and government officials feel the concept is incompatible with Western values of personal property. The law will be repealed in 1951.

1884–1894

LAND. Lands belonging to the Sauk, Fox, Potawatomi, Cheyenne, and Arapaho are taken from these tribes and occupied by white settlers. The United States opens Indian Territory to white settlement.

1885

ANIM. The last great herd of buffalo in the United States (northern herd) is nearly exterminated by hunters. The southern herd was nearly exterminated by 1880.

CONT. The Canadian Pacific transcontinental railroad is completed.

LAWS. Federal jurisdiction over major crimes is extended to Indian Territory and to reservations by the Congressional *Major Crimes Act*. This ends the practice of having tribal judicial systems handle major offenses (murder, manslaughter, arson, burglary, rape, larceny, and assault with the intent to kill) committed by one Indian against another. This is the first law to make Indians on tribally-held lands subject to U.S. law.

WARS. The Second Riel Rebellion joins the Canadian Indians and Métis (half-French and half-Indian) living along the Saskatchewan River in Canada. They are alarmed by the coming of white settlers and the disappearing of the buffalo herds. Louis Riel, a Métis political leader, forms a provisional government and defies the authority of the Canadian government. The Indian participants are led by the Cree Chiefs Poundmaker and Big Bear. Although the Canadian government ends the rebellion, some of the grievances of the Indians and Métis are remedied.

Cree Indians surrender to Dominion troops of Canada.

1886

ECON. Mohawk Indians of the Kahnawake (or Caughnawaga) Reserve in Quebec are trained in high-steel construction to help build a bridge across the St. Lawrence River. The Mohawk men are so adept at balancing on and climbing the high steel beams that construction companies begin hiring them as ironworkers on bridges and other steel structures. This starts a tradition among the Iroquois of high steel construction work.

WARS. Geronimo surrenders. The last major Indian war in the United States ends on September 4, when Chiricahua Apache war chief Geronimo (Goyathlay) is captured by U.S. troops after four years of fighting on the Mexican border. Geronimo had been captured earlier by Gen. George Crook, but he escaped from the San Carlos reservation in Arizona and was then recaptured by Gen. Henry Ware Lawton. Pursued by three-quarters of the standing U.S. Army, 4,000 Mexican troops, and 1,000 Apache scouts, Geronimo finally surrenders out of concern for the women and children in his band. Geronimo and several hundred Apaches are sent to Florida as prisoners, later transferred to Alabama, and finally settled on a reservation in Oklahoma. Indian hostilities cease in the Southwest.

1887

CONT. Anthropologist Frank Boas begins his extensive study of the Kwakiutl people of British Columbia, living among the tribe and discovering the complexity of their society. His publications

Geronimo in his camp before he surren-
dered to General Crook. Courtesy of Library
of Congress.

will promote the view that the cultures of Indians
are as sophisticated as those of white societies,
and not inferior or "primitive." Boas will edit a
significant linguistics work in 1911 titled *Handbook of American Indian Languages*, from the
Smithsonian Institution.

LAND. The *General Allotment Act* (also known as
the *Dawes Act*) is passed by Congress, which ends
communal ownership of reservation lands. This
allows the federal government to partition Indian
reservations and give parcels (or allotments) to
individual tribal members. This policy attempts
to establish private ownership by Indians of their
lands, to remove Indians from tribal influence,
and to assimilate them into American life. The
government distributes 160-acre "allotments" to
individual Indians who are heads of families and
smaller parcels to unmarried persons. When a reservation is allotted, the male head of each family
will receive U.S. citizenship with his allotment.
Many Indian reformers advocate allotment as the
best means of assimilating Indians and helping
them be independent. The lands left over will be
sold to non-Indians. The leftover lands total

around 60 million acres. As a result of this act,
Indian lands will be reduced from 138 million
acres in 1887 to 48 million acres in 1934, when
the *Wheeler-Howard Act* will end the allotment of
land. Many tribes oppose the act. Several large
tribes, including the Five Civilized Tribes, the
Osage, and the Seneca, are explicitly excluded
from the act because they have lobbied to retain
their tribally held lands and tribal governments.
The Dawes Commission will preside over the
allotment of 20 million acres of land to 90,000
individual Indian landowners from 1893 to 1905.
Citizenship rolls will be made up for each tribe,
and the land will be surveyed and assessed, with
more than 200,000 claims analyzed during this
time period.

LAWS. Congress passes an act stating that any
Indian woman can acquire citizenship by marry-
ing a U.S. citizen.

MIGR. The Tsimshian Indians of British Columbia
move voluntarily to a reservation on Annette Island,
Alaska. An Anglican missionary, William Duncan,
is instrumental in obtaining the land from the U.S.
government. The settlement formed by the Tsimshian becomes a model Alaskan community with
comfortable homes, a cannery, sawmill, church, and
a school.

1888

POLI. Representatives from 22 Indian tribes
along with 3,000 other attendees meet at Ft.
Gibson in Indian Territory to form an Indian
state. Federal officials, fearful that the tribes
might succeed, rapidly push for allotment of the
Creek and Seminole Indian lands who had hosted
the gathering.

1889

ARTS. Nampeyo (1860–1942), a Hopi-Tewa
Indian, reproduces traditional Pueblo Indian pot-
tery, beginning a cultural renewal among Southwest
Indian potters.

EDUC. Susan La Flesche, an Omaha Indian,
becomes the first female American Indian physician. She graduates first in her class at the Women's
College of Medicine in Philadelphia, and she

Sitting Bull, in 1889, talked to a white man he trusted—John Carnigan, a school teacher at Standing Rock Reservation: "Our religion seems foolish to you, but so does yours to me. The Baptists and Methodists and Presbyterians and the Catholics all have a different God. Why cannot we have one of our own? Why does the agent seek to take away our religion? My race is dying. Our God will soon die with us. If this new religion is not true then what matters? I do not know what to believe. If I could dream like the others and visit the spirit world myself, then it would be easy to believe, but the trance does not come to me. It passes me by. I help others to see their dead, but I am not aided" (Garland 1923, 254).

returns to work on the Omaha Reservation in Nebraska. The Bureau of Indian Affairs hires her as the sole reservation doctor, serving over 1,000 Indians.

LAND. Two million acres in the center of Indian Territory (which will become Oklahoma Territory in the following year) that have not been assigned to an Indian group are opened for distribution to white settlers for the Land Run. On April 22, more than 50,000 settlers claim plots of land in a single day.

The *Sioux Bill* is passed by Congress, dividing the Great Sioux Reservation established by the *Treaty of Fort Laramie* in 1868. Six smaller reservations are created: Standing Rock, Pine Ridge, Rosebud, Cheyenne River, Crow Creek, and Lower Brulé. The law opens millions of acres of land to white settlement.

RELI. Wovoka founds a new Indian religion, the Ghost Dance movement. The Northern Paiute (Numu) prophet named Wovoka has a fever-induced vision where he is given instructions from God on how Indians should live. This will lead to the establishment of the Ghost Dance revitalization movement, which will soon be embraced by many tribes in the Great Plains region.

1890

LAND. On February 10, Sioux lands in South Dakota that were ceded to the U.S. government are opened to settlement under terms of a presidential proclamation. Around 11 million acres are offered to homesteaders.

The western portion of Indian Territory becomes Oklahoma Territory under federal rules. The U.S. government begins allotting the reservations so that any surplus lands can be sold to whites. Indian Territory is now reduced to the large reservations of the Five Civilized Tribes (Cherokee, Choctaw, Chickasaw, Creek, and Seminole) and several small reservations located in the northeastern corner of the region.

POPU. By this time, the U.S. Indian population reaches a low point of less than 250,000. The Bureau of the Census states (in 1894) in their *Report on Indians Taxed and Not Taxed in the United States (Except in Alaska) at the Eleventh Census: 1890* that the Indian population is down almost 40 percent from census figures for 1850. Also, the 1890 census determines that what has been defined as frontier (i.e., habitable regions with less than two inhabitants per square mile) no longer exists.

RELI. The Ghost Dance movement, led by the Paiute prophet and medicine man, Wovoka, gains influence among the Lakota and other Plains and Western tribes. Defeated and demoralized by reservation life, diseases, and crop failures many tribes adopt the religion as a way to give them hope and lift them out of their despair. Wovoka, who claims to have been taken into the spirit world during an illness, foretells of the restoration of the Indian, the return of the buffalo, and the disappearance of the white man. These events will come true, he said, if the Indians will return to the old values and lifestyle and perform the Ghost Dance. The "ghost shirt" will be worn by adherents

A Sioux Ghost dance, c. 1890. Drawing by Frederic Remington. Courtesy of Library of Congress.

to the faith, and the shirt will be bullet-proof. However, at the massacre of Wounded Knee on December 29, this proves to be untrue, and the movement will decline shortly thereafter.

WARS. Sitting Bull, the Sioux chief famous for the 1876 Battle of the Little Big Horn, is killed at the Standing Rock Agency at Pine Ridge, South Dakota, on December 15. Government officials are fearful that Sitting Bull will lead Ghost Dancers in a resistance movement against whites. He is arrested in a skirmish with U.S. troops and is shot by an Indian police officer as Sioux warriors try to rescue him. Several followers of Sitting Bull, his son Crow Foot, and six Indian police are also killed, increasing tensions in South Dakota.

At Wounded Knee on December 29, U.S. troops massacre Lakota Sioux en route to a Ghost Dance celebration. This ends the last major Indian resistance to white settlement in America. Nearly 500 well-armed U.S. 7th Cavalry troops confront a band of Lakota Indians under Chief Big Foot near Wounded Knee Creek in South Dakota. The Indians are en route to a large Ghost Dance celebration and are near freezing and starvation. The army troops attempt to disarm Big Foot's people, treating the Indian women roughly and disrespectfully. As tensions rise, one warrior refuses to give up his gun. When the soldiers grab for it, the gun goes off and the troops begin firing on the Indians, massacring an estimated 100 Sioux men and 250 women and children. The fleeing Indians are chased down and shot. Bodies of babies, chil-

Wovoka to his followers: "My people, before the white man came you were happy. You had many buffalo to eat and tall grass for your ponies—you could come and go like the wind. When it grew cold you could journey to the valleys of the south, where healing springs are; and when it grew warm, you could return to the mountains of the north. The white man came. He dug up the bones of our mother, the earth. He tore her bosom with steel. He built big trails and put iron horses on them. He fought you and beat you, and put you in barren places where a horned toad would die. He said you must stay there; you must not go hunt in the mountains" (Armstrong 1972, 150).

dren, and women will later be found as far as three miles from the camp, riddled with bullets. Three days after the massacre, burial crews will gather the frozen corpses of 146 Indians at the site for burial in a mass grave. The Wounded Knee slaughter is one of the greatest tragedies in American Indian history, and it will become an emblem of the centuries of injustices inflicted on Indians. In the 1960s and 1970s, Wounded Knee will be a rallying cry for the Red Power Movement.

1891

ANIM. Reindeer are introduced into Alaska from Siberia by Sheldon Jackson, a Presbyterian missionary in Alaska. Jackson hopes that reindeer will take the place of whales (which are declining) for Inuit hunters. The 1,280 reindeer imported expand to an estimated 600,000 by 1938. However, the plan eventually fails to interest the Inuit.

LAND. Congress authorizes the leasing of allotted Indian lands by whites. The *General Allotment Act* of 1887 is amended to allow Indians to lease allotments to non-Indians and to give 80-acre allotments to every adult on the tribal rolls.

LAWS. Congress passes *The Act for the Relief of the Mission Indians* which offers federal protection to California Indians. The United States will establish 32 small reservations throughout southern California over the next 18 years.

PUBL. J. W. Powell's book titled *Indian Linguistic Families of America North of Mexico* is published. Powell groups the languages of the American Indians into about 50 families. These will later be arranged into six major language groups by the linguist Edward Sapir in 1929.

A Child of the Forest is published by Sophia Alice Callahan, a 23-year-old Creek woman. The novel is a story of a Creek woman who learns to live in both the Indian and white worlds.

WARS. Kicking Bear, the Oglala Sioux leader and advocate of the Ghost Dance Religion, surrenders his Sioux people to army troops at the Pine Ridge Reservation to avoid further bloodshed after the Wounded Knee Massacre from two weeks earlier. The peaceful surrender of about 5,000 Lakota Sioux is the last formal surrender by Indians to the U.S. Army in the Plains Indian Wars.

1892

LAWS. Through the *Intoxication in Indian Country Act*, Congress prohibits the sale or transportation of alcohol in Indian lands.

PUBL. George B. Grinnell publishes his book titled *Blackfoot Lodge Tales*, a collection of folk tales of the Blackfoot tribe. He was a sympathetic observer of Indians who fought vigorously against the unjust treatment of the Indians by the U.S. government.

1892–1897

EDUC. The federal government withdraws support for church school for Indians in favor of boarding schools for Indians.

1893

LAND. White settlers have been flooding into Oklahoma Territory. The U.S. government is pressured into opening the neighboring Indian Territory to settlers by allotting the reservations

---

Simon Pokagon (1830–1899), Potawatomi chief, reminisced about life as it was once: "In early life I was deeply hurt as I witnessed the grand old forests of Michigan, under whose shades my forefathers lived and died, falling before the cyclone of civilization as before a prairie fire. In those days I traveled thousands of miles along our winding trails, through the unbroken solitudes of the wild forest, listening to the songs of the woodland birds, as they poured forth their melodies from the thick foliage above and about me" (First People 2006).

of the Five Civilized Tribes. Congress forms the Dawes Commission on March 3 to evaluate the situation and negotiate allotment agreements with tribal leaders. The United States had purchased the lands forming what is now the panhandle of Oklahoma, known as the Cherokee Outlet, from the Cherokee Nation for $8.5 million in 1891. On September 16, 1893, one of the most spectacular land rushes in American history takes place when thousands of land-hungry American homesteaders rush to stake claims on the 165- by 58-mile Cherokee Strip, composed of 6.5 million acres.

1894

ARTS. Thomas Edison's film company produces the first film about American Indians titled *The Sioux Ghost Dance*. The company follows with *Eagle Dance* (1898) and *Serving Rations to the Indians* (1898), all successful short movies running less than a minute which are privately viewed on Kinescope machines. For many Americans this is their first glimpse of Indians.

1895

HUNT. The Bannock Indians travel from their reservation home in Fort Hall, Idaho, to go to Wyoming to hunt game under the provisions of the treaty of 1868. A conflict arises with the settlers in the Wind River Valley, and the U.S. Cavalry escorts the Indians back to Idaho. The court case *Ward v. Race Horse* rules that the Bannock had lost their hunting rights, and Congress will reimburse them for the loss.

1896–1898

CONT. The Klondike Gold Rush begins in August, 1896, in Yukon Territory and Alaska. A flood of white prospectors travel north into the lands of Alaska Natives, overrunning the native ancestral territories and committing acts of violence against the natives. In the next decade, more than $100 million worth of gold will be mined, but the Alaska Natives will not receive any of this money.

1897

ENVI. Oil is discovered on the Osage Reservation in northern Indian Territory. This will alert the tribe to insist on retaining mineral rights when their reservation is allotted in later years.

LAND. The Choctaw and Chickasaw finally agree to allotment of their lands in Indian Territory by signing the *Atoka Agreement*. After withstanding years of pressure to allotment, the tribes have made a far better deal than most other tribes received from the federal government. They negotiate for and obtain allotments of 320 acres (instead of the usual 160 acres) due to the clamor for settlers to obtain land in Indian Territory.

RECR. The first Cheyenne Rodeo is held in July, beginning an annual Wyoming tradition.

The first Indian baseball player in the major leagues is Louis Sockalexis, a Penobscot from Old Town, Maine. He joins the Cleveland Spiders, sometimes receiving racial taunts from fans. However, in 1914, when fans are asked to rename the Cleveland Spiders, they vote to name the team the Cleveland Indians in an attempt to honor Sockalexis. (Research conducted by a college professor in 1999 will debunk the myth that the Cleveland major league baseball team was named in "honor" of Louis Sockalexis.)

SOCI. The American Museum of Natural History, with the help of Kwakiutl Indian George Hunt, researches the Northwest Coast Indians.

1898

LAND. The *Curtis Act* passed by Congress extends the allotment policy to the Five Civilized Tribes (Cherokee, Choctaw, Chickasaw, Creek, and Seminole) and dissolves their tribal governments and courts. The act sets the stage for the formation of the state of Oklahoma from Indian Territory.

RECR. The Trans-Mississippi Exposition in Omaha, Nebraska, features a show of around 500 Indians from 23 tribes dressed in traditional regalia and performing traditional activities.

Hunting Bear (Silvester John Brito) had tried other forms of psychological counseling and medicine, which did not cure him. The peyote ceremony cleansed him "of all evil" and gave him "a new life. . .a rebirth" (Brito 1989, xii).

1899

EDUC. Fort Spokane becomes a school for Indian children.

PUBL. Potawatomi scholar Simon Pokagon's autobiographical novel is published shortly after he dies. *O-Gi-Maw-Kwe-Mit-I-Gwa-Ki* (Queen of the Forest) is one of a few novels by Indians published in the nineteenth century. Written in the Potawatomi language, it will be translated later into English.

RELI. By this time, Peyotism has spread through the Indians of Texas and the Southwest, such as the Carizzo, the Lipan Apache, the Mescalero Apache, the Tonkawa, and the Caddo, and to other Indians of the United States, such as the Kiowa, Kiowa-Apache, and the Comanche. Peyotism spreads quickly following the subsidence of the Ghost Dance, for which it largely substituted.

20TH CENTURY

C. 1900

HEAL. Many of the Indian tribes in the western United States are experiencing famine conditions. These conditions are partially relieved by the organization of a famine relief committee at Topeka, Kansas, which gathers and distributes food, clothing, and money.

LAND. The Crazy Snake uprising in Oklahoma Territory takes places under Chitto Harjo. Creek traditionalists break away from the primary Creek tribe and begin the Crazy Snake movement, a campaign against the allotment of the Creek Nation. The Crazy Snakes establish their own government with the capital in the town of Hickory Ground, establish laws that forbid allotment, and create a police force to enforce the laws. In the following year on January 27, 1901, federal officials will be sent in under request from the principal chief of the Creek to raid the Crazy Snake capital and arrest the rebel government leaders. This will not stop the movement entirely, however. In February, 1902, Chitto Harjo and nine other Crazy Snakes will be arrested for refusing to disband the movement and will be imprisoned in Leavenworth, Kansas, which puts an end to the uprising.

1900–1930

ARTS. Edward S. Curtis photographs western tribes.

1901

ARTS. The Indian Industries League is incorporated in Boston, Massachusetts, to encourage Indian crafts and industries such as beadwork, basketry, and leatherwork, and to find markets for the materials produced. The league supports the notion of Indians becoming self-sufficient and being able to leave reservations and become assimilated into mainstream American life.

POLI. The Sequoyah League is founded in New York and Los Angeles. This philanthropic group advocates the preservation of traditional Indian ways, opposing Indian schools and the allotment of Indian lands.

1902

ECON. The Secretary of the Interior makes the first oil and gas leases on Indian lands in Oklahoma.

HEAL. The entire Inuit (Eskimo) population of Southampton Island in Hudson Bay is wiped out by typhus.

LAND. The Five Civilized Tribes agree with the Dawes Commission to have their reservation lands allotted.

LAWS. Indian men are ordered by the Commissioner of Indian Affairs to cut their hair. In an effort to speed up Indian assimilation, Indian agents are ordered to prohibit Indian males from wearing their hair long.

"Certainly they (white men) are a heartless nation," said the uncle. "They have made some of their people servants—yes, slaves! We never believed in slaves, but it seems that these Washichu do. It is our belief that they painted their servants black a long time ago to tell them from the rest, and now the slaves have children born to them of the same color! The greatest object of their lives seems to be to acquire possession—to be rich. They are desirous to possess the whole world. For thirty years they were trying to entice us to sell our land to them. Finally, the Outbreak gave them all, and we have been driven away from our beautiful country." Charles Alexander Eastman (1858–1939) as a boy listening to his uncle (Eastman 1930, 282–83).

PUBL. Eva Emery Dye publishes her novel *The Conquest: The True Story of Lewis and Clark,* which promotes the legend of Sacagawea's role in the Lewis and Clark Expedition of 1804–1805. Dye portrays Sacagawea as a guide whom the expedition relied upon for its success.

Charles Alexander Eastman (1858–1939) publishes his first memoir titled *My Indian Boyhood,* an autobiographical story of his traditional Dakota Sioux upbringing. Eastman, born to a Sioux father and mixed-blood mother, is a graduate of Dartmouth and Boston College and is a physician and reformer. He will write several books and stories for non-Indians which promote respect for Indian cultures including *The Madness of Bald Eagle* (1905), *Old Indian Days* (1907), and *The Soul of the Indian* (1911).

SETT. The *Reclamation Act* encourages settlement of the West by whites through subsidies for water development. The act establishes the Reclamation Service to build irrigation projects in 16 western states.

1903

EDUC. The Museum of Natural History in New York City opens a Northwest Coast Indian exhibit.

MIGR. On May 12, the Cupeño Indians in present-day San Diego County, California, are removed from their ancestral village of Cupa at Warner Springs and relocated to the Pala Reservation in Luiseño territory, 40 miles away. This event, known as the Cupeño "long walk,"

disrupts the tribe and causes hardships to the 100 or more survivors.

TREA. The Supreme Court rules in *Lone Wolf v. Hitchcock* that Congress has "the power to abrogate the provisions of an Indian treaty." If Congress believes it is acting "in the interest of the country and the Indians themselves" it can ignore treaty agreements.

1904

ECON. Congress passes the *Pipelines Act,* which allows oil companies to construct pipelines to carry oil through Indian lands without permission of the reservation residents. This comes in response to oil being discovered in Oklahoma Territory and Indian leaders resisting the construction of pipelines through their lands.

RELI. The Feather Religion is founded by Klickitat Indian Jake Hunt in the Pacific Northwest.

1905

HUNT. An important Supreme Court case involving Indian fishing and hunting rights sets a precedent that will be cited many times in the future. In the case of *United States v. Winans* the court upholds Yakama (formerly Yakima) fishing rights in Washington State along the Columbia River in accordance with the *Yakama Treaty* of 1855 which states that the tribe retains the right to fish in "all usual and accustomed places." The fishing rights guaranteed in the treaty are ruled to be superior to the rights of the non-Indian owners of the fishing sites.

WATE. The Pyramid Lake Paiute's water rights are violated by construction of the Derby Dam on the Truckee River in Nevada. Pyramid Lake, fed by the Truckee, is reduced to half its size because of the dam, affecting the Paiute Indians living on the lake's banks. The Indians were not consulted about the building of the dam. In 1970, Indian activists will bring attention to the plight of the Paiute of Pyramid Lake, but the Department of the Interior will not change anything to help the tribe.

1906

LAND. The Federal government seizes 50,000 acres of wilderness land including Blue Lake in the mountains of New Mexico, sacred to the Taos Pueblo Indians, to become part of a national park.

The *Burke Act,* passed by Congress on May 8, amends the *General Allotment Act* (or *Dawes Act*). The intent of the act is to give control of Indian allotments held in trust to the federal government rather than to state governments, to extend the period in which allotments are held in trust if their Indian owners are deemed incompetent to handle their own affairs, and to reduce the trust period for Indians who can take on the full responsibility of land ownership. The act also slows down the process by which Indians gain citizenship under the *Dawes Act*. The effect of the law, however, often will result in many Indians becoming landless after being defrauded by unethical businessmen. In 1910, the *Omnibus Act* will allow the government to end the trust period on allotments owned by "competent" Indians.

The *Alaska Native Allotment Act* is passed by Congress on May 17 to extend the provisions of the *General Allotment Act* to Indian lands in Alaska, but there is little interest by non-Indians in putting the act into effect.

The *Osage Allotment Act* is passed, making the Osage the last tribe in Indian Territory to agree to allotment. The tribe negotiates for 500-acre allotments and is allowed to retain communally held mineral rights to their land. Rich oil deposits were discovered on Osage lands in 1899.

LAWS. On June 8, Congress passes the *Act for the Preservation of American Antiquities* (or the *Antiquities Act*), designed to protect ancient ruins and artifacts found on federally owned lands.

SOCI. A division occurs in the Hopi Tribe between the traditionalists and the progressives. The progressives (called "friendlies" by whites) welcome whites settling in their lands. The Hopi traditionalists (called "hostiles" by whites) oppose the presence of whites in their territory. The progressives eventually expel the traditionalists from the village of Oraibi, and U.S. officials arrest 75 of these "hostiles."

1906–1909

LAND. Troops are stationed at the Wind River Reservation in Wyoming during the time of allotment of lands on the reservation to prevent problems between the Shoshone Indians and the homesteaders.

1907

ECON. The Quebec Bridge collapses during construction on August 29, killing a total of 96 ironworkers, including 35 high-steel workers of the Mohawk Caughnawaga Band. This is the worst bridge-construction accident in history. In 1915, the Mohawk steelworkers will begin working in New York City.

LAND. Indian Territory and the Territory of Oklahoma are merged and become Oklahoma, which is admitted to the Union as the 46th state on November 16. With Oklahoma statehood, Indian Territory and the Indian nations within it cease to exist.

POLI. Charles Curtis, a one-eighth Kaw Indian and part Osage Indian from Oklahoma, becomes the first U.S. Senator with Indian ancestry. He previously served eight terms in the U.S. House of Representatives. In 1928, Curtis will be elected Vice-President of the United States on the Herbert Hoover ticket.

PUBL. *The North American Indian* by U.S. photographer Edward S. Curtis, 39, is published in its first volume. It will eventually be a 20-volume set (completed in 1930). Curtis (1869–1952) will spend 30 years taking photographs of Indians in the United States, British Columbia, and Mexico.

Lewis Tewanima, considered one of the greatest long distance runners in U.S. track history. Courtesy of Library of Congress.

He attempts to create a definitive pictorial record of Native North Americans, taking over 40,000 photographs from 80 different tribes, including many well-known tribal leaders such as Chief Joseph of the Nez Percé. J. P. Morgan pledged up to $75,000 to support Curtis in his work. His photographs are a romanticized portrayal of Indians with great appeal to non-Indians.

SPOR. Lewis Tewanima (Hopi; 1879–1969) is considered one of the greatest long distance runners in U.S. track history. He will be a member of the U.S. Olympic Team in 1908 and 1912. In the 1912 Olympics he will set a U.S. record for the 10,000 meter race, winning a silver medal. This record will be broken by Billy Mills (Oglala Lakota Sioux) in the 1964 Olympic Games. Tewanima also sets the world record for the indoor 10 mile at Madison Square Garden.

1908

WATE. The Supreme Court defines rights of the federal government to reserve water for use by Indian tribes. In the case of *Winters v. United*

States the Department of Justice files suit to protect the water rights of the Indians of the Fort Belknap Reservation in Montana. By the time of the lawsuit, the tribe is not receiving enough water to irrigate their fields for farming as is implied they should receive from an 1888 treaty. The case will become the basis for many water-rights claims of reservation populations.

1909

EXPL. Four Inuit men help explorer Robert E. Peary become the first white man to reach the North Pole.

HEAL. Geronimo, the famous military leader of the Chiricahua tribe of Apaches, dies of pneumonia on February 17 at Ft. Sill, Oklahoma.

LAND. Theodore Roosevelt, two days before leaving the presidency, issues eight executive orders transferring 2.5 million acres of timberland on Indian reservations to national forests.

The Pawnee Indians, who had never waged war on the United States, become the last Indian tribe to sign a formal agreement with the U.S. government to cede portions of their reservation in Oklahoma for homesteaders. The Pawnee had served as scouts with U.S. forces on many occasions against other Indian tribes. Their lands were gradually taken away by treaties signed in 1818, 1825, 1833, 1848, 1857, and 1876.

SPOR. The University of Wisconsin at Lacrosse gives its sports teams the name "Indians." This is the first school or sports organization to use a reference to Indians as their team or mascot.

1910

HEAL. The Bureau of Indian Affairs (BIA) starts the first regular Indian medical service. The Division of Medical Assistance within the BIA begins regular medical service for Indians.

RELI. The Federal government forbids the Sun Dance among the Plains Indians, citing the use of self-torture as the reason.

1911

CONT. Ishi, the last of the Yahi Indians of northern California, emerges from the foothills near Oroville. The rest of his tribe has evidently been killed by Americans or died from European diseases. Unable to communicate with the whites who find him, he is temporarily placed in jail for his protection. Soon, anthropologist Alfred Kroeber arranges for Ishi to come to live at the University of California where he will share his knowledge of the Yahi language and culture with researchers. He will live at the university museum until his death from tuberculosis in 1914. Several books will be published about Ishi, including *Ishi in Two Worlds* (1961) and *Ishi, Last of His Tribe* (1964), both by Theodora Kroeber.

EDUC. The Boy Scouts of America institutes an Indian lore merit badge, which constitutes one of the first organized efforts to teach non-Indians about American Indian history and culture.

Hopi children from the village of Hotevilla are forced to go to school. U.S. soldiers are called in to capture the children and take them to the Shonogopavi Day School.

LAND. The Hollywood Indian Reservation is established in west-central Florida by executive order. This is for the Seminole Indians who stayed in Florida and did not move to lands west of the Mississippi. In 1938, two more reservations will be established in southern Florida by executive order—Big Cypress and Brighton.

LANG. A significant work in linguistics is published by the Smithsonian Institution titled *Handbook of American Indian Languages,* edited by Franz Boas.

POLI. The Society of American Indians (SAI) is founded by a group of prominent, educated Indian men and women, holding its first conference in Columbus, Ohio, on October 12. The organization is committed to teaching respect for Native Americans and their ways, to promoting Pan-Indianism, to obtaining American citizenship for Indians, and to abolishing the Bureau of Indian Affairs. This important Indian political organization brings together influential Indian advocates, many who have been educated at BIA boarding schools. Instead of destroying their "Indianness," many of those who attended Indian boarding schools become leaders in Indian affairs.

1912

ARTS. Edward S. Curtis makes his first motion picture of Native Americans, *In the Land of the War Canoes.*

LAND. The anti-allotment Cherokees, Creeks, Choctaws, and Chickasaws form the Four Mothers Society and go to Washington to argue their case before Congress. The society is founded to preserve communal ownership of tribal lands and obtain approval from Congress to remove restrictions on the sale of allotments, and generally to improve the political situation of Oklahoma Indian traditionalists.

SPOR. Jim Thorpe, 24, a Sac and Fox athlete from the Carlisle School, wins the gold medals for the pentathlon and decathlon at the Fifth Olympic Games in Stockholm, Sweden. However, in the following year Thorpe will be stripped of the medals because he played one season of semi-professional baseball. The public disagrees with this decision made by the Amateur Athletic Union. The medals will be reinstated in 1984.

Louis Tawanima, a Hopi from the village of Shungopovi, places second in the Stockholm Olympics in the 10,000-meter run. In the 1908 Olympics in London, Tawanima finished ninth in the marathon.

1913

LAWS. The Supreme Court case of *United States v. Sandoval* determines that the federal government has total responsibility for the Pueblo Indians of New Mexico, throwing the land titles of the state into question.

MIGR. After 17 years of imprisonment, the Chiricahua Apaches who were led by Geronimo are given a chance to return to the Southwest. The majority agree to move to the Mescalero Apache Reservation in New Mexico.

POLI. The Indian-head nickel, issued by the U.S. Mint, reveals a composite profile of an Indian (created from three Indian chiefs) on one side and a buffalo on the reverse side. The design suggests that the Indian, like the buffalo, is doomed to become a casualty of westward expansion of the United States.

1914

HEAL. Fort Spokane becomes an Indian hospital and tuberculosis sanatorium.

1914–1917

WARS. World War I takes place, in which many Indians will enlist, fight, and die.

1915

ARTS. *The End of the Trail,* a bronze sculpture created by James Earle Fraser (1876–1953), reveals an exhausted Indian sitting slumped forward from the waist atop his horse. The weary old pony is so weak that its legs are buckling beneath the weight of its burden. The image is conveyed that the Indian, once noble, is now subdued by the forces of "civilization" and is a dying breed. It is one of many popular images of the demise of Indian peoples.

ECON. Mohawk steelworkers from the Kahnawake Reserve begin working in New York City. After a few months, the first Mohawk worker to get hired, John Diabo, falls from a high beam and drowns in the river below. In the decades to come, many more Mohawks will move to New York, settling primarily in Brooklyn, to become steelworkers.

EDUC. The Roe Indian Institute, the only Indian-run high school in the United States, is established in Wichita, Kansas. Founded by Henry Roe Cloud, a Winnebago educator and Yale University graduate, the prep school will later be renamed the American Indian Institute.

LAND. Congress authorizes the Bureau of Indian Affairs to buy land for landless natives in California.

POLI. American Indian Day is established by the Society of American Indians as the first Saturday in May of each year.

The Indian Defense League of America is founded.

1916

EDUC. The Museum of the American Indian is built in New York City by George Gustav Heye to house some of his vast collection of Indian artifacts.

PUBL. Yavapai physician Carlos Montezuma begins publishing the newsletter *Wassaja.* The Yavapai intellectual, a founding member of the Society of American Indians, uses the periodical to express his opinions on how Indian policy should be reformed, including why the Bureau of Indian Affairs should be abolished. He will continue to publish the newsletter until 1922.

1917

LAND. The Papago (Tohono O'odham) Indian Reservation in Arizona is the last to be established by executive order.

WARS. Some 16,000 Indians serve alongside white troops in WWI. About half of male Indians at this time are noncitizens and not subject to the draft. However, their participation in the war is at a rate nearly double that of the general population. All Indians will later on be made U.S. citizens in part due to the Indian troops' distinguished service in WWI.

1917–1920

LAND. The Bureau of Indian Affairs "Competency Commission" lifts restrictions on sales of Indian land. Any Indian landowner who is of less than half Indian ancestry or judged competent to manage his or her own affairs can be issued a patent to sell or lease his or her land. Thousands of patents will be issued, discontinuing federal guardianship of Indian lands, resulting in large amounts of Indian land passing into the hands of whites.

1918

ARTS. Maria Martinez and her husband, Julian Martinez, of San Ildefonso Pueblo in New Mexico, develop a black-on-black style of pottery that will become one of the most popular and valued of all Indian pottery. The black pottery will make Maria the most famous Indian potter in the world.

LANG. Indian code talkers are officially used for the first time in WWI by 14 Choctaws in Company E of the 142nd Infantry during the Meuse-Argonne Campaign against the Germans. The Choctaw and the Lakota Sioux provide code talkers similar to the Navajo and other tribes that will serve in WWII. The code talkers translate military communications into their native languages, confounding the enemy who cannot read the languages. The French government will honor the Choctaw code talkers in 1989 for their help in winning several key battles. The code talkers will be acknowledged and honored by the U.S. Congress in 1995. In 1919, Congress will grant citizenship to Indian veterans. All Indians will later be made U.S. citizens in part due to the Indian troops' distinguished service in WWI.

RELI. The Native American Church, with rites that include the sacramental use of peyote, is incorporated in Oklahoma by members of the Kiowa, Comanche, Cheyenne, Apache, Ponca, and Otoe tribes. Frank Eagle, a Ponca Indian,

serves as the first president. The new religion is a blend of Indian beliefs and Christianity and focuses on the sacramental use of peyote. By 1930, about half of the nation's Indians will be members of the new church. In 1944, the Oklahoma charter church will be amended resulting in a new name, the Native American Church of the United States. In 1955, the national organization of the church will be renamed the Native American Church of North America.

WARS. Iroquois Indians declare war on Germany. The tribe was not included in the 1919 Peace Treaty. They will renew their Declaration of War in 1941 to include Italy and Japan.

1919

POLI. Indian soldiers and sailors who enlisted to fight for the United States in World War I can now receive citizenship.

The Mission Indian Federation is founded in Riverside, California. The group is concerned with the past dealings of the federal government with California tribes, especially the absence of compensation for lands taken from them by treaties in exchange for reservations that the government never established.

1921

HEAL. The *Snyder Act* is passed by Congress in response to the dire health conditions in many Indian reservations and communities. Funds for health, social, and educational programs for Indians are the responsibility of the Department of the Interior.

ECON. Oil royalties on Osage lands in Oklahoma have reached approximately $20 million a year. Wealthy tribe members have become targets of crime and fraud. In a three-year period beginning in 1921, many Osage will be killed under mysterious circumstances, often with non-Indians named as their legal beneficiaries. With 24 murder cases left unsolved, Congress will pass the *Osage Guardianship Act* in 1925 to protect Osage accounts and expenditures.

Oil is discovered on the Navajo Reservation. In 1923, the Navajo tribe will form the Navajo Tribal Council, a legally-constituted body to represent the Navajo people in negotiations concerning oil and gas development leases.

1922

ARTS. The first Indian Fair takes place in Santa Fe, New Mexico, created by the Museum of New Mexico. This will develop into the Santa Fe Indian Market as part of the Southwest Association for Indian Arts, which takes place each August in Santa Fe as the largest and most highly acclaimed Native American arts show.

The powerful documentary film *Nanook of the North* is produced, showing Canadian Inuit acting out traditional activities before whites came to their lands in Canada's Hudson's Bay. Nanook, the central figure of the film, struggles to hunt for food in the Arctic environment. Two years after the filming he will die of starvation.

The first Gallup Inter-Tribal Indian Ceremonial is held in Gallup, New Mexico. Included in the event are Indian dances, a rodeo, and Indian arts and crafts booths. The ceremonial will become one of the largest annual Indian fairs in the country.

POLI. The Pueblo Indians of New Mexico unite to form the All Pueblo Council. This group will fight the *Bursum Bill,* pending in Congress, which would recognize the rights of white squatters on Pueblo lands and take some of the Pueblo territory away. The bill will be defeated in 1924.

The Iroquois Confederacy sends Cayuga Indian Deskaheh to the League of Nations in Geneva, Switzerland, to seek recognition of sovereignty of the Iroquois tribes. The organization declines to do so.

PUBL. *History of the Cherokee Indians* is published by Emmet Starr, after nearly 30 years of research and writing. This monumental history of the Cherokee and their culture highlights the important contributions and accomplishments of the tribe.

1923

POLI. The American Indian Defense Association is formed by a group of wealthy white liberals, with John Collier as executive secretary, to fight for a variety of Indian causes. The group includes influential writers, artists, reformers, anthropologists, and others interested in the preservation of Indian cultures. The organization will lobby Congress on important Indian issues in the next 10 years. At this time, the Indian Rights Association is the only nineteenth-century "Friends of the Indian" organization still active.

The Committee of One Hundred is appointed by Secretary of the Interior Herbert W. Work to review Indian policy. This group of eminent citizens will propose, advise on, and review Indian policy, such as issues concerning Indian health and education.

RELI. Indian dancing is restricted by the Bureau of Indian Affairs. The Commissioner of Indian Affairs, Francies E. Leupp, rules that reservation superintendents should only permit Indian dances once a month, that the dances should last no longer than one day, and that only Indians older than 50 should be allowed to attend. Indian dances are viewed by many whites as an obstacle to assimilation.

1924

HEAL. The Division of Indian Health is created with the BIA. In 1955, the United States will transfer total responsibility for Indian health from the Department of the Interior to the Public Health Service, a division of the Department of Health, Education, and Welfare (HEW), and rename it the Division of Indian Health. In 1958, the department will again be renamed as the Indian Health Service.

LAND. The *Pueblo Lands Act* settles land disputes between the Pueblo Indians and non-Indians living in their territory. The *Bursum Bill* that would have granted title to some non-Indians in the region is defeated in Congress.

LAWS. The *Indian Citizenship Act* grants full U.S. citizenship to all American Indians.

RELI. The last Big House Ceremony is held by the Lenni Lenape (Delaware) Indians near Copan, Oklahoma. This most sacred religious rite was traditionally held over 12 nights to celebrate the harvest and bring good fortune during the coming year. The ceremony will now be abandoned due to the elder religious leaders becoming too old to perform it, and the youth not allowed by their school teachers to participate.

1925

PUBL. Zane Grey publishes his novel *The Vanishing American* telling the dramatic love story of a Navajo man and a white woman. The book will be made into a film the following year.

1926

ARCH. Excavation of the Folsom archaeological site in New Mexico inaugurates the study of Paleo-Indians in North America. Bones and projectile points uncovered offer evidence of human habitation in the area during the Stone Age.

ECON. The Fred Harvey Company begins offering tours of Southwestern Indian lands. The company operates luxury hotels in the West, and now offers guided tours through such areas as the Hopi, Navajo, and Zuni reservations. When vacationers arrive by railroad, Harvey Company cars pick them up at the station, tour them through Indian lands, and return them to the comfort and luxury of a Harvey hotel at night. Tourists create a demand for Indian arts and crafts which Southwestern Indians start developing specifically for sale to whites.

POLI. The Indian Defense League of America is founded by Clinton Rickard, a Tuscarora chief, with the purpose of giving the Iroquois the right to travel freely across the American-Canadian border as stipulated in the *Jay Treaty* of 1794. The U.S. government will honor this right in 1928.

The National Council of American Indians is established by writer and activist Gertrude Bonnin (Zitkala-Sa). It will encourage Indians to vote and be active in politics.

PUBL. The journal titled *The American Indian* begins publication, covering articles concerning Oklahoma tribes and Indians across the country.

1927

ECON. To protect Indian oil royalties on their lands, Congress passes the *Indian Oil Leasing Act*. This law gives the Secretary of the Interior the ability to negotiate oil leases on behalf of Indian tribes. However, many tribes will be granted long-term leases that net fairly small royalty incomes.

POLI. The Seneca Nation retains tribal sovereignty in deciding who is a member of the tribe. In the Supreme Court case of *Patterson v. Seneca Nation* the Seneca tradition of tracing ancestry matrilineally (through the mother's line) and denying tribal membership to children with Seneca fathers and white mothers is upheld by the court.

RELI. A division occurs in the Indian Shaker Church. One group of the church wants to use the Bible in their services, and another group does not. The conflict makes its way to the superior court of Snohomish County, Washington, which formally divides the church. The anti-Bible faction continues with the name of Indian Shaker Church, while the pro-Bible group is now called the Indian Full Gospel Church.

1927–1941

ARTS. The federal government sponsors the carving of four president's faces on Mt. Rushmore in the Black Hills of South Dakota, land sacred to the Sioux Indians.

1928

ARTS. A new Indian painting style is developed by six young Kiowa art students at the University of Oklahoma. The students become known as the Kiowa Six. Under the encouragement and direction of Oscar Jacobson, the head of the art department at the university, they learn to use modern European materials and techniques to paint bold, brilliantly-colored figures that reflect American Indian values and beliefs. Most often their depictions are of warriors and dancers in ceremonies. Their work is promoted by Jacobson, and the students' paintings become known nationally and internationally.

ECON. The *Meriam Report,* prepared for the Institute for Government Research after a two-year commission, is published under the direction of Lewis M. Meriam on the status of American Indian living conditions. The 872-page report, officially titled *The Problem of Indian Administration,* describes the impoverished conditions of most Indian farmers and cattlemen, and lists reasons for these conditions such as the institution of the *General Allotment Act* of 1887, and the poor quality of land held by Indians. American Indians are described as the worst-off of all ethnic groups in the United States, and the report calls for the re-evaluation of federal Indian policies and an overhaul of the Bureau of Indian Affairs.

The Inuit have been trading white-fox fur pelts to the Hudson's Bay Company and other trading firms in northern Canada for the last three or four years. This has brought brief prosperity to the Inuit who abandoned their old ways to adopt new hunting technology learned from white traders. However, by the mid-1930s, the price of furs will drop dramatically, and the loss of income will devastate the Inuit.

POLI. Charles Curtis, who is part Kaw and part Osage and a U.S. Senator, is elected Vice-President of the United States with Herbert Hoover as President. He will serve in this position until 1933.

The U.S. Congress passes a law that exempts American Indians born in Canada from the rules of U.S. immigration laws. This clears up a controversy that goes back to the War of 1812 concerning the free passage of Iroquois Indians across the U.S.-Canadian border.

1928–1932

ECON. A Senate Investigating Committee on Indian Affairs conducts an extensive investigation into conditions of Indians in the United States, resulting in a 40-volume report. The investigation will lead to many beneficial laws and policies for Indians, including the 1946 Indian Claims Commission.

1932

ARTS. The first Southwest Indian Fair is held in Anadarko, Oklahoma, featuring extensive displays of traditional Indian arts and crafts. Organized by members of the Comanche, Kiowa-Apache, Caddo, Wichita, and Lenni Lenape (Delaware) Indians, the fair will become an annual event attracting thousands of Indians and non-Indians interested in Indian arts and crafts, songs, and

---

Black Elk, shaman of the Oglala Sioux, at Harney Peak in the Dakota Black Hills, in 1912, facing west, holding the sacred pipe before him in his right hand, sang his swan song to Wakan Tanka, the Great Mystery: "Hey-a-a-hey! Hey-a-a-hey! Hey-a-a-hey! Hey-a-a-hey! Grandfather, Great Spirit, once more behold me on earth and lean to hear my feeble voice. You lived first, and you are older than all need, older than all prayer. All things belong to you—the two-legged, the four-legged, the wings of the air and all green things that live. You have set the powers of the four quarters of the earth to cross each other. The good road and the road of difficulties you have made me cross; and where they cross, the place is holy. Day in, day out, forevermore, you are the life of things. Therefore I am sending you a voice, Great Spirit, my Grandfather, forgetting nothing you have made, the stars of the universe and the grasses of the earth. You have said to me when I was still young and could hope, that in difficulty I could send a voice four times, once for each quarter of the earth, and you would hear me. . .(later). . .Hear me, not for myself but for my people; I am old. Hear me, that they may once more go back into the sacred hoop and find the good road and the shielding tree" (Black Elk 1932, 209).

dancing. In 1935 the fair will be renamed the American Indian Exposition.

PUBL. *Black Elk Speaks,* an influential book about Sioux (Lakota) beliefs, sparks interest in Native American religion. In 1930, a Lakota Sioux medicine man, Black Elk, began discussing his life and Lakota religion, culture, and history with John C. Neihardt. Neihardt transcribed and organized Black Elk's story into a manuscript, which is now published as *Black Elk Speaks.* The book has wide appeal among whites who are sympathetic to Indian issues. The book will also become very popular during the Red Power Movement in the 1960s and 1970s.

1933

ANIM. The Navajo Indian Reservation is required to reduce their livestock. Due to overgrazing of sheep, cattle, and horses, erosion of the land has produced so much silt in the Colorado River that there is concern about the completion of Boulder Dam. In the next decade, tensions will arise between the U.S. government and the Navajo regarding the matter of reduction in sheep and livestock on the Navajo Reservation.

ECON. The Indian Emergency Conservation Work (IECW) program is established by the federal government as part of Franklin D. Roosevelt's New Deal program the Civilian Conservation Corps (CCC). The program hires Indian laborers to work on conservation projects on Indian lands, to benefit American Indians. Under this program, herds of deer, buffalo, elk, and antelope are developed, continuing into the 1970s. In 1937, the IECW will be renamed the Indian Civilian Conservation Corps (ICCC) and will last until 1942 when it will be disbanded. The new program will also offer more on-the-job training and vocational education for Indian laborers.

POLI. Ethnologist John C. Collier is appointed to the position of U.S. Commissioner of Indian Affairs by President Roosevelt, beginning a new era for the BIA. He will serve until 1945, instituting many needed reforms in government policies toward the Indians. His direction leads to the passage of the *Indian Reorganization Act* in 1934.

1934

EDUC. The *Johnson-O'Malley Act* passed by Congress authorizes the Secretary of the Interior to contract with states or territories to offer various services to Indian groups. The most significant impact will be on the public school education of Indians, but the act will also address the needs of health care, agricultural assistance, and social services for tribes.

POLI. The *Indian Reorganization Act* (IRA; also known as the *Wheeler-Howard Act*) reverses the U.S. policy of allotment as specified by the *Dawes Act* of 1887, providing for tribal self-government, constitutions, and landholding, and launching an Indian credit program. The act, developed by John C. Collier, the new Commissioner of Indian Affairs, is perhaps the most significant legislation affecting Indians in the twentieth century. Now, land is to be owned by the tribe as a whole. Some of the land that had been sold to whites is bought back by the Bureau of Indian Affairs with federal funds and deeded to the tribes. A loan fund of $10 million is created to assist tribal councils in promoting economic development. Scholarships are also provided for Indians attending vocational and trade schools. In addition, the IRA guides tribes who want to write constitutions and reorganize their government. Indians are to be given preference in hiring for BIA jobs, also. More than the required two-thirds of tribes vote to accept the IRA, with the notable exception of the Navajo Tribe. In 1936, Congress will extend provisions of the IRA to Alaska natives in the *Alaska Native Reorganization Act.*

The American Indian Federation (AIF) is formed in Gallup, New Mexico, by several wealthy Indian conservatives. The group advocates assimilation of Indians and the dismantling of the Bureau of Indian Affairs (BIA). It will last through the mid-1940s, failing to end the BIA.

1935

ARTS. The Indian Arts and Crafts Board is established by Congress to assist Indians in marketing their Indian-made products and promote commercialization of aspects of Indian culture. It also makes it a crime for non-Indian artisans to market their

"They sent the Indians to Oklahoma. They had a treaty that said 'You shall have this land as long as grass grows and water flows.' It was not only a good rhyme but looked like a good treaty, and it was till they struck oil. Then the government took it away from us again. They said the treaty only refers to 'water and grass; it don't say anything about oil.' " Will Rogers in a 1928 syndicated column (Rogers 2002).

works as Indian-made. In 1990, the *Indian Arts and Crafts Act* will be passed by Congress to further protect Indian-made products.

The Southwest Indian Fair in Anadarko, Oklahoma, is renamed the American Indian Exposition, an annual event attracting large numbers of Indians and non-Indians interested in traditional Indian arts and crafts.

RECR. On August 15, part-Cherokee humorist Will Rogers dies in a plane crash in Alaska. Born on November 4, 1879, on a ranch in Oolagah, Indian Territory, Rogers became the most famous American Indian in the country and a beloved performer in the 1920s and 1930s.

C. 1935–1940

LANG. A Navajo system of writing is devised, known as the Harrington-La Farge alphabet.

1936

ARTS. The Indian Actors Association is established in Hollywood, California. Affiliated with the Screen Actors Guild, the new association seeks to protect the interests of Indian actors, specifically lobbying for better pay and benefits and encouraging casting agents to hire real Indians to perform in Indian roles in motion pictures.

POLI. On May 1, Congress passes the *Alaska Native Reorganization Act* which extends the provisions of the *Indian Reorganization Act* of 1934 to Alaska native groups. This new law designates that any Alaskan land that had been reserved for Indian or Inuit (Eskimo) use by an 1884 U.S. law can now be designated as an Indian reservation by the Secretary of the Interior, along with a majority approval of the Indians or Inuit of the area. New

federal programs are also established for Indian self-government and economic development.

On June 26, Congress passes the *Oklahoma Indian Welfare Act* which extends to the large Indian tribes of Oklahoma the same benefits that the *Indian Reorganization Act* (IRA) provided to the rest of the American Indian population. These Oklahoma tribes, specifically the Five Civilized Tribes, had their governments dissolved when the territory became a state, and now this act includes them in the new programs and changes offered by the IRA.

PUBL. Chief Tantaquidgen of the Algonquian tribe of the eastern United States called the Mohegans (or Mohicans), is believed to be the last of his tribe. He is presented with a copy of the novel *The Last of the Mohicans* by James Fenimore Cooper. The Mohegans had formed as a tribe when they split from the Pequots in the seventeenth century and were soon afterward defeated by the Mohawks. By the time of European contact, scholars estimate the population of the Mohegans was between 8,000 and 25,000. By the early 1700s, disease, war, and alcoholism had reduced their numbers to only four or five hundred. With the loss of their lands to the European settlers, the Mohicans were mostly forgotten and "vanished." Mohegan Indians will survive, however, with around 1,700 enrolled members of the tribe in the year 2005 (after being federally recognized in 1994). In 2005, Gladys Tantaquidgeon (the tribal medicine woman) will die at the age of 106, and will also be called one of the last Mohegans, as she was one of the last traditional, full-blood Mohegans and the oldest member of the tribe.

SOCI. A new Congressional act called the *Oklahoma Indian Welfare Act* is drafted to fill a void created when the governments of the Five Civi-

"My relatives didn't come over on the Mayflower, but they met the boat." http://willrogers.org

lized Tribes were dissolved, and when the Oklahoma Indians were excluded from the U.S. *Indian Reorganization Act* of 1934. This will lead to the reorganization of many Oklahoma tribes and restoration of tribal legal identity.

1937

ECON. The Shoshoni (Shoshone) Indians of Wyoming are granted permission by Congress to sue the federal government for the value of the Shoshoni Reservation's land and natural resources, which were given to the Arapaho Indians in 1876. With the lawsuit, the Shoshoni receive $4 million, and the Arapaho land holdings are legalized.

1938

ECON. Congress passes the *Indian Lands Mining Act* which permits reservation lands to be leased to commercial mining companies. This good-intentioned act is urged for passage by John C. Collier, the Commissioner of Indian Affairs, who believes the leases will provide jobs and royalties for Indians on reservations. However, many of the leases will not provide much royalty income to tribal members, but instead, end up leading to the destruction of Indian resources.

1939

ARTS. The Sioux Museum and Crafts Center is created in Rapid City, South Dakota, sponsored by the U.S. government's Indian Arts and Crafts Board.

Seneca artists have been experiencing an artistic renaissance for the last 3–4 years. The Federal Works Progress Administration program has engaged Seneca artists to produce woodcarving, basketry, quillwork, painting, and drawing. The works of Seneca artists such as Jesse Cornplanter, Ernest Smith, and Sarah Hill are displayed at the World's Fair in New York City from April to October in the New York State Pavilion.

1940

ANIM. The *Eagle Protection Act* is passed by Congress, which restricts the killing of bald eagles or the taking of their parts. However, the law makes it difficult for many Indian groups to practice their native religions, because eagle feathers are used to make sacred religious paraphernalia. The law will be amended in 1962 to allow Indians to obtain a special eagle hunting license to obtain the needed feathers for religious purposes.

ARTS. The swastika motif is formally rejected by Southwest Indian artists to protest the Nazi Party in Germany. Artisans from the Navajo, Hopi,

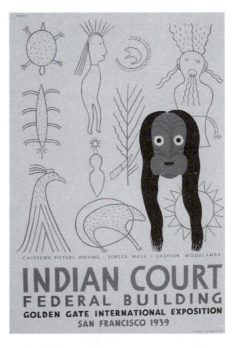

A Works Progress Administration poster advertising Seneca art at the 1939 Golden Gate International Exposition. Courtesy of Library of Congress.

Papago, and Apache tribes sign an agreement to stop using swastika designs in their work. The swastika used to be a common design motif in Southwestern silverwork, basketry, and pottery, representing such things as prosperity and good fortune. The swastika has been a religious symbol used throughout the centuries in many countries, cultures, and religions, including the Aryan people, a prehistoric group who settled in northern India and Iran. The Aryans considered themselves a pure race, superior to other surrounding cultures. When the National Socialist Party was formed in 1919 in Germany, it adopted the ancient symbol, destroying the good symbolism that it held for thousands of years prior to the Nazis.

ECON. Uranium ore is discovered on Navajo lands. In 1948, uranium will first be mined on the Navajo Reservation by an outside company.

LAWS. In October, Congress passes the *Nationalities Act* granting citizenship to all American Indians without impairing tribal authority. For the first time in American history, all young American Indian men are called upon to register for the draft as the United States prepares to enter World War II. Because Indians did not receive U.S. citizenship until 1924, most were not subject to the draft during WWI.

WARS. In August, BIA Commissioner John Collier meets with the Selective Service to determine how to register Indians for military service.

1941

ARTS. Native American sculptor John Gutzon de la Mothe Borglum is attempting to complete Mount Rushmore National Monument in South Dakota when he dies of a heart attack on March 6 at age 73.

The Museum of Modern Art in New York City opens an influential Indian art exhibit in cooperation with the Indian Arts and Crafts Board titled "Indian Art in the United States." Indian-made objects are presented as works of art and not only as objects for anthropological study. The curator explains that new forms and techniques used by Indians do not always mean repudiation of tradition but are often sources of its enrichment.

RELI. The Sun Dance is revived among the Crow Indians in Montana. In an effort to preserve Indian traditions in the modern era, a Crow named William Big Day participates in the Shoshone's annual Sun Dance on the Wind River Reservation in Wyoming. He is taught how to stage the ceremony by a Shoshone religious leader, and he brings the Sun Dance to the Crow Reservation, leading to a revival of the dance among his own people.

1941–1945

WARS. World War II draws many Indians to fight. When the Japanese attack Pearl Harbor on December 7, 1941, there are around 5,000 American Indians in the armed forces. Before the end of WWII, more than 25,000 Indians will serve on active duty in the U.S. military, with around 45,000 more serving in wartime industries. Navajo (Dineh), Choctaw, and Comanche code talkers use their native languages as a battlefield code. A special unit of Navajo code talkers develop a more complex code based on their Athabascan language, which is never broken by the Japanese.

Some Indians, including some Iroquois and Hopi, resist the draft based on their traditional religious teachings or their belief in tribal sovereignty. But, the U.S. government can now force military conscription on Indians. On November 24, a U.S. Court of Appeals in New York in *Ex Parte Green* rejects a suit by an Iroquois who sought the release of an Indian from the U.S. Army. The court rules that Indians of the Six Nations (Cayuga, Mohawk, Oneida, Onondaga, Seneca, and Tuscarora) are citizens of the United States and therefore affirms the federal government's right to draft Indians. Some Indians are jailed as draft resisters.

1942

ARTS. Maria Tallchief, an Osage Indian, begins her career as a prima ballerina.

CONT. In March, construction begins on the Alaska Highway by the U.S. Army Corps of Engineers. The 1,500-mile stretch from Dawson Creek, British Columbia, to Fairbanks, Alaska, will open traffic through Native lands in 1947, bringing epidemics of non-Indian diseases and disrupting Native societies.

HUNT. In the state of Washington, a Yakima man named Tulee is sued for fishing outside of the Yakima Reservation without a fishing license. In the case of *Tulee v. Washington,* Tulee argues that he is not subject to state law because he is an Indian. In the state court he is convicted, but the Supreme Court will overturn the verdict. This case will be cited as a precedent in later lawsuits upholding Indian fishing and hunting rights.

LAND. A Japanese internment camp is constructed on the Colorado River Reservation of the Mojave and Chemehuevi Indians. The camp is one of 10 internment camps built to hold Japanese Americans during the war. The government will finance land improvements and an irrigation system on the reservation in exchange for permission to build the camp.

A gunnery range is made out of part of the Pine Ridge Reservation in South Dakota. A 341,726-acre area of the Lakota Sioux reservation is seized by the U.S. government to use as an aerial gunnery range. The area will be used extensively from 1942–1945 as air-to-air and air-to-ground gunnery ranges. For safety, 125 Indian families are relocated from their farms and ranches in the 1940s. Some Indian residents will remain nearby, dodging shells by diving under their tractors out in the fields while cutting hay.

PUBL. *The Handbook of Federal Indian Law* is published for the first time by Felix S. Cohen, a lawyer with the U.S. Department of the Interior. This work systematically organizes the 5,000 federal Indian laws, 372 ratified Indian treaties, court cases, and other less formal agreements with Indians and the federal government. The book is a much-needed comprehensive resource on Indian law which will be used often over the years in court cases and legal challenges.

RELI. The Lakota Sioux of the Standing Rock Reservation hold a Sun Dance for the first time in 50 years. Participants pray for an Allied victory in WWII and for the safe return of the Lakota Sioux,

of whom about 2,000 are serving in the armed forces.

WARS. In January, the Selective Service reports that 99 percent of all eligible American Indians have registered for the draft, setting a national standard. About 44,000 Indians will serve in combat in WWII.

On July 18, the Six Nations tribes of the Iroquois Confederacy (Mohawk, Oneida, Seneca, Onondaga, Cayuga, Tuscarora) send a delegation to Washington, D.C., to declare war on the Axis powers (Germany, Italy, Japan). Many Iroquois have resisted the draft, and the Iroquois feel the U.S. military conscription laws violate the autonomy of the Six Nations. This public relations event is to show the patriotism of the Indians.

Japanese military forces occupy the islands of Attu and Kiska in the Aleutians as part of WWII. Around 45 Aleut inhabitants of the island are taken as prisoners to Hokkaido, Japan, where they will remain until the war is over in 1945. After this action, the U.S. military decides to evacuate the Aleut's villages on the Pribilof Islands. With only hours notice and limited to one suitcase each, the evacuees are sent to live in abandoned canneries, without heat, in southeastern Alaska for the remainder of the war. The harsh conditions take a toll on the Aleuts, with many falling victim to disease. In May 1944, the Pribilof Island Aleut will be allowed to return home, but their homes will have been vandalized and destroyed by U.S. soldiers.

1942–1945

LANG. Indian code talkers are influential in helping end World War II. They are famous today for having used their native languages to transmit messages in a form that the enemy could not decipher. Although the Navajo (who had around 420 code talkers) and the Comanche code talkers will later get most of the attention, code talkers participate in Europe and the Pacific from at least 18 tribes, including the Cheyenne, Cherokee, Ojibwe (Chippewa), Cree, Hopi, Kiowa, Menominee, Muskogee, Oneida, Osage, Pawnee, Pima-Papago, Sac and Fox, Sioux (Dakota, Lakota, and Nakota dialects), Seminole, and Winnebago. During the war, the Navajo code talkers fight with the Marines throughout the Pacific and are credited with making possible the invasion of Iwo Jima.

1943

POLI. The Indian Affairs Committee of the U.S. Senate recommends that the Bureau of Indian Affairs be terminated. This is the first time an official suggestion is made that Indian tribes should be without federal government supervision and services.

RELI. The Catholic Church honors Kateri Tekakwitha, a seventeenth century Mohawk nun renowned for her devoutness, by declaring her to be "venerable." Tekakwitha died in 1680, and is the first Native American to be so honored by the Catholic Church. In 1980, Tekakwitha will be beatified (declared blessed, one step closer to sainthood) by the Catholic Church. The Tekakwitha Movement embraces an integration of Catholicism and Indian religious traditions.

1944

MIGR. The Inuits (Eskimos), Aleuts, and Indians of Alaska step up their migrating from outlying villages to urban centers, where war-related job opportunities are available.

POLI. In November, the National Congress of American Indians (NCAI) is founded in Denver, Colorado, by 50 tribes, becoming the first effective pan-Indian association in the United States.

WARS. The Pribilof Island Aleut are returned home by the U.S. government after nearly two years in exile. The Japanese had attacked the village of Annu in June, 1942, and taken the Aleut residents to Japan. The U.S. government then forcibly removed the Aleut from their villages on the Pribilof Islands and held them against their will in an unsanitary camp in southeastern Alaska in harsh, cold conditions. In their absence from their villages, many of the Aleut houses were looted and destroyed by U.S. military personnel. As a result, they will abandon several of their ancient villages.

1945

LAND. On March 12, the U.S. Supreme Court rejects a suit by a Shoshone Indians for $15 million for damages caused by the occupation of lands in Idaho, Utah, and Nevada by white settlers. *The Box Elder Treaty* of 1863 was ruled inadequate for the Shoshone claiming the land.

LAWS. The Alaska Territorial Legislature passes a law forbidding the exclusion of Alaskan natives from public places.

POLI BIA. Commissioner John Collier resigns in January after years of political controversy, having served from 1933 to 1945. William A. Brophy takes over the position.

WARS. Around 44,000 American Indian men and women served in the armed forces during WWII, including 420 Navajos who served as code talkers in the Marine Corps. Indians are awarded two Congressional Medals of Honor, 34 Distinguished Flying Crosses, 47 Bronze Stars, 51 Silver Stars, and 71 Air Medals for their service in the war.

On February 24, 1945, Ira Hayes helps raise the American flag on the island of Iwo Jima marking the American victory after a pivotal battle. The Pima Indian, a Marine Private First Class, is one of the first American soldiers to reach the summit of Mount Suribachi, an extinct volcano at the southern tip of Iwo Jima. The photograph of Ira Hayes and five other Marines raising the flag, by Joe Rosenthal of the Associated Press, will become one of the most famous images of WWII. Hayes will die of exposure at the age of 33 after a night of drinking on the Gila River Reservation in Arizona on January 23, 1955.

1946

LAND. The Bureau of Land Management (BLM) is formed by the federal government from the General Land Office and the Grazing Service. The BLM is charged with overseeing the use of federal lands and its natural resources, and is also given responsibility for dealing with Indians on issues concerning reservation land, water rights, and mineral rights.

The *Indian Claims Commission Act* is passed by Congress, creating the Indian Claims Commission (ICC) to review and resolve outstanding Indian land claims. The commission is meant to free the U.S. Court of Claims from hearing Indian land claims, which has been inundated with more than 200 cases since 1881. The ICC is charged with settling once and for all the ongoing disputes that have been smoldering for nearly a century over lands taken by the whites. The Commission is charged with hearing tribal land and accounting claims against the government derived from treaties, agreements, and government trust responsibilities for Indian resources. Claims must be filed within a five-year period, which results in the filing of 588 claims by tribes. The Commission will be extended, however, until 1967.

POLI. The U.S. Commission on Civil Rights is established under President Harry S Truman, which urges more humanitarian consideration for American Indians.

1947

POLI. A termination timetable is submitted to Congress in February by the Acting Bureau of Indian Affairs Commissioner, William Zimmerman, Jr. This lists tribes that might be severed from federal supervision right away or after 10 years. Listed as ready for termination in 1947 are the Flathead, Hoopa, Klamath, Menominee, Mission, Six Nations, Osage, Potawatomi, Sacramento, and Turtle Mountain tribes, totaling 40,000 Indians. Zimmerman also testifies before a Senate committee, urging termination of federal services to "advanced tribes."

The Hoover Commission on the Reorganization of Government recommends termination of federal-Indian trust relationship and a policy of rapid integration into American life for Indians. To accomplish the integration of the Indian into American life, the commissioners urge the federal government to terminate social services to the tribes and to turn all treaty obligations over to state governments. In 1950, the federal programs of termination and relocation, and urbanization for reservation Indians will be instigated.

WARS. U.S. Army Indian Scouts are discontinued as a separate military unit of the U.S. armed forces. The Indian Scouts were reduced to patrolling Fort Huachuca, Arizona, and to guiding Interior Department survey teams, even though they had earned Congressional Medals of Honor in various wars. During the Indian Scouting Service's 77-year history, Indian Scouts served in several of the U.S. foreign wars, including the Spanish-American War and WWI.

1948

ARTS. The grandson of Geronimo, Allan Houser, wins a Guggenheim Fellowship for sculpting and painting. Houser is affiliated with the Haskell Institute and becomes known for his canvas murals in the penthouse of the Department of the Interior in Washington, D.C.

Korczak Ziolkowski, a non-Indian sculptor from Boston, begins his life's major work carving a gigantic monument of Lakota Sioux warrior Crazy Horse into the Black Hills of South Dakota. In 1939, the sculptor was first invited by Lakota Chiefs to create the Crazy Horse memorial. The massive monument is located on top of Thunderhead Mountain in the Black Hills National Forest near Custer. Because Crazy Horse was never photographed, Ziolkowski works from his imagination, having the warrior sitting astride

In 1875, when the U.S. government attempted to buy the Black Hills of the Sioux, Crazy Horse would not even be part of the discussions. "One does not sell the earth upon which the people walk" Crazy Horse (1842–1877; U.S. Commissioner of Indian Affairs 1875, 188).

a stallion with his arm outstretched and finger pointing to his burial site. The sculptor wants this to be the largest monument created on earth. The four heads of the nearby Mount Rushmore Memorial are much smaller than this one that will span 563-feet high by 641-feet long. After Ziolkowski's death in 1982, his widow and children will take over the nonprofit project, which is projected to continue for many years into the twenty-first century. The face of Crazy Horse will be completed and dedicated in 1998.

ECON. Uranium is first mined on the Navajo Reservation with the Kerr-McGee Company. The reservation lacks health regulations and has a large available labor force which needs jobs. Many Navajo returning from service in WWII will work in the uranium mines, suffering exposure to radioactive ore and radon gas. Eventually, a large number of these workers will die of cancer. In 1979, radioactive material will escape from a Navajo Reservation mine and contaminate the Rio Puerco with radioactive waste.

On May 7, Congress passes the *Indian Loans Act,* which authorizes Indians to receive loans from the revolving loan fund administered by the Secretary of the Interior.

The Bureau of Indian Affairs develops a program to encourage Navajo to move to cities for jobs. Concern is that their reservation economy cannot support the growing Navajo population. Participants are sent to Los Angeles, Denver, and Salt Lake City where BIA employees try to place them in jobs. This program will lead to the expanded relocation policy of the federal government beginning in 1952.

EDUC. The Bureau of Indian Affairs begins a non-repayable Higher Education Grant Program to encourage Indians to go to college. These grants are for college tuition and fees. A similar program was started by Congress in 1930 for Indians pursuing college degrees, but many graduates did not repay their loans so Congress stopped authorizing money for the fund. By the 1990s, the program will grow to become the primary source for federal funding for Indian students going to college.

LAND. On May 14, Congress passes the *Indian Land Sales Act,* providing for a more flexible Indian land policy. The act authorizes the Secretary of the Interior to issue patents-in-fee and to remove prohibitions against transfer of ownership or title on individually-owned lands held under the *Indian Reorganization Act* of 1934 and the *Oklahoma Indian Welfare Act* of 1936. The law also allows the sale of individually-owned lands to non-Indians. The transfer or disposal of tribal lands continues to be governed by Congress.

POLI. Indians gain the right to vote. In separate court decisions, the Indians of New Mexico and Arizona win the right to vote as in other states, thus making Indians enfranchised in all states. On July 15, the Arizona Supreme Court rules in *Harrison v. Laveen* that Indian residents have the right to vote in local and state elections, reversing a 1928 ruling that Indians should not be allowed to vote because they are under the guardianship of the federal government. On August 3, a federal court in Santa Fe declares that a New Mexico constitutional provision denying Indians the vote is contrary to the 15th Amendment of the U.S. Constitution.

TRAD. Inuits (Eskimos) in Alaska frequently visit Siberia to hunt and trade. The Soviet Union repudiates a 1938 agreement allowing Inuits to

Henry Standing Bear, Sioux chief, in a 1939 letter to Korczak Ziolkowski, made a request that inspired the sculptor to begin his mammoth project of carving a statue of Crazy Horse out of a mountain in the Black Hills: Standing Bear: "My fellow chiefs and I are interested in finding some sculptor who can carve a head of an Indian chief who was killed many years ago. . .My fellow chiefs and I would like the White man to know that the Red man had great heroes, too" (O'Driscoll 1998, 10A).

visit Siberia without visas, and a party of Inuits is held for two months in the Soviet Union.

WATE. The Oahe Dam floods more than 160,000 acres on the Standing Rock and Cheyenne River Reservations of the Lakota Sioux. The dam is built near Pierre, South Dakota, as part of the federal government's damming of the Missouri River. The flooded area includes the Lakota's prime rangeland and farms and most of their timberlands.

1949

ARTS. The Gilcrease Museum opens in Tulsa, Oklahoma. Established by Creek businessman Thomas Gilcrease, the museum will come to house one of the largest collections of Native American art and artifacts in the world.

ECON. The three affiliated tribes of the Berthold Reservation in North Dakota receive payments of $12,605,625 by the U.S. government for being displaced by the Garrison Dam and Reservoir Project.

The Association of Indian Affairs issues a statement on August 31 describing broken families, delinquency, hopeless poverty, and slum squalor among the Winnebago, Omaha, Santee Sioux, and Ponca Indians of the Nebraska reservations.

EDUC. Emory Sekaquaptewa, Jr., is the first full-blooded Indian to go to the U.S. Military Academy at West Point. He is a 19-year-old Hopi from Oraibi, Arizona.

HEAL. Due to record snowstorms, the U.S. government sends aid, food, and medicine to the Navajo and Hopi reservation Indians in Arizona.

POLI. The BIA establishes 11 area offices throughout the country to streamline its organization.

1950

ARTS. The motion picture *Broken Arrow* is released, offering a more balanced view of Indian-white relations. The film represents a new type of Hollywood western, with a complex Indian character in Cochise. The motion picture expresses a degree of sympathy for Chochise's desire to save his people's land from being taken over by whites, and it includes a controversial scene in which the white adventurer, Thomas Jeffords (played by James Stewart), marries an Indian woman.

ECON. Indians of the Pribilof Islands, off the coast of Alaska, are cited as an example of exploitation by the U.S. government. In a report released on March 2 by Rowland Watts, national secretary of the Workers Defense League, and prepared for the United Nations Commission of Inquiry into Forced Labor, the U.S. government is accused of tolerating forced labor practices on the Indians living on St. Paul and St. George Islands, who had no way to make a living except to sell sealskins for one dollar to a company with an exclusive contract with the Department of the Interior. The company would sell the skins at $20 each to the Department of the Interior, which would sell the processed skins for $70 each. Indians on the islands were forced to work for the company, and were even told they would not be allowed to return to the islands if they left, even to visit relatives.

The *Navajo-Hopi Rehabilitation Act* is signed into law by President Harry S. Truman on April 19. Over $88 million is authorized by Congress to improve the Navajo and Hopi Reservations' infrastructure over a 10-year period, and therefore help to alleviate the desperate conditions of around 94,000 Navajo and Hopi. The money is intended to improve health conditions, schools, roads, soil and water conservation, irrigation, off-reservation employment opportunities, and resettlement of some Southwestern tribes.

MIGR. The new commissioner of the Bureau of Indian Affairs is Dillon S. Myer, who institutes a relocation program for reservation Indians, encouraging their migration to urban centers, and starting the movement to terminate tribes from their reservations.

POLI. The first Indian to be called for jury duty in the United States is Francis Garcia, of Santo Domingo Pueblo, New Mexico, in the District Court in New Mexico. He is sworn in on May 22.

SPOR. Jim Thorpe, a Sac and Fox Indian, is named the greatest all-around athlete of the past 50 years by an Associated Press poll of 381 sportswriters and sportscasters. He is the first choice of 252 respondents in the poll. In 1954, a Pennsylvania town will vote to change its name to Jim Thorpe.

WARS. Two Indian soldiers serving in the Korean War will later be awarded the Medal of Honor for heroic acts costing their lives in the war. Mitchell Red Cloud, Jr., a Winnebago soldier who is standing guard, sights a Communist force preparing to attack his company. He sounds an alarm and proceeds to hold off the attacking enemy with an automatic rifle long enough for his fellow soldiers to prepare to defend themselves. He is killed while fighting. In another battle, Charles George, a Cherokee, dies when he throws himself on a grenade to protect his fellow soldiers.

1950–1953

WARS. In the Korean War, Indians serve in integrated units along with African-Americans and other minority groups.

1951

ARTS. Canyon Records is established in Phoenix, Arizona, as the first recording company to market American Indian music to an Indian audience. Their catalog will eventually comprise over 400 contemporary and traditional recordings, including those of R. Carlos Nakai, the Navajo-Ute flutist.

DEAT. Sgt. John R. Rice, a Winnebago Indian from Nebraska, was killed in action in Korea on September 6, 1950. His non-Indian wife purchased a burial plot in a "whites only" cemetery in Sioux City, Iowa. When Rice's casket was about to be lowered into the grave, cemetery officials stopped the burial, which unleashed a barrage of protests. U.S. President Harry S Truman interceded and had Rice buried in Arlington National Cemetery with full military honors on September 5, 1951. The cemetery in Sioux City later apologized for the incident.

LAND. A group of 50 Paiute Indians bring charges before the Indian Claims Commission on January 24 that the white man "stole" the sites of

Jim Thorpe, shown here playing baseball for the New York Giants, was named greatest all-around athlete of the past 50 years in 1950. Courtesy of Library of Congress.

Reno, Carson City, and Winnemucca, Nevada, Boise, Idaho, and Burns, Oregon. Claiming to represent approximately 5,000 Paiutes, they demand $1 billion as their share of the Comstock Lode silver mine.

The Menominee tribe of Wisconsin receives an $8.5 million settlement for the federal government's mismanagement of their forest lands. The suit was filed in 1934. The government will terminate the tribe in 1953.

The federal government chooses Western Shoshone land in Nevada as the official site for the testing of nuclear bombs.

SOCI. The diary of an eighteenth-century historiographer, located after a 30-year search, reveals that the Iroquois Confederacy was established in 1552. This will prompt the Six Nations Indians of the Iroquois Confederacy to celebrate the 400th anniversary of their group during the New York State Fair in 1952.

1952–1957

ECON. The Bureau of Indian Affairs expands the relocation program encouraging Indians to move to cities. It offers an employment assistance program to help Indians relocate to urban areas, find employment on or near reservations, receive adult vocational training, or get into on-the-job-training programs. The government hopes the relocation program will reduce the high cost of maintaining the reservation system. During this period, more than 17,000 Indians will receive assistance from the BIA's relocation services, with some establishing good jobs and others living in urban poverty.

1953

DEAT. Chief Sitting Bull (Tatanka Iyotake) is reburied in South Dakota on April 8, after 63 years of being buried in North Dakota. The new burial site is closer to Sitting Bull's home, and nearer to his place of death. The reburial was accomplished through the efforts of Clarence Grey Eagle, who was 16 years of age and present when Sitting Bull was killed in 1890.

EDUC. An emergency education program for Navajo and Hopi Indians is initiated by the Bureau of Indian Affairs. The program includes providing dormitories in communities near the reservations so the Indians can attend public schools, creating small temporary schools, and setting up trailers or hogans for education in areas where the Indian population is too small to sustain schools. In two years, the school enrollment will increase by 8,000 Navajo and Hopi students attending schools.

LAND. On January 13, the U.S. Court of Claims rejects an Oklahoma Cherokee claim for compensation for 14.6 million acres of land in Arkansas that was promised in an 1817 treaty. The court ruled that an 1828 treaty giving them land in Oklahoma satisfied the earlier treaty.

LAWS. The most significant legislation indicating the intent of the federal government to terminate federal supervision of Indians since WWII is passed in Congress as *Concurrent Resolution 108* by the House and Senate. This legislation urges an end to Indians' status as wards of the United States and indicates that all tribes in California, Florida, New York, and Texas should be terminated "at the earliest possible time." The legislation also lists tribes for termination including the Flathead, Klamath, Menominee, Potawatomi, and Turtle Mountain Chippewa (Ojibwe). This begins the formal policy of government termination of tribes.

On August 15, Congress repeals special Indian alcohol prohibition laws (first established in 1802). Liquor sales will now be subject to tribal regulations and local opinions. Many reservations will institute their own bans on liquor sales and consumption.

Public Law 280 is passed by Congress, transferring jurisdiction over civil and criminal matters of Indians from federal courts to state courts in California, Minnesota, Nebraska, Oregon, and Wisconsin. This law is passed without the consent of the tribes and despite their appeals for a presidential veto. Indian rights groups see the law as a major threat to tribal self-government. In 1968, the *Indian Civil Rights Bill* will partially change this legislation.

RECR. The first Miss Indian America is crowned at the All Indian Days festivities in Sheridan,

Wyoming. Arlene Wesley James, a Yakima Indian, is Miss Indian America.

1954

ARTS. Maria Tallchief, the Osage ballerina, appears on the cover of *Newsweek* magazine. She is now the highest-paid ballerina in the world.

EDUC. On September 23, New York State schools begin the integration of Indian and white students. The program moves 1,535 Indian children from reservation schools to public schools, and brings other reservation schools under the control of local school districts.

HEAL. Dr. James R. Shaw of the Department of the Interior provides a list of statistics concerning Indian health for a committee of the U.S. House of Representatives. Included are the following: an average Navajo life-expectancy of less than 20 years (compared to the white average of 68.4 years); a tuberculosis death rate 9.3 times greater than that for whites; a dysentery death rate 13 times greater; and a measles death rate 25 times greater than whites.

The *Parran Report,* published after a survey commissioned by the Department of the Interior, relates the bleak health conditions, hunger, and poverty of the Inuits, Indians, and Aleuts of Alaska.

LAND. The U.S. government authorizes the Cheyenne River Sioux Tribe to receive $10,644,014, and the Yankton Sioux Tribe to receive $218,985, as compensation for being displaced by the Oahe and Fort Randall Dam and Reservoir projects in South Dakota.

POLI. In order to determine which tribes might be terminated from federal supervision and services (in accordance with Congressional *Concurrent Resolution 108* of 1953) a special joint subcommittee on Indian affairs is formed to conduct a survey of Indian tribes.

The federal government's policy at this time is to terminate tribes from federal trusteeship. The Confederated Salish and Kutenai tribes of the Flathead Reservation of Montana defeat a move by the U.S. government to terminate their tribes.

The U.S. government terminates recognition of two of the largest and most prosperous tribes: the Menominee Indians of Wisconsin, and the Klamath Indians of Oregon. The Menominee tribe will be federally recognized again in 1973, and the Klamath tribe will be reestablished as a federally recognized tribe in 1986.

The newly-elected (November 21) president of the National Congress of American Indians, Joseph R. Garry, is a Coeur d'Alene Indian and a leading opponent of the government policy of terminating federal services for Indians.

Indians in Maine are given the right to vote. Previously they were barred from voting on grounds that they were not under federal jurisdiction.

SPOR. Jim Thorpe, the great Indian athlete, is buried in the town of Jim Thorpe, Pennsylvania, which was created from the small boroughs of Mauch Chunk and East Mauch Chunk, Pennsylvania.

1954–1962

POLI. During these years, Congress strips 61 Indian tribes, bands, and communities of federal services and protection.

1955

HEAL. Progress is made in treating Navajo patients with tuberculosis with new antibiotic drugs at the hospital at Fort Defiance, New Mexico, under a team from Cornell Medical School in Ithaca, New York.

The federal government transfers responsibility for Indian health care from the Bureau of Indian Affairs to the Public Health Service within the U.S. Department of Health, Education, and Welfare. Indian health problems have been much greater than the population of the United States as a whole, and much greater than among other minority groups. Funding for Indian health care will increase over the next several decades.

LAND. Criticism is aimed at a new policy of the Bureau of Indian Affairs that allows individually-owned Indian lands to be sold to non-Indians. The National Congress of American Indians adopts a resolution asking Congress for authority to make tribal purchases of trust lands rather than allow them to pass to individuals.

1956

DEAT. The Wyandot Indians of Oklahoma succeed in acquiring two acres of land in the center of Kansas City, Missouri, that was a sacred Indian burial ground and is now on the city's main thoroughfare. Congress allows the land to be ceded to the Wyandot during the rush of the closing legislative session, fulfilling a 66-year-old goal of the tribe.

EDUC. The BIA's adult vocational training program is established for Indians with an emphasis on service, trade, and clerical jobs.

LAWS. Congress passes the *Lumbee Recognition Act,* which recognizes the Lumbee Indians of North Carolina as an Indian tribe, but denies them services from the BIA.

TREA. The Canadian government rules that Mohawk Indians crossing the U.S. and Canadian border are subject to the same customs duties as whites. The Mohawk had refused to pay duties on modern household appliances, basing their claim to exemption on the *Jay Treaty* of 1794, which exempts "usual" personal items from customs.

WATE. The proposed Kinzua (Pennsylvania) Dam and Reservoir Project is opposed by Seneca Indians of the Allegany Reservation. They contend that this project would flood land that is guaranteed to them by a 1794 treaty. The Indians prevent U.S. Army engineers from surveying on their reservation.

The Dalles Dam on the Columbia River floods the ancient spiritual and trading center at Celilo Falls. This area, sacred to many northwestern Indian tribes, is destroyed by the dam as well as significant fishing sites guaranteed to the Umatilla, Nez Percé, Yakima, and Warm Springs tribes.

President Eisenhower vetoes a proposed $5 million payment to the Crow Indians of Montana for land taken by the government for the Yellowtail Dam Project in the Missouri River Basin, saying the amount is more than a "just" payment.

1957

POLI. Utah becomes the last state to prevent Indians to vote. The Utah Supreme Court had

ruled the previous year in *Allen v. Merrill* that Indians living on reservations did not meet residency requirements as stipulated in state law. This year the Utah legislature repeals the statute and abolishes its discriminatory method of withholding suffrage from Indian people.

On March 1, four Paiute bands, the Shivwits, Koosharem, Indian Peaks, and Kanosh, have federal supervision and services terminated by the U.S. government.

WATE. The Tuscarora Tribal Council refuses permission for soil tests by the engineers of the New York State Power Authority. This is the first step the engineers would take toward construction of a dam that would flood around 1,300 acres of the Tuscarora Reservation. A new phase of active resistance is begun by Indians to protect their lands.

1958

FAMI. The BIA, in cooperation with the Child Welfare League of America, launches a campaign to encourage white families to adopt Indian children.

POLI. A delegation from the Six Nations (Cayuga, Mohawk, Oneida, Onondaga, Seneca, and Tuscarora) and the Micosukee Indians from Florida visit Fidel Castro in Cuba as a move to help unite the Indians of North, Central, and South America. The delegation is led by Wallace "Mad Bear" Anderson of the Six Nations.

The president of the National Congress of American Indians (NCAI), Joseph R. Garry, criticizes the Eisenhower administration's Indian policy as the worst since 1887. Garry's remarks are made at the opening session of the NCAI annual meeting, specifically attacking the government's policy of terminating federal services and supervision of Indians.

At the same NCAI meeting, Montana Democratic Congressman Lee Metcalf accused the Bureau of Indian Affairs (BIA) of using "duress, blackmail, and pressure" to get Indians to consent to termination. Thirty-six California Indian groups agree to termination this year, which will seriously damage their social and cultural unity in the years ahead.

On September 18, the Secretary of the Interior, Fred A. Seaton, announces that termination without tribal consent is ended in spirit, and that the main policy of the government toward Indians will now be improvements in health, education, and economic development rather than assimilation.

WARS. The Lumbee Indians of North Carolina arm themselves and drive off a Ku Klux Klan (KKK) meeting held on January 18 on Lumbee land in Robeson County. The KKK rally is probably a response to rumors of a romantic relationship between an Indian woman and a white man, which violates the informal segregation of the county's Indian, white, and black populations. When approximately 75 Klansmen gather, they are approached by several hundred Lumbees, some armed with rifles, who run the Klansmen off the Lumbee lands.

WATE. The federal government authorizes monies for three Sioux tribes in North and South Dakota for their losses due to the Oahe and Fort Randall Dam and Reservoir projects amounting to about $14.8 million, mostly going to the Standing Rock Sioux of North Dakota. Some monies are given to the Crow Creek and Lower Brulé Sioux tribes of South Dakota, with more payments provided in 1962 for new displacements.

The New York State Power Authority offers $3 million to the Tuscarora Reservation Indians to expropriate land for the building of the Kinzua Dam, but the tribe rejects the offer and continues to block officials from surveying the land. The dam is intended to control flooding along the Ohio and Allegheny Rivers, but its reservoir would flood two Seneca reservations, one in Pennsylvania and one in New York. In 1960, the Tuscarora tribe will lose their fight in the Supreme Court to prevent the building of the dam, and the U.S. government will start construction of the dam in 1964.

1959

HEAL. On July 31, the U.S. Public Health Service is authorized by Congress to build water, drainage, sewage, and waste disposal systems on Indian lands. The bill is intended to end the poor sanitary facilities and unsafe drinking water on reservations.

LAND. In August, the Indian Claims Commission rules that the federal government must pay California tribes for the 64 million acres taken from them since 1853. The California Indians were demanding that the land be returned to them.

Alaska is admitted to the United States as the 49th state with the passage of the *Alaska Statehood Act*. This adds a population of about 43,000 Inuits, Aleuts, and Indians to the U.S. population. The act allows the new state to appropriate 108 million of the 375 million acres within Alaska's borders for the state's own use. Alaska Natives claim most of this land is theirs and should be returned to them.

POLI. A United Indian Nation is formed in Florida on March 31, composed of 36 representatives of the tribes of the Onondaga, Ute, Tuscarora, Mohawk, Seneca, Oneida, Cayuga, Ojibe (Chippewa), Lenni Lenape (Delaware), and Micosukee Indians. The purpose of the group is to stop the encroachment of white men on their lands.

The termination of federal services for the Wyandot, Peoria, and Ottawa Indians of Oklahoma ends in August.

A six-man delegation of traditional Hopi leaders from Arizona visits the United Nations in New York. They relate Hopi prophecies regarding an impending war between the forces of good and evil and inform the United Nations of the betrayal of treaties and other rights of the Hopi by the United States.

1960

PUBL. *The Navajo Times,* a weekly newspaper published by the Navajos at Window Rock, Arizona, is begun. The newspaper will be published by the Navajo Nation until 2004 when it will become independent of tribal government and become a for-profit corporation published by the Navajo Times Publishing Company.

HUNT. In Florida, the Micosukee Seminole Indians are granted year-round hunting, fishing, and frogging rights on over 143,000 acres of the Everglades.

POLI. John F. Kennedy, the President-elect, sends a telegram to the National Congress of American Indians on November 17 at the NCAI annual meeting stating that he intends to do something about the conditions of poverty and disease which afflict so many American Indians.

POPU. The U.S. Census Bureau, for the first time, allows Americans to report heir own racial origins as "Indian." Approximately, 513,500 people identify themselves as Indian. The Lumbee Indians of North Carolina are listed in the U.S. Census as Indians, although their origin remains a mystery.

1961

ECON. The federal *Area Redevelopment Act* is passed and intends to provide economic assistance for depressed areas in the country. This includes grants for Indian tribal governments which can build new tribal headquarters and community facilities.

EDUC. The Navajo Tribal Museum is established at Window Rock, Arizona.

LAND. Under a new federal policy announced on December 4 by the BIA regarding land sales on Indian reservations, tribes will now have the first chance to purchase individually-owned Indian land before it is allowed to pass from Indian ownership. This counters the Termination policy. Federal loans are available to assist tribes in making such purchases.

POLI. The new Commissioner of the Bureau of Indian Affairs is Philleo Nash, succeeding Glenn L. Emmons who served from 1953 to 1961. Nash will be a popular commissioner who stands for Indian rights, wants a shift away from termination, and desires a "new trail" for Indians emphasizing maximum self-sufficiency and full-participation in American life.

Tribes terminated of federal supervision and services this year include the Modoc, Snake, Clackamas, Kusa, Rouge River, and Umpqua Indians of Oregon, and the Modoc Indians of Oklahoma and Missouri.

The National Indian Youth Council is formed in New Mexico in August with Mel Thom, a Paiute, elected as the first president. The group of young, Indian, college-student activists rejects the idea of Indian assimilation. In 1964, the council will sponsor "fish-ins" along rivers in Washington State in support of fishing rights of Pacific Northwest tribes.

The American Indian Chicago conference takes place from June 13–20 at the University of Chicago. This is the largest gathering in decades of Indian tribal representatives meeting to work on the formulation of Indian policy. Around 500 representatives from 90 Indian communities begin a new era of Indian activism.

SPOR. The first World Eskimo-Indian Olympics are held in Fairbanks, Alaska. This will become an annual event.

At the American Indian Chicago conference in June 1961, around 500 Indians representing 90 tribes issued a "Declaration of Indian Purpose." From its conclusion: "In the beginning the people of the New World, called Indians by accident of geography, were possessed of a continent and a way of life. In the course of many lifetimes, our people had adjusted to every climate and condition from the Arctic to the torrid zones. In their livelihood and family relationships, their ceremonial observances, they reflected the diversity of the physical world they occupied. The conditions in which Indians live today reflect a world in which every basic aspect of life has been transformed. Even the physical world is no longer the controlling factor in determining where and under what conditions men may live. In region after region, Indian groups found their means of existence either totally destroyed or materially modified. Newly introduced diseases swept away or reduced populations. These changes were followed by major shifts in the internal life of tribe and family. The time came when the Indian people were no longer the masters of their situation" (*Declaration of Indian Purpose* 1961, 16).

1962

ARTS. The Institute of American Indian Arts is established at the Santa Fe Indian School. This is the first government-sponsored Indian art school, created by the Indian Arts and Crafts Board and the Bureau of Indian Affairs.

ECON. The Council of American Indian Nations is formed in Hawaii to provide assistance for Indians living in Hawaii.

HEAL. The Atomic Energy Commission (AEC) begins dumping nuclear waste on Inuit land near the village of Point Hope in Alaska. The Inuit of Point Hope strongly object to the project. The AEC dumps 15,000 pounds of radioactive waste into holes in the ground and covers it with gravel, without using protective containers. This mishandling of radioactive material will not be made public until the 1980s, when the secret waste dump is connected to the very high incidence of cancer suffered by the Point Hope Inuit.

LAND. The U.S. Senate extends the Indian Claims Commission to 1967, with 468 tribal claims pending. The commission offers compensation for lands taken by whites from the Western Shoshones. After a 15-year court battle, this ruling divides the tribe, with some accepting monetary compensation for the land and others holding out to fight to regain their land, led by sisters May and Carrie Dann.

The Navajo-Hopi land dispute, which began in the late nineteenth century, continues with the federal court ruling in *Healing v. Jones*. This case determines that most of the 2 million acres of disputed land belongs to both the Hopi and the Navajo, angering both sides and not settling the ongoing conflict. In 1975, Congress will pass the *Hopi-Navajo Land Settlement Act* to divide the Joint Use Area. Roughly half of the 2-million-acre area will be granted to the Navajo, with the transfer to take place in 1977. In 1980, the *Hopi-Navajo Relocation Act* will be passed to purchase new lands for Navajo families living on the Hopi Reservation who will be relocated.

POLI. The U.S. Supreme Court rules against the Creek Indians who claim they are owed $167,323 under five treaties in the nineteenth century by the U.S. government.

The Catawba tribe of North Carolina is terminated by the United States. Many in the tribe desire to be free from their status as wards of the federal government, while others want deeds to their land allotments so they can obtain loans to improve the property. After termination, the tribe will remain united by sharing the 630-acre state reservation and by their connection to the Mormon Church.

PUBL. *The Tundra Times* newspaper is established under the ownership of the Inuit, Indian, Aleut Publishing Company. The weekly paper will become an advocate for native land claims.

Edward Spicer publishes his influential book *Cycles of Conquest: The Impact of Spain, Mexico, and the United States on the Indians of the Southwest, 1533–1960*. His emphasis on the persistence of Indian traditions counters views that Indians are a "vanishing race."

WATE. The Navajo Indian Irrigation Project is authorized by Congress to transport water from the San Juan River to land near Farmington, New Mexico, for the use of 6,500 Navajo farm families. However, the project will be delayed for many years.

The Crow Creek and Lower Brulé Sioux tribes of South Dakota are awarded payments by the federal government for displacements caused by the Big Bend Dam and Reservoir Project.

1963

ARTS. The American Indian Arts Center opens in New York City to promote quality Indian arts and crafts to non-Indian collectors.

LAND. The Indians of California are offered $29.1 million for some 64 million acres taken from them by the United States since 1853. This amounts to 47 cents per acre. Most tribes agree to accept the settlement. The Pit River Indians vote overwhelmingly to reject the offer and to continue seeking return of their land, which they say amounts to 3,368,000 acres.

POLI. Navajo leader Annie Dodge Wauneka receives the Presidential Medal of Freedom from President John F. Kennedy at a ceremony at the

White House on December 2. This is the highest honor the federal government can award a civilian. Mrs. Wauneka, a political leader and health care advocate, is described as the most honored Indian woman of modern times.

WATE. A significant water rights case is determined in the Supreme Court case of *Arizona v. California*. Five tribes living along the lower Colorado River are determined to be entitled to enough water for irrigation of their lands. The court determines the Indians' share of the water by multiplying their reservations' acreage by the amount of water needed to make one acre farmable. This method will be used in several future water-rights cases to define tribal shares of water.

1964

ARTS. Storyteller dolls are first exhibited as a new Indian art. Helen Cordero, a potter from Cochiti Pueblo, exhibits her "storytelling dolls" at the New Mexico State Fair. She developed the clay dolls from early Pueblo effigy figures. The figurines show a storyteller, with eyes closed and mouth wide open, who has several smaller figures of children crawling on her. The clay dolls are so popular that their creation will become an industry for future Pueblo artists. Many variations of the dolls will be developed over the years.

Buffy Sainte-Marie, the Cree Indian folk singer, releases her first album, *It's My Way*. Her popularity allows her to protest the mistreatment of Native Americans and bring attention to a variety of Indian causes. Her song "Universal Soldier" will become popular as the unofficial anthem of the Vietnam War protest movement.

CIVI. Six Lakota Sioux men take over the closed federal prison on Alcatraz Island in San Francisco Bay to protest the seizure of Indian lands. The protesters cite the *Treaty of Fort Laramie* (1868) between the Lakota and the U.S. government, which includes a provision stating that ownership of federal lands abandoned by the government is to revert back to the Indians. Although treated lightly by the press, this takeover sets the stage for the later long occupation of Alcatraz by the Indians of All Tribes beginning in November, 1969.

ECON. The *Economic Opportunity Act,* passed by Congress and President Lyndon Johnson, includes Indians in its "War on Poverty."

HUNT. Washington State Fish and Game Department officials arrest members of the Nisqually, Yakima, Muckleshoot, and Puyallup tribes over fishing rights.

POLI. The U.S. *Civil Rights Act* prohibits discrimination for reasons of color, race, religion, or national origin.

The first Indians to serve in the state government of New Mexico in 350 years of white rule are elected. Monroe Jymm and James Atcitty are elected to the New Mexico House of Representatives.

The American Indian Historical Society is founded in San Francisco. Its goal is to seek justice for Indians in academic circles, improve the image of Indians in history textbooks, and produce materials about Indian issues and history from the Native American perspective. In the next two decades, the society will publish several significant periodicals *(The Indian Historian, Wassaja,* and *The Weewish Tree),* and operate the Indian Historian Press beginning in 1970.

PUBL. Thomas Berger's book *Little Big Man* is published. The movie version will be produced in 1970, starring Dustin Hoffman.

RELI. The California State Supreme Court rules that the use of peyote in Navajo religious ceremonies is not a violation of California state law. The ruling protects the ceremonial use of peyote, setting aside the 1962 convictions of three Navajos who maintained that the state drug law violated their religious freedom under the Constitution. In 1967, the Navajo Tribal Council will lift its ban (begun in 1940) on the ceremonial use of peyote by members of the Native American Church.

SPOR. On October 14, Billy Mills, a Lakota Sioux from the Pine Ridge Reservation in South Dakota, wins an Olympic gold medal in Tokyo in the 10,000-meter run. He also sets an Olympic record in the event.

WATE. The Seneca tribe of the Allegany Reservation in New York is authorized by the federal government to receive $15 million for land, damages, and rehabilitation as a result of the Kinzua Dam and Reservoir Project.

1965

LAND. The Indian Claims Commission rules that the Taos Pueblo Indians of New Mexico were unjustly deprived of sacred ancestral lands in what is now Carson National Forest. In 1906, the federal government took 48,000 acres surrounding Blue Lake in northwestern New Mexico and made it part of the Kit Carson National Forest. The Commission is not allowed to return lands, but instead offers compensation and 3,000 acres. However, the Taos Pueblo leaders refuse this offer and vow to continue to fight for the return of the lake and all the land that was confiscated. In 1970, the land and the lake will be returned to the tribe.

POLI. The *Voting Rights Act of 1965* ensures equal voting rights for all, regardless of state law voting limitations and other discriminatory laws.

1966

ARTS. Mohawk actor Jay Silverheels, best known for his portrayal of Tonto on the *Lone Ranger* television series, establishes the Indian Actor's Workshop in Los Angeles. The workshop will focus on more accurate portrayals of Indians in television and motion pictures, and encourage the casting of Indians in Indian roles. In 1979, Silverheels will be honored with a star on the Hollywood Walk of Fame.

EDU. The Rough Rock Demonstration School is established for the Navajo as the first American Indian school completely controlled by Indians. Funded by the BIA and the Office of Educational Opportunity, the school will be a great success and inspire other tribes around the country to start their own contract schools.

LAND. Secretary of the Interior Stewart Udall institutes a "land freeze" in Alaska until Alaska native land claims are settled. This prevents disposal of land and resources claimed by Inuits, Aleuts, and Alaska Indians (amounting to most of the state) until the land claims are dealt with.

POLI. The *Report of the Commission on the Rights, Liberties, and Responsibilities of the American Indian* is published by the Fund for the Republic, compiled by William A. Brophy and Sophie D. Aberle, two supporters of Indian causes. The short title of the report is *The Indian: America's Unfinished Business.*

The Bureau of Indian Affairs holds a conference on policy and reorganization in Santa Fe, New Mexico, in April. Indians are initially prevented from attending, but representatives of 62 tribes are eventually admitted to the conference and to meetings with Stewart Udall, the Secretary of the Department of the Interior.

The Alaska Federation of Natives is formed in an attempt to create a unified social and political organization for the native population of the state, representing Inuit, Aleut, Tlingit, and Athabascans. The Alaska Federation of Natives will bring attention to the land claims of Alaska natives, and its lobbying efforts will lead to the passage of the *Alaska Native Claims Settlement Act* in 1971.

The new Commissioner of the Bureau of Indian Affairs is Robert L. Bennett, an Oneida from Wisconsin. Bennett is the second Indian to be named Commissioner, with the first being Ely S. Parker in 1869.

1967

ARTS. Maria Tallchief, the popular Osage ballerina, is named winner of the 1967 Indian Achievement Award presented by the Indian Council Fire Organization. The award was established in 1933.

ECON. 900,000 acres of Alaska's North Slope land, of which most is claimed by Inuits, Aleuts, and Indians, is leased by the state to U.S. oil companies.

EDUC. The American Indian Law Center is established at the University of New Mexico. It will offer courses in Native American law and provide tribal governments with legal assistance.

LAWS. The *Indian Resources Development Act* (called the *Omnibus Bill*), submitted to Congress by the Interior Department in May, is rejected by Congress, with no Senator or Congressman signing the bill. The act would have vested final authority over Indian land transactions to the

Department of the Interior. The Indians want more input on what the bill will contain.

1968

CIVI. The *American Indian Civil Rights Act,* an amendment to the *Civil Rights Act,* is signed into law on April 18 by President Lyndon B. Johnson. The act extends the U.S. Constitution's Bill of Rights to include reservation Indians and requires tribal consent before states can assume jurisdiction of Indian criminal and civil cases.

A protest is launched by 41 Mohawks who attempt to block the St. Lawrence Seaway International Bridge because the Canadian government does not honor the *Jay Treaty* of 1794, which established free travel between the United States and Canada for the Indians. Canadian police arrest the protestors, but none are prosecuted. The following February, the Akwesasne Mohawk of Canada will be issued passes to cross the bridge at no cost.

The Georgia-Pacific Company has its logging operations stopped in Indian Township, Maine, by a group of protesting Passamaquoddy Indians. The company had received state approval but not tribal approval to cut timber from these lands. A group of Passamaquoddy dressed up in traditional war attire and staged an attack on the logging crews, scaring the workers away and confiscating their expensive equipment. The dispute over the 1,900 acres of land is settled with the Indians retaining control, and the start of tree-cutting operations by all-Indian crews.

ECON. A trans-Alaska pipeline is proposed by three oil companies after large oil deposits are discovered on Prudhoe Bay in northern Alaska. The project is opposed by Native Alaskan groups who have outstanding land claims in the area.

HUNT. Fishing rights continue to be argued in Washington State. The U.S. Supreme Court rules on May 27 that the Puyallup and Nisqually Indians are guaranteed the taking of fish in the usual and accustomed grounds by an 1854 treaty. However, the state might still regulate the manner and purpose of Indian fishing. The Supreme Court will rule in 1973 that the Indians do have fishing rights and that the state can regulate only under reasonable and flexible conditions.

LAWS. The National Council on Indian Opportunity is created by a Presidential executive order on March 6. The Council, headed by the Vice-President and including seven Cabinet members and six Indian representatives, will try to coordinate federal Indian programs, involve Indians in decision-making and policies, and resolve conflicts in Indian affairs.

POLI. President Lyndon B. Johnson states new Indian policy goals in a special message to Congress on March 6. He cites the need to raise the standards of living for Indians, states his opposition to the government relocation policy, and states his desire for Indians to experience "full participation in modern America." To promote his self-determination policy for Indians, Johnson establishes the National Council on Indian Opportunity, charged with recommending reforms to increase Indian involvement in federal programs aimed to benefit them.

The American Indian Movement (AIM) is founded on July 29 in Minneapolis, Minnesota, in response to police brutality of Indians and to deal with other problems faced by relocated urban Indians. Led by Dennis Banks and Clyde Bellecourt, the group is modeled after the Black Panthers organization. AIM will attract attention

One Indian talking to another Indian about fishing rights: "The white man, he took over, see, after he saw there was money in fish. He just took over, you know, just steal— like stealing off the Indian. And that's how they got it. And that's why they don't want the Indian to fish, because there's big money for them. Indian is nothing to the white man. He's nothing" (Davis 1969, 108).

for its success in reducing the number of Indian arrests in Minneapolis by 50 percent.

The U.S. Postal Service honors Chief Joseph, the nineteenth-century leader of the Nez Percé Indians, by issuing a postal stamp with his portrait. This is the first stamp of an Indian chief.

PUBL. The Mohawk of the Akwesasne Reservation in New York begin publication of the *Akwesasne Notes*. The newspaper reprints stories concerning Indian issues and will become an influential source of information for the Red Power Movement during the late 1960s and early 1970s.

1969

ARTS. Floyd Red Crow Westerman, a Dakota activist, records his first album as a folksinger-songwriter titled *Custer Died for Your Sins/The Land is Your Mother*. His songs are about the lives of contemporary Indians and the efforts of non-Indians to dictate Indian conduct.

ECON. Cochita Pueblo, New Mexico signs a 99-year lease in April with Great Western Cities, Inc. to develop 6,500 acres next to Cochiti Lake, 35 miles north of Albuquerque, into a recreational city of 50,000. Housing and recreational facilities were to be built with Cochiti Pueblo Indians receiving rental income and employment. However, the company will go bankrupt in 1985, greatly limiting the development of the area.

The largest employer of Indians is Fairchild Semiconductors. The company dedicates a new rocket component factory on September 6 on the Navajo Reservation at Shiprock, New Mexico, employing nearly all Indians in their 1,200-person workforce.

EDUC. The National Indian Education Association (NIEA) is founded in Minneapolis, Minnesota, to improve the quality of schooling for American Indian and Alaska native students. NIEA will become the largest Indian education organization in the country.

The "Kennedy Report on Indian Education" is issued by the U.S. Senate. Officially titled *Indian Education: A National Tragedy—A National Challenge,* the document concludes that Indian students are poorly served by Indian schools, and several changes are recommended. The report resulted from hearings of the Special Senate Subcommittee on Indian Education chaired by Senators Robert F. Kennedy and Edward Kennedy.

The Navajo Community College opens its doors to Navajo students as the first Indian-controlled and reservation-based postsecondary school in the United States. Included in the curriculum are courses in Navajo history, language, and culture.

POLI. On July 4, the Commissioner of the Bureau of Indian Affairs, Robert L. Bennett, resigns, stating that the Nixon administration ignores Indians. Bennett was the first Indian commissioner of the BIA since 1869. In August, he will be replaced by Louis R. Bruce, Jr., a Mohawk-Sioux.

The National Congress of American Indians (NCAI) votes in favor of keeping the Bureau of Indian Affairs within the Department of the Interior.

PUBL. N. Scott Momaday (b. 1934) a Kiowa author, is the first Indian to win a Pulitzer Prize. On May 5, his fiction novel titled *House Made of Dawn* is awarded the Pulitzer Prize for literature. Through its nonlineal structure, the book uses traditional American Indian styles of storytelling. Momaday will publish many successful novels and books of poetry in forthcoming years.

Vine Deloria, Jr. (Sioux author), publishes *Custer Died for Your Sins; An Indian Manifesto,* a book offering a scathing account of the injustices committed against Indians throughout American history. The book will become a classic for the Red Power Movement. Deloria will publish many influential and successful books in his career until his death in 2005.

SPOR . Dartmouth College abandons its Indian mascot for its sports teams, bowing to student pressure to make the change.

1969–1971

CIVI. Alcatraz Island in San Francisco Bay is occupied by "Indians of All Tribes," a group of Red Power activists, on November 14, 1969, to call attention to the many of the problems of contemporary Indians. Alcatraz, the former maximum-security federal prison, was first

Vine Deloria, Jr., Sioux, in 1969 and 1970 became a spokesman for many American Indians. "When one examines the history of American society one notices the great weakness inherent in it. The country was founded in violence. It worships violence and it will continue to live violently. Anyone who tries to meet violence with love is crushed. . .yes, violence is America's sweetheart" (Deloria 1969, 225–226).

occupied by 14 Indian college students who were persuaded to leave by the U.S. Coast Guard. However, within two weeks, 78 Indians took their place led by Adam Fortunate Eagle and Richard Oakes, claiming the land for Indians and beginning a 19-month occupation of the island until June 1971. The Indians call themselves "Indians of All Tribes," and want the island to replace the San Francisco American Indian Center (which had burned down on November 1, 1969) and to establish a Center for Native American Studies, an American Indian Spiritual Center, and other uses for Indians. The Alcatraz occupation will attract international media attention and public sympathy for the plight of Indians in urban areas and on reservations.

1970

ARCH. The Makah Indian village of Ozette is uncovered in northern Washington State following a severe storm. Assisted by Washington State University, the Makah people will eventually uncover more than 55,000 well-preserved artifacts from the site. The village had been destroyed in a mudslide before the Makah came into contact with whites. This will constitute the largest collection of artifacts located from a pre-contact site.

CIVI. Indian activists occupy lands and protest government policies: (1) Alacatraz Island in San Francisco Bay continues to be occupied by Indians. Water and electricity are cut off to the island by federal officials; (2) On March 8, Indians march on the California state capitol in Sacramento to draw attention to the shooting death of an Indian student at the University of California, Los Angeles; (3) On March 8 and again on March 15, a group of Indian activists calling themselves the United Indians of All Tribes takes over Fort Lawton, federal government land south of Seattle, Washington, claiming it as surplus land; (4) Indian protesters seize the Bureau of Indian Affairs office in Denver, Colorado, on March 14 to protest BIA hiring practices. The Denver protest sparks a wave of demonstrations and sit-ins at BIA offices throughout the country; (5) On March 16, Indian protesters from 14 tribes fail in an attempt to take over Ellis Island of New York City and set up a camp there; (6) On March 28, 40 of the Alcatraz Island protesters travel to Nevada to support the Pyramid Lake Paiute in their struggle over water issues; (7) On April 27, members of the American Indian Movement in Minneapolis, Minnesota, organize a protest of the premier of the film *A Man Called Horse* which they say portrays the English gentleman (played by Richard Harris) as superior to the Lakota, and misrepresents the Sun Dance ceremony and ritual; (8) On May 1–3, Pomo Indian protesters take over the land that is their ancient burial grounds on Rattlesnake Island near Clear Lake, California. The island is owned by the Boise-Cascade Lumber Company, which plans to develop the area as a vacation resort; (9) On June 2, a fire breaks out in the former prison on Alcatraz Island, currently being occupied by Indian activists, and destroys the warden's quarters, the doctor's quarters, the infirmary, and the inside of the lighthouse; (10) Pit River Indian protesters, joined by members of the American Indian Movement, occupy lands in Lassen National Forest in northern California on June 6, but they are stopped by federal officials; (11) In the fall, Indian activists protest Mount Rushmore in South Dakota; (12) Lakota Sioux protesters establish a protest camp at South Dakota's Badlands National Monument, demanding the return of Sheep Mountain to the tribe; (13) In October, Pit River Indian activists, who were arrested in June in Lassen National Forest, are on trial. Indian supporters establish a camp at Four Corners, near Burney, California, and a team of federal troops, U.S. marshals, and U.S. Forestry Service officials storm the camp, forcing the Indians out; (14) Indian activists take over land near Davis, California, that is owned by the University of California, to protest the university's plans to build a primate research center on the site instead of allowing the land to be used for an Indian-run college; (15) On November 26, American Indian Movement (AIM) activists stage a protest at Plymouth, Massachusetts. Led by Russell Means and Dennis Banks, the protesters declare Thanksgiving "a national day of mourning" and paint the historic Plymouth Rock red. They also take over *Mayflower II,* a replica of the ship that brought the Pilgrims to America, using the ship as a podium to speak on contemporary Indian grievances. Indian protests will continue to be strong throughout the 1970s.

LAND. Florida Seminoles reject an award of $12.3 million from the Indian Claims Commission for lands taken in 1823 and 1832 by the U.S. military, and by the *Indian Removal Act* of 1840. For many years the Seminoles had been trying to get $47 million compensation from Congress for their Florida land. Only about 1,500 Seminoles are now living in Florida, with the majority now living in Oklahoma.

Alaska's native groups reject a proposal by the U.S. Senate Interior Committee to settle native land claims, which offers $500 million, two percent royalties on minerals located on public land, and 4 million acres of land to the Inuit, Aleut, and Indian groups. The native groups say the amount of land offered is too little and want more details regarding the organization of Native Development corporations.

The U.S. government returns Blue Lake and 48,000 acres of sacred ancestral land to the Taos Pueblo Indians of New Mexico on December 15, ending a 64-year legal battle. This is a landmark case in the history of Indian land claims, being the first time the United States has ever returned land to an Indian group. Taos Pueblo had been fighting for return of the land to the tribe since 1906, when the land was taken by the U.S. government and made into part of the

Carson National Forest. When the Indian Claims Commission offered money and some land in compensation for the Blue Lake area in 1965, the tribe refused and continued to fight for the return of the land.

POLI. The Native American Rights Fund is founded with a grant from the Ford Foundation. It is created to provide legal aid to Indians and Indian groups that cannot afford to hire lawyers.

The federal Indian policy of self-determination is formulated. On July 8, President Richard M. Nixon addresses Congress in a special message concerning his Indian policy. He states his program is based on the premise of "self-determination without termination." Nixon asks Congress to repeal the termination policy resolution of 1953. Other proposals concern tribal control of federally-funded programs, new economic development, health and education assistance, and other rulings to move Indians forward economically and independently.

The Commissioner of the BIA, Louis R. Bruce, Jr., begins a thorough reorganization of the BIA, announcing the goal of giving Indians greater control over their affairs. Indians are skeptical of BIA promises.

SPOR. The Little Red Mascot is abolished by the University of Oklahoma as its sports mascot due to protests by Indian students against the stereotyping. Activists protest the use of mascot "Chief Wahoo" by the Cleveland Indians professional baseball team. Between now and the end of the century, many more name changes will be made for mascots and sports teams bearing Indian names and references by colleges, universities, public schools, and professional sports teams.

1971

ARTS. Chief Dan George, a Salish Indian actor, is nominated for an Academy Award for Best Supporting Actor for his portrayal of Old Lodge Skins in the movie *Little Big Man.* Although he does not win the Academy Award, he will be honored as Best Supporting Actor by the New York Film Critic's Circle.

CIVI. The Alcatraz Island occupation ends on June 11 when U.S. marshals remove the last of the Indians who have been occupying the island since November, 1969. Indian demands for use of the island are not met, but international and national awareness has heightened concern for a wide variety of Indian issues.

White vigilantes beat Oglala Dakota Raymond Yellow Thunder to death in Gordon, Nebraska. A ruling of death by suicide causes protests by more than 1,000 Lakota Sioux from the Pine Ridge Reservation. Officials, forced to perform an autopsy, change their finding to manslaughter. Two of the killers are subsequently tried and convicted. These are the first whites in Nebraska sentenced to a jail term for the murder of an Indian.

EDUC. The BIA begins a 5-year pilot project to teach English as a second language to Alaska's Inuit children.

Deganawida-Quetzalcoatl University (also known as D-Q University) is established near Davis, California, and opens for classes on July 7. It is unique as an Indian-operated university. D-Q is not located on a reservation or affiliated with a single tribe, but is intended to serve indigenous peoples throughout North and Central America. The university is named for Deganawida, the great Peacemaker of the Iroquois, and Quetzalcoatl, the god of several of the Mesoamerican peoples, including the Toltec, Maya, and Aztec.

LAND. The historic *Alaska Native Claims Settlement Act* (ANCSA) is signed by President Nixon on December 18. The act establishes the Alaska Native Fund of $962.5 million, which will be made available over a period of 11 years to eligible Indians, Inuits, and Aleuts for land claims. Also, 44 million acres of land in Alaska is made available for Native peoples. In a radical departure from earlier government policies, the Native lands in Alaska are not made into reservations held in trust by the U.S. government, but instead are granted to the Native Alaskan groups in fee simple patents. Their 44 million acres are set up to be managed by for-profit corporations with the shares communally owned exclusively by the Native peoples. The ANCSA calls for the creation of 12 regional corporations and about 200 village corporations. In 1987, the ANCSA will be amended to permit shareholders to vote on whether to offer new shares to Native children born after 1971, to give additional shares to elderly shareholders, and to extend restrictions on the sale of shares.

POLI. The National Tribal Chairmen's Association is formed to give tribal chairmen more of a voice in federal Indian policy.

PUBL. *Bury My Heart at Wounded Knee,* by Dee Brown, is published and becomes an immediate best-seller. The book documents the systematic destruction of Indian nations and cultures in the latter half of the nineteenth century and informs readers of the Wounded Knee Massacre.

1972

CIVI. Richard Oakes, a Mohawk Indian activist, is shot and killed. He was a leading spokesperson for the Indians of All Tribes during its occupation of Alcatraz Island.

The "Trail of Broken Treaties" formulates a 20-point position paper concerning the plight of Indians. On October 30, about 700 Indians representing more than 80 tribes arrive in Washington, D.C., for a demonstration for reforms in government policies on Indian affairs. They call this protest the "Trail of Broken Treaties." Government officials do not welcome them or have an agenda prepared for them, although presidential representatives do make promises to hear grievances and study the problems. During November 2–8, the "Trail of Broken Treaties" protesters will occupy the headquarters of the Bureau of Indian Affairs in Washington, D.C. Around 500 Indians under the direction of Dennis J. Banks and Russell C. Means, the American Indian Movement leaders, protest the BIA for unkept promises to Indians and destroy BIA files.

EDUC. The *Indian Education Act* (also known informally as Title V) is passed by Congress to address major reforms in Indian education. The act provides extra funds to public schools with a large number of Indian students, gives educational grants to tribes and other nonprofit organizations serving Indians, allocates money for adult job training programs, and establishes an Office of Indian Education within the U.S. government.

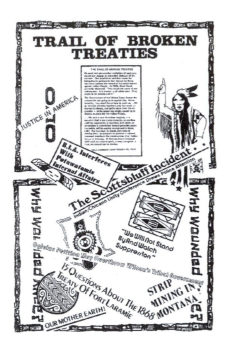

Backed by a 20-point paper called "The Trail of Broken Treaties." Approximately 700 Indians from 80 tribes protested for government reform on Indian affairs in 1972. Courtesy of Images of American Political History.

LAND. On May 20, 21,000 acres of forested land are returned to the Yakama tribe in central Washington State by executive order of President Nixon. This includes Mt. Adams, a mountain of great religious importance to the Yakama. The land was part of the Gifford Pinchot National Forest.

In September, a lawsuit is filed by a coalition of over 300 Indians from California tribes against the federal government. The $15 billion damage suit charges that the tribes were deceived in the 1964 settlement of their claims to two-thirds of California, in which they accepted $29.1 million for approximately 64 million acres.

POLI. Due to long-standing conflict over Indian affairs officials and tribes, several federal officials are removed or resign. In December, President Nixon accepts the resignations of BIA Commissioner Louis R. Bruce, Jr., and one of his deputies. Nixon also dismisses the Assistant Interior Secretary for Public Land Management,

who was overseer of Indian affairs for the Interior Department.

SPOR. The American Indian Athletic Hall of Fame is established at Haskell Indian Nations University in Lawrence, Kansas, to celebrate the achievements of Indians in football, baseball, basketball, and track.

1973

CIVI. On February 6, about 200 members of the American Indian Movement (AIM) travel to the town of Custer, South Dakota, to protest the case of Wesley Bad Heart Bull, a young Indian man who was stabbed to death by a white man at a local bar. After the assailant was charged with involuntary manslaughter rather than murder, the protesters confront the police at the Custer courthouse. A riot breaks out and several of the protesters are beaten and charged with rioting, including Sarah Bad Heart Bull, the mother of the victim.

AIM activists take over Wounded Knee on February 27. Members of the American Indian Movement (AIM) and about 200 armed Oglala Sioux occupy the site of the Wounded Knee Massacre on the Pine Ridge Reservation in South Dakota. The siege will last for 71 days, from February 27 to May 8. Under the leadership of Russell Means and Dennis Banks, the Indians demand a change in tribal leaders, a review of all Indian treaties, and a full-scale investigation of the treatment of Indians. The takeover particularly intends to bring attention to the campaign of terror launched by Lakota tribal chairman Dick Wilson against traditional Indians and his political opponents on the Pine Ridge Reservation. The morning after the takeover, federal marshals surround the site, and a siege results with outbreaks of gunfire. By the time the Indians surrender with a promise of future negotiations on Indian grievances, two Indians will have been killed and one federal marshal seriously wounded. The FBI will push for the arrest of 562 people involved in the protest, but only 15 will be convicted of a crime. Although much worldwide attention is brought to Indian problems with the government by the Wounded Knee takeover, the effort fails to end tribal chairman Dick Wilson's harassment of Indian traditionalists on the Pine Ridge Reservation. In the next three years, 69 people affiliated with the resistance effort will be killed, and each case will remain unsolved by the FBI.

ECON. Despite the opposition of Alaska Native organizations, in a national television address on November 7, President Nixon urges Congress to speed passage of legislation to authorize a trans-Alaska oil pipeline. This is the result of a severe national energy crisis.

The American Indian National Bank is established to help Indian businesspeople and tribes with needed funds.

LAND. On June 11, the U.S. Supreme Court rules that the Klamath Indians in northern California are the legal owners of the land in their reservations, despite an 1892 Congressional homestead act that opened the area to white settlers.

In a Senate Indian Affairs Subcommittee hearing on June 16, two former BIA officials testify that the BIA was grossly negligent in protecting Indian land and water, and deliberately under funded programs designed to assist Indians in developing their natural resources.

LAWS. Arizona is told no state income taxes can be levied against reservation Indians. In the U.S. Supreme Court case of *McClanahan v. Arizona State Tax Commission,* the court confirms that Indians are exempt from state taxes.

On May 1, the U.S. Interior Department lowers the voting age of Indians to 18 years in order to conform to the 26th Amendment of the Constitution, which lowered the national voting age in June 1971.

POLI. Congress repeals the termination of the Menominee tribe of Wisconsin with the *Menominee Restoration Act.* This ends a 12-year struggle to restore federal recognition to the tribe. The successful fight was led by Indian activist and leader, Ada Deer. Other tribes will soon regain federal recognition.

On December 3, Morris Thompson becomes the new Commissioner of Indian Affairs. An Athabascan from Alaska, Thompson, 34, is the youngest person to serve as commissioner.

1974

ARCH. The *Archaeological Recovery Act* sets aside monies to recover or salvage Indian burial grounds and other significant archaeological sites that are endangered by the construction of dams and other federal government projects. This is the first major legislation concerning the protection of Indian sites of historical and cultural significance.

CIVI. In St. Paul, Minnesota, the first trial takes place concerning the 1973 occupation of Wounded Knee, South Dakota. The trial results in hostilities between the Indians and the police in the courtroom, with six police officers and four militants injured and the courtroom left in shambles. Federal judge Fred J. Nichol dismisses charges against Russell Means and Dennis Banks from the Wounded Knee occupation, causing much controversy and inciting hostilities with local and state government officials.

ECON. The *Indian Financing Act* establishes loans for Indian-run businesses. Indians have had difficulty borrowing money from banks because banks will not accept tribal lands as collateral because the lands are held in trust by the federal government.

"My people are not concerned about a phony economy like the Caucasians. We have our land and it has been good to us. The sea has been good to us. The Bureau of Indian Affairs has given us enough education to read about what has happened in the lower forty-eight states…Now they want to come up here and rape our land." Joe Upicksoun, president of the Arctic Slope Native Association, on the proposed pipeline across Alaska (Armstrong 1972, 161).

HUNT. In the U.S. District Court in Washington State, a landmark victory results for Indian fishing rights in the case of *United States v. State of Washington* (known as the Boldt Decision, after the presiding judge George Boldt). A long series of protests and court battles concerning fishing rights culminates in this court decision that determines the state of Washington cannot impose rules on Indian fishers regarding their fishing methods, and that treaties allow the Indian groups to fish at their "usual and accustomed areas."

LAND. The *Navajo-Hopi Land Dispute Settlement Act* establishes permanent boundaries between the two tribes on and around Big Mountain in Arizona.

SHEL. The *Housing and Community Development Act* provides Indian housing.

1975

CIVI. A shoot-out on the Pine Ridge Reservation between AIM members and FBI agents results in the death of two agents and one Indian activist. Two FBI agents are shot and killed while delivering arrest warrants against four Indians on the Pine Ridge Reservation in South Dakota on June 26. Tensions have been running high between the reservation police under tribal chairman Dick Wilson and AIM members who have allegedly been victims of violence and assaults by the police. The Indians are charged with kidnapping, robbery, and assault. As the FBI agents drive onto the reservation in two cars, they are ambushed and shot at from a house and two nearby buildings. The gunfire continues between FBI reinforcements and the Indians until dark when the 16 suspects escape, leaving the body of one Indian inside the house. In November, four Indians (Leonard Peltier, Robert Eugene Robideau, Darrell Dean Butler, and James Theodore Eagle) are indicted on charges of murdering the two FBI agents. Leonard Peltier is convicted. His verdict remains controversial today. In 1979, Peltier will escape from prison but be recaptured after a short while. Seven years will be added to his sentence.

On July 26, Dennis Banks, a leader of the American Indian Movement (AIM), is found guilty of rioting and assault in the Custer County,

South Dakota, Courthouse on February 6, 1973. The Custer Chamber of Commerce was burned and two other buildings damaged by fire during the riot. In August, Dennis Banks is declared a fugitive after failing to appear in Custer County Circuit Court for the riot and assault charges. The judge issues a warrant for Bank's arrest. In 1978, Governor Jerry Brown will give Banks sanctuary in California.

LAND. The Hopi and Navajo tribes share a 2-million-acre area of the Hopi Indian Reservation called the Joint Use Area. The conflict over sharing the land has been going on for many years. Congress passes the *Hopi-Navajo Land Settlement Act* partitioning the Joint Use Area, giving half the land to the Navajo, with the transfer to take place in 1977. This division of land calls for the eventual relocation of nearly 5,000 Navajo and several hundred Hopi. In 1980, the *Hopi-Navajo Relocation Act* will be passed to fund the purchase of new lands for Navajo families living on the Hopi Reservation. In 1992, a federal court will determine that some Navajo families living on the Hopi reservation can stay in their homes under lease agreements. In 1996, the *Navajo-Hopi Land Dispute Settlement Act* will require the Navajo living on the Hopi Reservation to lease their land from the Hopi or move from the area.

The Havasupai Indians win title to a portion of the Grand Canyon after a 66-year legal struggle.

LAWS. The *Indian Self-Determination and Education Assistance Act* permits tribes to participate in all federal social programs and services relating to Indians and to provide funds for public schools on or near reservations.

1976

CIVI. Two AIM members (Robert Robideau and Darrell Butler) are found not guilty by a federal court jury of the Pine Ridge shootings of July 13, 1975, where two FBI agents were killed.

AIM leader Anna Mae Aquash, a Micmac Indian activist, is found shot to death on the Pine Ridge Reservation in South Dakota. Her murder is never solved.

In September, Yurok Indians barricade the Klamath River with ropes and nets to block sport fishermen who the Indians say are on their land. In the previous year, the U.S. Supreme Court gave the Yuroks reservation rights to the riverbed and to a mile-wide strip on either side of the Klamath River. The court also ruled favorably on the controversial use of gill nets by the Indians, which were previously banned under state laws.

LAWS. The *Major Crimes Act* is amended to add five new crimes to the list of major crimes committed on a reservation for which an Indian will be tried in federal court: kidnapping, statutory rape, incest, assault with intent to commit rape, and assault with a deadly weapon.

POLI. Fred Gabourie, 53, becomes the first full-blooded American Indian named to a California judgeship. Gabourie, an attorney from Burbank, California, is a Seneca who speaks Sioux and Muskogee.

Vermont Governor Tom Salmon grants the Abenaki Indians state recognition. The Vermont Abenaki had failed to meet four of the seven criteria for federal recognition by the BIA. In the following year, the new Vermont governor, Richard Snelling, will rescind the state recognition.

RECR. The first Indian National Finals Rodeo is held in Albuquerque, New Mexico. The best participants from around 150 regional all-Indian rodeos in the country are brought together for this rodeo, which will become an annual event.

1977

ARCH. The Native American Heritage Commission is created in California and dedicated to preserving important Indian sites in the state. Governor Jerry Brown appoints 10 California Indians to the new state commission.

ARTS. The Native American Public Broadcasting Consortium is founded to fund and produce public television programs about American Indians.

CIVI. In November, attorneys for Governor Jerry Brown appeal to the California Supreme Court to set aside the court order requiring the governor to extradite Indian activist Dennis Banks to South Dakota. Banks fears he will be killed if he returns to South Dakota.

Indian activists present a resolution to the International Human Rights Conference in Geneva, Switzerland, asking the United Nations to recognize Indian tribes as sovereign nations. The International Treaty Council created by the activists is recognized as a nongovernmental organization by the United Nations.

Leonard Peltier, an American Indian activist, is put on trial for the murder of two FBI agents that took place on the Pine Ridge Reservation in 1975. He is found guilty and sentenced to two consecutive life terms. The verdict is controversial with charges of misconduct launched against the prosecution. His case will elicit an international following of supporters who claim he is being held as a political prisoner by the U.S. government.

LAND. In June, the Agua Caliente Band of Cahuilla Indians of Palm Springs, California, is granted zoning control over 1,750 acres of valuable unimproved land in the city of Palm Springs. The ruling by the Department of the Interior gives the Indians greater freedom to develop the properties.

POLI. The Inuit Circumpolar Conference (ICC) is founded as a political organization to protect the rights of all Inuit peoples and promote self-sufficiency within their communities.

PUBL. Leslie Marmon Silko's novel *Ceremony* is published. Silko is a Laguna Pueblo poet and writer whose innovative narrative style interweaves the protagonist's story with retellings of traditional Pueblo legends. She will publish many books in the years ahead.

TREA. The Comanche and Ute Nations make an official peace between the tribes at a tribal meeting in Ignacio, Colorado. This resolves a long-standing conflict going back to the early 1700s.

1978

ARTS. The first Native American Film and Video Festival is held.

CIVI. In April, Navajo protestors seize control of the Texaco Montezuma Creek (Utah) oil complex, claiming job discrimination against the Indians, harassment, and environmental damage by the oil companies. After a two-week occupation, the companies and Indians come to some agreements for change, ending the siege.

In May, Chumash Indians occupy a proposed liquefied natural gas construction site near Point Conception, California, claiming the site overlooking the Pacific is sacred to the tribe. The Chumash demand protection of the site, which is the location of their ancient burial grounds. The utility company agrees to allow six Chumash to oversee the excavation and to allow the tribe to have access to the area for religious purposes.

The "Longest Walk" protest takes place from February to July, when a group of Indian activists, led by AIM founder Dennis Banks, walks 3,000 miles from San Francisco to Washington, D.C., to draw attention to Indian issues. Around 1,500 Indians representing 90 tribes participate in the walk, with around 100 completing the walk in Washington, D.C. On July 25, they hold a rally near the Washington Monument. They came to Washington to protest the *Native American Equal Opportunity Act* and other Congressional bills that would abolish the reservation system and eliminate many of the Indians' special rights to land, water, fishing, and other resources. After the walk, the House of Representatives overwhelmingly adopts a resolution making it a national policy to protect the rights of Indians. A similar walk will take place in 1994, called the Walk for Justice. This 3,800-mile spiritual walk will take five months, beginning in San Francisco on February 11, at Alcatraz Island, and ending at Washington, D.C. It will draw attention to the 18-year prison ordeal of Leonard Peltier as well as other Indian issues.

California governor Jerry Brown refuses to extradite Dennis Banks to South Dakota. AIM leader Dennis Banks had fled South Dakota to escape imprisonment for rioting and assault. The governor of California cites undue hostility toward AIM members in South Dakota and refuses to send Banks back. The California Supreme Court upholds the governor's decision.

EDUC. Congress passes the *Tribally Controlled Community College Act* to help finance colleges run by tribal governments as well as elementary and secondary public schools with large numbers of Indian students.

FAMI. The *Indian Child Welfare Act* states that Indian children should be adopted by Indian adults whenever possible. The act gives preference first to a child's extended family, next to families with the same tribal affiliation as the child, and finally to families of other tribes. The act also establishes standards for federal foster programs and provides assistance to tribes for child and family service programs.

HEAL. The Navajo reservation is soaked by torrential rains, sleet, and snow in March, stranding Indians on the reservation and reducing movement to horseback, foot, or helicopter. Army and National Guard helicopters from three states airlift food, medicine, and animal food to thousands of Navajos.

HUNT. In September, U.S. Fish and Wildlife agents clash with Yurok fishermen near the mouth of the Klamath River in northern California over the Indians' right to fish salmon during a ban on such fishing due to the low population of the salmon. The Indians argue that logging and damming the river as well as foreign offshore fishing are destroying the salmon, and not the Indian net fishing.

LAND. A group of Florida Seminole Indians reject a 1976 final award of $16 million for lands taken from them by Andrew Jackson in the early 1800s, stating their right to the land could not be traded for money.

The Indian Claims Commission (ICC) ceases after 32 years of operation (since 1946) in resolving Indian land claims. It heard around 300 cases and awarded Indian groups approximately $800 million in compensation for lost lands, with tribes winning awards in about 60 percent of claims filed. There are 66 claims still pending, which are referred to the U.S. Court of Claims for resolution.

LAWS. The U.S. Supreme Court rules that Indian tribal courts do not have inherent power to try non-Indians for crimes committed on reservations, according to the ruling in the case of *Oliphant v. Suquamish Indian Tribe.* David Oliphant, a non-Indian, assaulted a Suquamish police officer and was arrested by tribal police. The court states that the Suquamish tribal court cannot try Oliphant because he is a non-Indian. The controversial ruling weakens Indian control on reservations and challenges the concept of Indian sovereignty.

The right of tribes to set criteria for tribal membership is confirmed in the Supreme Court case of *Santa Clara v. Martinez.* Julia Martinez is a Santa Clara Pueblo tribal member who wants to will her house to her daughters. The tribal council says her daughters cannot inherit property within the pueblo because their father is a Navajo. Martinez argues that it is Pueblo tradition to trace ancestry through the mother's line. The court rules that, as sovereign governments, Indian tribes have the right to determine their own criteria for tribal membership. This decision ends most future claims against tribal governments.

RELI. The *American Indian Religious Freedom Act* passed by Congress establishes a goal of federal Indian policy to protect and preserve Indian religions. Religious freedom is guaranteed to Indians, Eskimos, Aleuts, and Native Hawaiians by the First Amendment to the U.S. Constitution, and these groups have the right to access religious sites, to possess and use sacred objects, and to worship through traditional ceremonies and rites.

1979

ANIM. The U.S. Supreme Court rules in November on laws affecting Indian artifacts that contain eagle feathers. Two federal laws banning traffic in eagles and other rare birds do apply to Indian artifacts that contain feathers, even if the objects were made before the laws were passed.

ARCH. The *Archaeological Resources Protection Act* regulates excavations on federal lands to prevent archaeological looting of Indian remains, sacred objects, and other artifacts. This act strengthens the 1906 *Act for the Preservation of American Antiquities.*

ARTS. Jay Silverheels, a Mohawk actor and co-star of the *Lone Ranger* television series, becomes the first American Indian to receive a star on the Hollywood Walk of Fame. Silverheels (b. 1912), son of a Mohawk chief, will die next year on March 5.

ECON. President Carter's administration offers a $24 million program for developing Indian energy projects in the West.

ENVI. One of the largest nuclear accidents on American soil occurs on July 16 when more than 11,000 tons of uranium mining wastes escape from a mine on the Navajo Indian Reservation. The radioactive material contaminates the nearby Rio Puerco River, which is measured as having 7,000 times the acceptable level of radioactivity for drinking water.

HEAL. In March, a U.S. District court judge orders the U.S. Indian Health Service (IHS) to spend more money on California Indians as is provided to tribes in other states. The 50,000 eligible California Indians make up 10 percent of the IHS population, but they were only receiving a little over 1 percent of the funds annually.

1980

ARTS. Maria Martinez (b.1887), world famous potter from San Ildefonso Pueblo, New Mexico, dies. Born Maria Antonia Montoya, she married Julian Martinez (traditionally the men of the pueblo do the painting), and together they created a unique black-on-black pottery style from recreating pottery shards discovered in 1908 and 1909 from an excavation of an ancient pueblo site near San Ildefonso. Her pottery style is one of the most sought-after by collectors around the world.

EDUC. Little Big Horn College in Crow Agency, Montana, is established as a public, two-year community college chartered by the Crow Tribe of Indians.

LAND. On June 30, the U.S. Supreme Court settles the Sioux's Black Hills case that started in 1923. In *United States v. Sioux Nation of Indians,* the federal government awards the Sioux Indian nation about $106 million as compensation for taking the Black Hills of South Dakota in 1877. The court upholds the earlier award to the Indians of $17.5 million plus interest, totaling $106 million. This is the largest Indian land claims settlement for any tribe, but the Indians decide to reject the award and continue to fight for the return of the Black Hills.

The Catawba Indians claim 144,000 acres of land in three counties in South Carolina, stating that the 1790 *Non-Intercourse Act* invalidates any land transactions not made solely with the federal government and tribes. A state treaty had been made in which the Indians relinquished 144,000 acres in York, Lancaster, and Chester counties of South Carolina, and this was deemed invalid due to the 1790 act. In July, a state commission will recommend that the Catawba be allowed to expand their reservation to 5,450 acres and that each tribal member receive a cash payment.

LAND. The Eastern Branch of the Cherokee loses a lawsuit to stop construction of the Tellico Dam in Tennessee, which will flood the sites of the capital of the Cherokee Nation before the tribe was driven from Tennessee in the 1830s. The U.S. Court of Appeals rules that the sites are not essential to the religious practices of the Cherokee.

By the *Hopi-Navajo Relocation Act* Congress allocates funds to purchase new lands for Navajo families living on the Hopi Reservation. This is to help resolve the long-standing conflict dating from the formation of the Hopi Indian Reservation in 1882.

The state of Maine awards the Penobscot and Passamaquoddy $81.5 million to settle the tribes' claims to 12.5 million acres of land in the state. In the protracted legal battle, the tribes maintained that Maine had illegally confiscated two-thirds of the state's lands from the Penobscot and Passamaquoddy Indians, in violation of the *Trade and Intercourse Act of 1790*. The money is divided into $27 million to be put into a federal trust fund and $54.5 million for the purchase of 300,000 acres of land.

POLI. In January, The Ramapough Mountain Indians are recognized as a tribe by the state of New Jersey. They live on Stag Hill, 20 miles from New York City, in an economically depressed area. The Ramapough trace their ancestry to the Iroquois and Algonquin nations and have been characterized as a conglomeration of peoples since the American Revolution.

1981

ARTS. Actor Chief Dan George dies on September 23 at the age of 82. The Canadian Indian was nominated for an Academy Award for his role as the Indian chief in the motion picture *Little Big Man*. He also appeared in other films and was an eloquent spokesman for Indian rights.

The first All Nations Indian Powwow takes place at Knott's Berry Farm in Buena Park, California, in September. Over 600 Indian families, representing over 17 tribes, show their dancing and traditions.

CIVI. In March, a federal appeals court overturns the charges against Leonard Peltier, the Indian activist, for his July 20, 1979, escape from Lompoc Federal Prison. Peltier was serving two consecutive life sentences for the murders of two FBI agents in South Dakota in 1975. He maintains that he had to escape prison, because there was a government plot to kill him. The new ruling makes it possible to have a retrial of his December, 1979, trial regarding his escape.

AIM sponsors the occupation of a part of the Black Hills (Paha Sapa) to press demands that the sacred area be returned to the Lakota Sioux.

Crow Indians barricade the bridge over the Big Horn River to protest the Supreme Court decision to allow non-Indian fishing and hunting of the river where it passes through their reservation.

DEAT. When the California Department of Parks and Recreation turns over much of its archaeological Indian skeletal collection to California Indians for reburial, a group of professional archaeologists protest the move by filing a lawsuit to stop the reburials.

HUNT. The Bureau of Indian affairs plans a crackdown in December on a multimillion dollar black market in illegally-caught salmon along the West

Coast. In 1983, three Indians from the Pacific Northwest will be convicted for illegally selling Columbia River salmon to undercover agents.

POLI. President Ronald Reagan proposes massive cuts in federal funding for Indians and transferring responsibilities for Indian education and resources to state governments. Most of the proposed measures will not be passed, although during the Reagan years in the White House over $100 million in Indian programs will be slashed.

PUBL. The *Lakota Times* weekly newspaper begins publication on the Pine Ridge Reservation in South Dakota. In 1992, the newspaper will be renamed *Indian Country Today* to reflect its coverage of Indian affairs nationwide.

RELI. Little Sun Bordeaux, an eight-year old Jewish boy, and the grandson of the late Dallas Chief Eagle Bordeaux, becomes the new hereditary chief of the Teton Sioux. He is a direct descendant of Chief Crazy Horse and is considered by the tribe to be a reincarnation of Crazy Horse.

1982

CIVI. Some Sioux American Indian Movement (AIM) activists continue to occupy 800 acres in the Black Hills National Forest of South Dakota. Begun in April, 1981, the 18-month occupation heightens racial tensions in the region between whites and Indians. The Black Hills, traditional Sioux lands, were allowed by the federal government to be kept by the Sioux in 1868, but taken back in 1876 when gold was discovered in the area. In 1980, the U.S. Supreme Court will rule that the land, about 100 square miles, was illegally taken from the Sioux by the federal government, and the tribe will be offered a $106 million land claim settlement, which the tribe will turn down.

ECON. The U.S. Supreme Court rules in January that Indian tribes have the power to impose severance taxes on oil, gas, and minerals produced on their reservations.

Two acts are passed by Congress (the *Federal Oil and Gas Royalty Management Act* and the *Indian Mining Development Act*) to help tribes

with energy-rich lands to receive fair royalties for oil, natural gas, uranium, and coal.

Through the *Indian Tribal Governmental Tax Status Act* Congress confirms that Indian tribes are not taxable entities. Also, the act gives tribes many of the same tax benefits available to state and local governments.

ENVI. The *Nuclear Waste Policy Act* calls for the development of repositories for radioactive waste, allowing for negotiations with Indians tribes for use of reservation lands.

POLI. The U.S. Post Office issues a Crazy Horse stamp.

RELI. A Cherokee prisoner wins the right to wear his hair long. A Cherokee inmate refuses to allow prison authorities to cut his hair, maintaining that his long hair has religious significance for him. In the subsequent Supreme Court case of *Gallahan v. Holyfield,* the court rules in favor of the prisoner, primarily because the prison has not justified its policy of cutting the inmates hair for security reasons.

The National Indian Youth Council campaigns for Indian religious freedom. The organization protests the destruction of sacred sites on public lands and the lack of protection by the Interior Department in protecting the sacred sites.

WARS. President Ronald Reagan names August 14 "National Navajo Code Talkers Day" with Presidential Proclamation 4954. The Navajo code was declassified in 1968.

1983

CIVI. Dennis Banks, the AIM leader, still under indictment in South Dakota for the 1973 Wounded Knee occupation, takes refuge on the Onondaga Reservation in New York State. In 1984, Banks will surrender to officials in South Dakota and be sentenced to three years in prison.

The National Tribal Chairman's Association asks President Reagan to fire Secretary of the Interior James Watts for "callous disregard" for Indians. In a television interview on January 19, Watts states that Indian reservation "socialism" has led to "alcoholism, unemployment, venereal disease, and drug addiction." Watts will apologize in the opening session of the National Congress of American Indians in January for remarks he made characterizing reservation life in grossly negative terms.

DEAT. The great grand-daughter of the Indian Chief Sitting Bull, Little Flower May V. Sharp, dies in June. She was a full-blooded Hunkpapa Sioux.

ECON. In July, the U.S. Supreme Court rules that state governments have the power to license and regulate the sale of liquor on Indian reservations. The ruling applies to approximately 100 tribes throughout the country.

A federal appeals court in Denver rules in August that Navajo Indians have the right to tax oil and gas leases and mineral sales on their Utah reservation.

FOOD. In February, severe cold and wet weather on the Navajo Reservation leaves three people dead and 1,400 families stranded. Food is delivered in rescue helicopters to the isolated families near Window Rock, Arizona.

HUNT. An appellate court in San Francisco affirms a lower court decision to allow the Klamath Indians to hunt and fish on state-owned land without being bound by state fish and wildlife regulations, because Congress did not specify otherwise when the Klamath tribe ceded 617,000 acres to the federal government in 1901.

The U.S. Court of Appeals rules in *Lac Courte Oreilles Band of Lake Superior Chippewa Indians v. Voigt* (known as the Voigt decision) that the Ojibwe of Wisconsin have the right to fish, hunt, and gather wild foods in their former homeland, even though the area was ceded to the United States by treaty.

In New Mexico, the Mescalero Apache are given the right to regulate hunting and fishing on the tribe's reservation in the Supreme Court case of *New Mexico v. Mescalero Apache Tribe*.

POLI. The Pequot Indians of Connecticut win federal recognition.

PUBL. Peter Matthiessen publishes *In the Spirit of Crazy Horse*. The book is about contemporary Indian life on reservations in South Dakota, the history of the struggles of the Lakota Indians with the U.S. government, and a scathing indictment of the FBI's dealings with the American Indian Movement on the Pine Ridge Reservation in South Dakota in the 1970s. In 1984, a lawsuit against Matthiessen will be brought by one of the FBI agents who holds that the book defames his character. The lawsuit also blocks the publication of the book in a paperback edition and in foreign editions. A federal court of appeals will dismiss the lawsuit in 1989, and the book will be offered for sale for the first time since its original publication.

WATE. The Supreme Court makes a ruling in the case of *Arizona et al. v. San Carlos Apache Tribe* that tribes can be forced to settle water rights disputes in state courts rather than in federal courts. This is significant because state courts are usually less sympathetic to the position of tribes than federal courts.

1984

CIVI. In the summer, Indian activist Dennis Banks organizes the Jim Thorpe Longest Run while living as a fugitive on the Onondaga Reservation in New York State. Teams of Indian runners run a relay from the reservation in New York to Los Angeles, California, where they end at the site of the summer Olympic Games. At the Olympics, the Indians hold a powwow to honor Jim Thorpe, the great Sac and Fox athlete who won gold medals in the 1912 Olympics.

Dennis Banks, an AIM activist, surrenders to state and local officials in Rapid City, South Dakota, on September 13, and is sentenced to three years in prison. He will serve 18 months. Banks (Anishinabe/Ojibwa), was born on April 12, 1937, on Leech Lake Indian Reservation in northern Minnesota. He has been one of the foremost Indian rights activists since the early 1960s, co-founding the American Indian Movement (AIM) in 1968, and actively involved in many protests including the Alcatraz occupation of 1969 and the siege of Wounded Knee in 1973. He will also become known in the years ahead as a teacher, lecturer, author, artist, musician, and actor. His autobiography *Ojibwa Warrior: Dennis*

Banks and the Rise of the American Indian Movement will be published in 2004. He will play small roles in several motion pictures including *War Party* (1988), *The Last of the Mohicans* (1992), and *Thunderheart* (1992). Banks will continue to organize "sacred runs" in many locations around the country and the world to support peace and other worthy causes. *Sacred Run 2006* will take place from February 11 to April 22, 2006, from San Francisco to Washington, D.C.

ECON. The Commission of Indian Reservation Economies accuses the BIA of excessive regulations and incompetent management. The BIA is found to spend more than two-thirds of it annual budget on itself.

POLI. The Native American Journalists Association is founded in Minneapolis by Indian journalists working in print, radio, and television.

PUBL. Louise Erdrich publishes her first novel, *Love Medicine,* which becomes a best seller and receives the National Book Critics Circle Award and the *Los Angeles Times* Book Prize. Erdrich is an Ojibwe (Chippewa) fiction writer and poet who will publish many popular books over the coming years.

Leaders of the two Cherokee nations—the Cherokee Nation based in Tahlequah, Oklahoma, and the Eastern Band of Cherokees in Cherokee, North Carolina—meet in a joint council for the first time since the "Trail of Tears" separated them. Approximately 10,000 Cherokee gather in Red Clay, Tennessee, in this first full Cherokee Council since 1837.

1985

ARTS. The first annual Indian Summer Festival takes place in Milwaukee, Wisconsin. Organized by Indian Summer Festivals, Inc., a nonprofit organization, the festival is dedicated to strengthening the American Indian community and educating the general public on the history and the unique and diverse cultures of the American Indian by providing a forum to celebrate and showcase traditional and contemporary American

Indian culture. It will become one of the largest annual Indian events in the country.

ECON. The U.S. Supreme Court rules that the Navajo tribe may impose taxes on business activity on Navajo land, whether by Indian or non-Indian businesses, without the prior approval of the federal government.

The National Indian Gaming Commission (NIGA) is created to protect and preserve the welfare of tribes involved in Indian gaming.

LAND. The U.S. Supreme Court upholds the right of the Oneida Indian Nation in upper New York State to sue for damages for land taken from them in 1795 and sold to the state of New York. In the case of *County of Oneida v. Oneida Nation,* approximately 100,000 acres of Oneida Indian territory was found to have been seized without federal approval as required by a 1793 law. This landmark case will encourage other eastern tribes to sue for lands taken from them in the eighteenth and nineteenth centuries. The tribe and New York State are not able to negotiate a land settlement, however, for many years. In 1998, the U.S. government will join the Oneida in a suit to spur the state on to reach an agreement. The 20,000 landowners living in the disputed area are outraged, some of whom already resent the Oneidas' casino in the area and the nontaxable income they receive from it.

The Alaska Native Review Commission was formed in 1983 to study the effects of the *Alaska Native Claims Settlement Act.* Based on interviews with 15,000 Alaska Natives in 62 villages throughout Alaska, the commission publishes its findings in *Village Journey.* The transcribed testimony of the Natives comprises 98 volumes. The commission recommends that the land titles be transferred to tribal governments in order to regulate land and water use in alignment with traditional beliefs and customs.

POLI. Wilma Mankiller becomes the first woman Principal Chief of the Cherokee Nation of Oklahoma on December 14. She was an Indian activist in earlier years and held the position of deputy chief of the Cherokee Nation since 1983. Mankiller will prove to be a highly popular chief and be re-elected in 1987 and 1991 with a wide margin of votes.

RELI. The Catholic Church declares Junipero Serra venerable, despite Indian objections. Serra was the Franciscan priest who led the development of the mission system in California. The Catholic Church will declare Serra beatified in 1988. Indians object to these honors, charging that Serra and the Franciscans advocated seizing Indian land, forcing Indians into virtual slavery, converting the Indians by force, and suppressing their traditional religions.

1986

BURI. On September 19, Harry J. W. (Jimmy) Belvin, Principal Chief of the Choctaw Nation, dies in Durant, Oklahoma. During the 27 years he served as chief he was influential in obtaining more autonomy for the Choctaw and other Oklahoma tribes from the Interior Department.

PUBL. Paula Gunn Allen, scholar and novelist, publishes *Sacred Hoop: Recovering the Feminine in American Indian Traditions*. The collection of essays examines the central role of women in tribal traditions and their long-ignored significance in the cultural and literary history of Indians. The book will influence the teaching of American Indian cultures and literatures. She will publish many books of fiction and nonfiction in the years ahead.

RELI. Donald E. Pelotte, an Abnaki Indian from Maine becomes the first American Indian bishop of the Roman Catholic Church, as bishop coadjutor of the Diocese of Gallup, New Mexico.

WARS. On November 10, a plaque is dedicated at Arlington National Cemetery in Washington, D.C., commemorating the Native American Vietnam Veterans Memorial. This is the first national memorial for Native American veterans, and it begins with a plaque near the grave of Ira Hayes, the WWII Indian hero, with an inscription honoring American Indian Vietnam veterans.

1987

ARTS. The American Indian Dance Theater is established to provide a showcase for Indian dance.

Representing many tribes, the dancers employ traditional dances as well as powwow "fancy" dances to audiences throughout the United States and other countries.

ENVI. Congress and President Reagan come close to passing legislation to open the Arctic National Wildlife Refuge to oil drilling. The 20-million acre refuge is one of the largest protected wilderness areas in the United States and home to the Gwich'im people who survive on subsistence hunting of caribou. The *Exxon Valdez* disaster in 1989 will temporarily weaken support for further oil development in Alaska.

LAWS. A significant court case opens the door for Indian casinos. In the case of *California v. Cabazon Band of Mission Indians,* the U.S. Supreme Court rules that California cannot prohibit or regulate bingo and poker games on Indian reservations, because it allows them on non-Indian lands. The decision establishes that Indian tribes throughout the country can operate unregulated gaming as long as the same types of gambling are legal in their states.

POLI. Marine Sgt. Clayton J. Lonetree is sentenced to 30 years in prison and fined $5000 for spying for the Soviet Union. Lonetree, of Ho-chunk and Navajo heritage, receives a 25-year sentence, but he will be released in 1996 after serving only nine years.

RELI. Pope John Paul addresses a conference in Phoenix, Arizona, with approximately 1,600 American Indian leaders, asking them to forget the Church's past mistakes and wrongs in its dealing with Indians, and to now focus on its current efforts for Indians' rights.

1988

CIVI. Russell Means, cofounder of the American Indian Movement, announces his retirement from AIM. Means, born November 10, 1939, on the Pine Ridge Reservation near the Black Hills of South Dakota, has been one of the foremost Indian rights activists over the years. He is also an artist, musician, and actor. He will act in several motion pictures including *Last of the Mohicans* (1992) and *Natural Born Killers*

(1994). His autobiography, titled *Where White Men Fear to Tread,* will be published in 1995.

POLI. The federal government formally ends the termination of Indian tribes. *Public Law 100–297* repeals *House Concurrent Resolution 108,* passed in 1953, which allowed the government to terminate Indian tribes. Termination was the predominant Indian policy of the 1950s with the U.S. government attempting to sever its financial responsibilities to more than 100 tribes.

Congress passes the *Indian Gaming Regulatory Act* acknowledging that Indian gaming operations are a means of promoting tribal economic development and self-sufficiency. The act comes in response to last year's Supreme Court ruling *California v. Cabazon Band of Mission Indians,* which held that Indian gaming could be regulated only by a congressional act. The *Indian Gaming Regulatory Act* divides games into three classes. Class I games are traditional games to be regulated only by tribes. Class II includes bingo and lotto games, which are to be regulated by the National Indian Gaming Commission (established in 1985). Class III includes all high-stakes and casino-style games and may only be used by tribes when the games are not prohibited by the state in which the Indian group lives. The Indian group must also negotiate a formal agreement with their state that outlines rules for operating any Class III game.

On December 12, President Reagan meets with 16 American Indian leaders to soften tensions that had grown because of disparaging remarks he made last May in the Soviet Union regarding Indians and reservations. At a meeting with Russian students on May 30, Reagan stated that the United States should not have "humored" Indians by letting them "live a primitive lifestyle" (Darst 1988, A4).

1989

ARTS. Northwest Coast tribes stage the "Paddle to Seattle" event to revive canoe building among tribes who traditionally made and used canoes. Participants from 17 Indian groups travel in dugout canoes from their communities to Seattle, Washington.

ECON. The first American Indian reporter to appear on national television is Hattie Kauffman (Nez Percé) of ABC News.

EDUC. The National Museum of the American Indian is chartered by Congress as the 16th museum of the Smithsonian Institution with the *American Indian Act.* It will be the first national museum dedicated to Native American history, culture, arts, and life. The museum comprises three facilities, in Washington, D.C., Suitland, Maryland, and New York City. On September 28, 1999, groundbreaking will take place for the construction of the museum building on The Mall in Washington, D.C., and the museum will open to the public on September 21, 2004.

ENVI. The *Exxon Valdez* oil spill destroys much Aleut land and sea life. After the oil tanker runs aground on March 24, 11 million gallons of oil begin to spill out of a massive hole in the supertanker and into Prince William Sound near the Aleut village of Chignik. Eventually, the oil-slick will extend 470 miles southwest from Bligh Reef reaching 11,000 square miles, including 1,300 miles of shoreline. It is considered the number one spill worldwide in terms of damage to the environment. Much of the area's sea life, on which the Aleut depend for food, will be killed.

FAMI. The U.S. Supreme Court rules that tribes have jurisdiction over child custody cases involving Indian babies born off the reservation. In the case of *Mississippi Band of Choctaw Indians v. Holyfield et al.,* the court maintains that the provisions of the *Indian Child Welfare Act* of 1978 give the tribe the right to be involved in the adoption of two Choctaw children born outside the Choctaw reservation. The tribe wants the Choctaw children to be adopted by Indians.

LANG. The French government honors the Choctaw code talkers, who used their native language as a code for communicating top secret messages and were instrumental in the Meuse-Argonne campaign in France in 1918 during WWI. In appreciation of the Choctaw soldiers, officials of the French government honor Choctaw leader Hollis E. Roberts with a Chevalier de l'Ordre National du Mérite (a Knight of the

National Order of Merit), their country's highest honor.

POLI. Peter MacDonald, Sr., former leader of the Navajo Tribe, is charged with over 100 counts of bribery, fraud, conspiracy, and other crimes by the tribe.

1990

ARTS. Kevin Costner's film *Dances with Wolves* is released. The three-hour motion picture epic opens to wide acclaim from the public and the critics. Many Indians praise the film for its sympathetic view of the plight of the Lakota Indians in the nineteenth century, and for its casting of Indian actors such as Wes Studi (the toughest Pawnee), Graham Greene "Kicking Bird," Rodney A. Grant "Wind in His Hair," Floyd Red Crow Westerman "Ten Bears," Jimmy Herman "Stone Calf," Nathan Lee Chasing His Horse "Smiles a Lot," Michael Spears "Otter," Jason R. Lone Hill "Worm," Tantoo Cardinal "Black Shawl," and Doris Leader Charge "Pretty Shield."

Graham Greene (b. June 22, 1952), an Oneida actor, plays the role of Kicking Bird in *Dances with Wolves*. Born on the Six Nations Reserve in Ontario, Canada, Greene also acted in the film *Pow Wow Highway* (1988), and will go on to play key roles in future motion pictures: *Thunderheart* (1992), *Grey Owl* (1998), *The Green Mile* (1999), *Lost and Delirious* (2001), and *The Quiet American* (2002).

The *Indian Arts and Crafts Act* of 1990 is passed by Congress which prohibits misrepresentation in marketing of American Indian arts and crafts within the United States. All products must be marketed truthfully regarding the authenticity of the Indian heritage and tribal affiliation of the producers, so as not to mislead the consumer. This act intends to prohibit non-Indians from marketing their arts and crafts as Indian art. This legislation is a revision of the 1935 *Indian Arts and Crafts Act*.

DEAT. The *Native American Graves Protection and Repatriation Act* (NAGPRA) is signed by President Bush to protect American Indian grave sites and to return Indian remains and cultural artifacts to the tribes. Guidelines are established for the return of remains and sacred items from museums and universities, excluding the Smithsonian Institution for now. However, the Smithsonian Institution announces later in the year that it has adopted a new policy and will return Indian artifacts as requested by tribes.

LANG. The *Native American Language Act* reverses the government's policy of suppressing American Indian languages and cultures.

POLI. Peterson Zah is elected Navajo tribal president, replacing Peter MacDonald, Sr., who was convicted of bribery, fraud, conspiracy, and ethics violations and sentenced to serve 450 days in jail.

PUBL. Mary Crow Dog's *Lakota Woman* is published telling of the activist's involvement in the American Indian Movement in the 1970s. Co-authored by non-Indian author Richard Erdoes, it becomes an immediate popular and critical success.

RELI. The U.S. Supreme Court maintains that Oregon's laws against peyote use do not contradict the First Amendment's protection of religious freedom. In the case *Employment Division, Department of Human Resources of Oregon v. Smith*, two Indian drug and alcohol counselors are denied unemployment compensation after being fired from their jobs because of their peyote use in a ceremony of the Native American Church. The court rules in favor of the state of Oregon against peyote use. In the following year, however, the state of Oregon will allow Indians to use peyote for religious ceremonies.

WARS. The 100th anniversary of the Wounded Knee massacre is marked with about 400 people attending ceremonies in South Dakota. In October, Congress passes a joint resolution expressing "deep regret" for the massacre, but not including reparations or establishing a national monument, as Indian groups had requested.

1991

LAND. As a result of the *Nunavut Land Claims Agreement*, Canada declares that it will create the territory of Nunavut. It will be composed of

2 million square kilometres of land in the eastern half of the Northwest Territories, and about 85 percent of the population of the new territory will be Inuit. Nunavut will be officially created in 1999 as a new Canadian territory encompassing one-fifth of the country.

POLI. The Custer Battlefield National Monument is renamed Little Bighorn Battlefield National Monument. A $2 million memorial will be dedicated in 2003.

Larry Echohawk (Pawnee) is the first American Indian to be elected as a state attorney general in the United States. He was elected to the Idaho House of Representatives in 1982 and 1984.

PUBL. Sherman J. Alexie, Jr. (b. 1966, Spokane/Coeur d'Alene), a writer and director, publishes his first book, *The Business of Fancydancing: Stories and Poems*. In the years ahead he will publish many successful novels, poems, short stories, and screenplays including *The Lone Ranger and Tonto Fistfight in Heaven* (1993), *Indian Killer* (1996), *Smoke Signals* (motion picture, 1998), and *The Business of Fancydancing* (motion picture, 2002).

SPOR. Indians protest the Atlanta Braves baseball team logo at the World Series.

WARS. The first Native American casualty of the Persian Gulf War is Pfc. Michael A. Noline (San Carlos Apache). Noline is also the first casualty from Arizona, dying in action on January 26.

1992

ARTS. The First Americans in the Arts awards ceremony is instigated in Beverly Hills, California, honoring American Indian actors in movies and television and other fields of the performing arts.

BURI. Lucy Lewis, one of the best known Southwestern potters, dies around the age of 95. Lewis was born around 1897 at Sky City, Acoma Pueblo, New Mexico. Her beautiful and innovative pottery style earned her the title of matriarch of Acoma pottery.

ECON. The Mashantucket Pequot tribe opens their Foxwoods Resort and Casino complex on

their reservation in Connecticut. It will become the world's largest casino, bringing in enormous amounts of cash to the tribe and becoming one of the largest employers in the state.

LAND. The Hopi and Navajo tribes reach an agreement over long-disputed land. After more than a century of discord, an agreement is mediated in federal court with the Hopi agreeing to allow about 450 Navajo families to stay in their homes on the Hopi Reservation by leasing the land for 75 years from the Hopi. In exchange, the Hopi will be given around 400,000 acres of land in the San Francisco Peaks area. The U.S. government also agrees to settle several outstanding lawsuits with the Hopi for $15 million. In 1996, the *Navajo-Hopi Land Dispute Settlement Act* will require the Navajo living on the Hopi Reservation to either lease their land from the Hopi or move from the area.

POLI. Ben Nighthorse Campbell, a Northern Cheyenne, is elected U.S. Senator from Colorado, the first American Indian senator in 60 years. Campbell has also served in the Colorado legislature and the U.S. House of Representatives.

SPOR. Indians protest the Washington Redskins football team logo at the Super Bowl.

WARS. On September 17, 35 Marine veteran code talkers are honored at the Pentagon in Washington, D.C., at the Navajo Code Talker Exhibit that is on display.

1993

HEAL. A hantavirus epidemic breaks out on the Navajo Reservation during May to July. A young Navajo man is rushed to the hospital in Gallup, New Mexico, with severe flu symptoms and soon dies. Several similar cases show up claiming the lives of 16 Navajos. Doctors consult the Centers for Disease Control (CDC), which determines the mysterious illness as hantavirus, which has never before caused disease in humans in the Americas. The virus is traced to the wild deer mouse, whose population has grown tremendously after rains produced a large crop of the piñon nuts on which the animals feed. A campaign is launched to inform residents how to avoid contamination.

POLI. Ada Deer, Menominee scholar and activist, becomes the new assistant secretary for the Bureau of Indian Affairs and the first woman in this position, serving until 1997.

The Lumbee Indians of North Carolina are formally recognized by the U.S. House of Representatives. Recognized by the state of North Carolina in 1885, the tribe has been seeking full federal recognition since 1890. They are now permitted to adopt a constitution, but are not eligible to receive federal funding.

The United States restores federal recognition to the Catawba tribe after 13 years of negotiations between the tribe and the federal government. The tribe is made eligible for government services and awarded $50 million to purchase land, fund economic and social programs, and make payments to tribal members.

RELI. The *Native American Free Exercise of Religion Act* strengthens rights as defined in the *American Indian Religious Freedom Act* of 1978.

1994

CIVI. The state of Minnesota bans Indian names as liquor brands. Indians had protested the use of names of famous Indian leaders as liquor brands such as the Original Crazy Horse Malt Liquor and Chief Oshkosh Beer. In 1996, the Minnesota Court of Appeals will rule that the state law banning the sale of Original Crazy Horse Malt Liquor violates the freedom of speech of the company that distributes the product, and the court therefore overturns the ban.

The Walk for Justice takes place from San Francisco to Washington, D.C., where activists speak on Native American issues before a Senate caucus. Led by Dennis Banks, the group of walkers from around the world and 21 Indian nations leaves from Alacatraz Island in San Francisco Bay on February 11 for a five-month, 3,800-mile walk to Washington, D.C. The purpose of the walk is to bring attention to many tribal issues, including the incarceration of Leonard Peltier, the AIM activist.

POLI. President Bill Clinton invites leaders of all 547 federally-recognized American Indian and Alaska native tribes to the White House, the first-ever meeting of its kind. Representatives from over 300 tribes convene at the White House, where they are asked to discuss the most important issues concerning their people. Tribal leaders and U.S. officials identify issues for follow-up conferences.

RELI. The use of peyote in the Native American Church is upheld by an amendment to the *Native American Religious Freedom Act*. The act is in response to contradictions between state laws and federal policy regarding the use of peyote.

A white buffalo calf is born at a farm in Janesville, Wisconsin, which draws Indians from throughout the country. The calf is seen by some Indians as the embodiment of White Buffalo Calf Woman, a sacred figure in stories told by many Plains tribes. White Buffalo Calf Woman gave Indians the pipe, then turned into a white buffalo calf and ran away, promising to return one day.

1996

ARCH. Kennewick Man is discovered in Washington State. Archaeologists excavate the most complete human skeleton ever found in the Pacific Northwest, and estimate its age to be 9,300 years old. A legal battle ensues between scientists, Indians, and a group called the Asatru Folk Assembly that claims the skeleton as a Norse ancestor. Indians maintain that the *Native American Graves Protection and Repatriation Act* (1990) gives them the right to bury the remains, who they consider an ancestor. Scientists say the skull has Caucasoid features and believe that a skeleton as old as Kennewick Man cannot be traced back to a modern tribe in the area. In 1998, a court will order the skeleton to be transported to the Burke Museum of the University of Washington for examination by scientists under the supervision of the Department of the Interior. In 2000, Kennewick Man will be given by the U.S. government to five northwestern tribes who wish to bury him by tribal rites.

ARTS. Maria Tallchief, the popular Osage ballerina, is honored at the Kennedy Center for the Performing Arts in Washington, D.C., for a lifetime achievement award. Attended by President

Bill Clinton, the awards honor Americans who have made significant contributions to the performing arts.

CIVI. A federal court in Casper, Wyoming, rejects a request by Indians for a rock climbing ban at Devils Tower, a sacred Indian site.

ENVI. Coeur d'Alene Indians bring a $1 billion suit against mining companies for dumping toxic wastes into the Coeur d'Alene River basin. The affected area, stretching over 1,500 square miles, is one of the largest contaminated areas in the United States. The contamination is the result of 100 years of mining and ore processing activities, and it will take many years for the environmental cleanup.

LAND. The *Navajo-Hopi Land Dispute Settlement Act* requires the 3,000 or so Navajos living on the Hopi Indian Reservation to either lease their land from the Hopi or move from the area by the end of the year. After December 31, Navajo who have neither signed a lease nor moved from the reservation can be forcibly evicted by the Hopi Rangers.

LAWS. The Supreme Court case *Seminole Tribe v. Florida* addresses the role of states in Indian gaming. The Seminole Tribe sued Florida to force the state to negotiate with them concerning a gambling parlor it wants to open. The state claims it cannot be sued without its consent. In a controversial decision over state's rights, the court declares states are immune to prosecution for violating federal law that requires the states to negotiate with tribes according to the *Indian Gaming Regulatory Act*.

POLI. The Bureau of Indian Affairs is sued by the Native American Rights Fund for mismanaging funds held in trust for Indians in Individual Indian Money (IIM) accounts. This is the largest class action lawsuit ever initiated against the U.S. government for financial incompetence. The suit holds that billions of dollars owed to individual Indians from oil, gas, grazing, and timber leases have been misplaced due to poor record keeping over the years. In 1999, a federal judge will order an overhaul of the Indian trust fund system.

Winona LaDuke becomes the vice-presidential candidate on the Green Party ticket with Ralph Nader. The 37-year-old Colorado Ojibwa activist is the founder of the White Earth Land Recovery Project, which purchases land to regain the Ojibwa's original homeland for tribal use. Nader and LaDuke will win 0.6 percent of the popular vote in the November election. In 2000, LaDuke will run again for vice-president on the Green Party ticket with Ralph Nader.

POLI. Lynda Morgan Lovejoy (Navajo) is the first American Indian woman elected to the House of Representatives in the state of New Mexico.

PUBL. Vine Deloria, Jr., a Dakota lawyer and journalist, publishes *Red Earth, White Lies,* an analysis of the inherent racism in much of the research conducted by non-Indians into the origins of Indian people. Deloria, who published *Custer Died for Your Sins* in 1969, will publish 20 books on Indian issues before he dies in 2005.

1997

ARTS. The first Native American Music Awards ceremony takes place at the Pequot tribe's Foxwoods Resort in Connecticut. The program recognizes excellence in the growing Native American music movement.

HUNT. Whaling resumes by some Indian groups. On August 17, the Inuit in the eastern Arctic perform the first legal whale hunt since the Canadian government began regulating their bowhead hunting in 1976. In October, the Makah Indians of Washington State are given permission by the International Whaling Commission to hunt whales off the coast of Neah Bay. A treaty made by the tribe with the United States in 1855 gave the Indians the right to continue their traditional whale hunts, but a 1926 ban on whaling in the region was imposed by the commission due to over-hunting by non-Indians. The Makah will hunt their first gray whale on May 17, 1999. Animal-rights groups and whale-watching organizations will strongly criticize the hunting and killing of the California gray whales, especially because the Indians use nontraditional hunting methods.

POLI. California tribes seek support for their right to operate casinos on reservations without interference from the governor. Tribes are required by the *Indian Gaming Regulatory Act* to negotiate compacts with a state before opening a gambling operation in that state. California Governor Pete Wilson will only offer very restrictive compacts with California tribes, and many California tribes have opened casinos without state approval. Wilson has countered by shutting down gambling operations and confiscating slot machines.

Sally Ann Gonzales (Yaqui) and Debora Norris (Navajo) are the first American Indian women to be elected to the Arizona House of Representatives.

RELI. The first American Indian to be named archbishop in the Roman Catholic Church is Charles J. Chaput (Prairie Band Potwatomi) who assumes leadership of the Denver archdiocese.

The U.S. military announces on April 15 that it will allow American Indian soldiers to use peyote in their religious services.

1998

ARTS. The granite carving of Crazy Horse, started in 1939, is unveiled in the Black Hills of South Dakota, 15 miles from Mount Rushmore.

The motion picture *Smoke Signals* is released by Sherman Alexie.

EDUC. The Mashantucket Pequot open a $193 million museum and research center in Mashantucket, Connecticut. At 308,000 square feet, it is larger than the planned Smithsonian Institution's Museum of the American Indian scheduled to open in Washington, D.C., in 2002.

1999

DEAT. Iron Eyes Cody, Cherokee/Creek Indian actor, dies around age 94 on January 5. He became known during the 1970s for his tearful face in the "crying Indian" television ads for Keep America Beautiful. He shed a single tear upon watching people litter. Cody appeared in over 100 motion pictures and television shows. There is controversy over whether or not Cody was American Indian. Even though he married an Indian woman and adopted two Indian boys, and lived his life representing Indians and Indian causes, research points to his actually being an Italian-American, born Espera DeCorti in 1904 in Kaplan, Louisiana. He published his autobiography in 1982 titled *Iron Eyes: My Life as a Hollywood Indian.*

EDUC. Bill Gates of the Microsoft Corporation launches a program through his private charity that will provide $1 billion in scholarships for minority students, including American Indians. Over the next 20 years, the Gates Millennium Scholars Program will offer scholarships to undergraduate and graduate students in math, science, engineering, education, and library science.

The Lilly Endowment gives $30 million to the American Indian College Fund, the largest private donation ever received by an American Indian organization. The money will primarily be spent on constructing new buildings at 30 tribal colleges.

HUNT. The U.S. Supreme Court rules on March 24 to uphold a treaty from 1837 with the Chippewa Indians allowing hunting and fishing on 13 million acres of public land in Minnesota.

Makah Indians legally hunt and kill a gray whale in Neah Bay, Washington State, their first whale hunt in 75 years.

POLI. The Nunavut Territory and government come into existence on April 1 as a result of the *Nunavut Land Claims Agreement* and the *Nunavut Act* (1993). Comprising one-fifth of the country of Canada, this is the largest aboriginal land claims settlement in Canada's history. For millennia a major Inuit homeland, this new territory in

"Smoke Signals, drawn from stories by Sherman Alexie, was a groundbreaker—both artistically, as a work of sophistication and maturity, and creatively, as the first feature film written, produced, and directed by Native Americans" (Thomas 2002, E12).

"It would be difficult to find a more historically mismanaged federal program." U.S. District Judge Royce Lamberth, regarding the mismanagement of the Indian trust fund system by the BIA, and the billions of dollars missing that is owed to Indians (Melmer 2000, A1).

Canada's Arctic spans 2 million square kilometers north and west of Hudson's Bay to the North Pole, and is now home to almost 30,000 residents, 85 percent of whom are Inuit.

The Sacagawea coin is unveiled in a ceremony at the White House. The new one-dollar coin features the face of Sacagawea, the Shoshone interpreter and guide for the Lewis and Clark Expedition. The coin will be issued next year.

A class action lawsuit is filed by 34 Indian tribes against tobacco companies to recover billions of dollars the tribes have spent treating smoking-related illnesses. The legal action follows a successful lawsuit last year by 46 states that were awarded $206 billion in compensation from tobacco companies, but Indian tribes were excluded from this settlement.

President Bill Clinton visits the Oglala Sioux Pine Ridge Reservation in South Dakota on a four-day tour of the poorest communities in the United States. This is the first time a U.S. President has visited a reservation since the Roosevelt administration. Clinton promises the government will investigate new ways to alleviate reservation poverty.

A federal judge orders an overhaul of the Indian trust fund system. The Native American Rights Fund brought the class action suit against the government on behalf of 300,000 Indians in 1996 for mishandling of Indian trust funds for monies Indians should have received over the years for oil, gas, grazing, and timber leases. It is disclosed by a federal judge that the U.S. government officials who were charged with mismanaging the trust funds for Indians had shredded 162 boxes of records related to the case in 1998.

RECR. The Miccosukee Indians open their $50 million Resort and Gaming center along the southeastern edge of the Florida Everglades.

21ST CENTURY

2000

ARTS. The Grammy Awards add a category for Native American music. The National Academy of Recording Arts and Sciences vote to create a new award to honor each year's best Native American music.

DEAT. Clarence Basil Cuts The Rope (b. April 12, 1935), artist and member of the Gros Ventre Tribe, dies on March 29 in Montana.

ECON. California tribes win the right to operate casinos. *Proposition 1A* is passed on March 7 by California voters which amends the state's constitution to allow Las Vegas-style gambling on Indian land in California. Indian casinos will flourish in the state in the coming years.

Low-cost telephone service is to be made available on Indian reservations. As part of a $17 million government initiative to help low-income communities access the Internet, President Bill Clinton announces a plan to offer dollar-a-month phone service to around 300,000 Indians across the country. Clinton travels to Shiprock, New Mexico on the Navajo reservation to deliver his announcement. Only about 22 percent of Navajos have phone service on the reservation.

LAND. On January 14, the U.S. Department of Energy announces its intention to return 84,000 acres of land in northern Utah to the Northern Ute tribe. The land return is the largest made to any tribe in the continental United States in over a century. The land was taken by the federal government in 1916, because it contained oil reserves

that the United States thought might be needed by the navy during WWI, but the land was never used.

The Torres-Martinez Band of Desert Cahuilla Indians receives $14 million in compensation for reservation lands flooded by the Colorado River in 1906. After 18 years of litigation, Congress grants the money to the 659 tribal members who plan to use the settlement to purchase 11,000 acres of land and build a casino in Riverside County, California.

The Timbisha Shoshone Indians are granted 7,600 acres around Death Valley, by the *Timbisha Homeland Act,* which includes 314 acres within Death Valley National Park.

POLI. The Bureau of Indian affairs issues a formal apology to American Indians on September 8. As part of a ceremony commemorating the 175th anniversary of the BIA, the apology by Kevin Grover (head of the BIA) is for "ethnic cleansing" of tribes, forcing Indians from their lands, undermining their cultures, and failure of the agency to alleviate alcoholism, violence, and other problems plaguing Indian communities.

2001

ARTS. Paula Gunn Allen (b. 1939, Laguna Pueblo/Sioux), a writer, poet, and novelist, receives a Lifetime Achievement Award from the Native Writer's Circle of the Americas. Some of the other Native writers to have received this prestigious literary award are N. Scott Momaday (1992), Leslie Marmon Silko (1994), Joy Harjo

(1995), Vine Deloria, Jr. (1996), and Louise Erdrich (2000).

DEAT. Jamake Highwater, an award-winning Native American author of many books for both adults and children, dies at the age of 59.

POLI. On his last day in office, January 20, President Clinton does not pardon Leonard Peltier, the AIM activist, as many hoped he would do.

WARS. Fifty-six years after serving in WWII, Congress and President George W. Bush honor 29 Navajo code talkers with the Congressional Gold Medal. President Bush presents medals to four of the five living code talkers, including Chester Nez, and presents the relatives of 24 others with the medals.

2002

ARTS. The motion picture *Windtalkers* is released, starring Nicholas Cage, Christian Slater, Roger Willie, and Adam Beach. Directed by John Woo, it portrays a story about two Navajo code talkers and how the code is to be protected at all costs. By this time, there are over 100 books, children's books, novels, motion pictures, and documentaries about the code talkers.

POLI. President George W. Bush proclaims the month of November to be National American

Deputy Secretary of Defense John J. Hamre (2nd from right) speaks with participants in an observance honoring Native American military contributions. Samuel Tso, a WWII Navajo code talker, sits on the left. Courtesy of Department of Defense.

Indian and Alaska Native Heritage Month, recognizing the many remarkable contributions American Indians and Alaska natives have made to our national identity. By this time, there are 562 Federally Recognized Indian tribes in the United States.

2004

DEAT. The first American Indian woman to die in the Iraq War is Army Spc. Lori Piestewa (Hopi), 23, from Tuba City, Arizona. Her death on March 23 makes her the first American Indian woman killed while fighting for the U.S. military. Piestewa was a single mother, who left behind a four-year-old son (Brandon) and a three-year-old daughter (Carla).

EDUC. The National Museum of the American Indian, located on the National Mall in Washington, D.C., opens to the public on September 21. The museum, chartered by Congress in 1989 as the 16th museum of the Smithsonian Institution, is dedicated to the Native peoples of North, South, and Central America. The museum's mission is to preserve, present, and celebrate the Native cultures of the Americas.

POLI. Cecilia Fire Thunder is elected President of the Oglala Sioux Tribe of South Dakota, beating out Indian activist and actor Russell Means for the position.

2005

ARTS. The first annual Indian Summer Music Awards take place on September 10 as part of the annual Indian Summer Festival in Milwaukee, Wisconsin, North America's largest Native American festival. The awards are to recognize, honor, and promote the best commercially produced American Indian music from the previous year.

DEAT. The last of the Comanche code talkers from WWII dies on July 20. Charles Chibitty (b. 1921), 83, was one of a group of Comanches from the Lawton, Oklahoma, area who were selected for special duty in the U.S.

Alphabet	Navajo Word	Literal Translation
A	wol-la-chee	ant
B	na-hash-chid	badger

Words	Navajo Word	Literal Translation
Lt. Colonel	che-chil-be-tah-besh-legai	silver oak leaf
Fighter plane	da-he-tih-hi	humming bird
Cruiser	lo-tso-yazzie	small whale
About	wola-chi-a-moffa-gahn	ant fight
Which	gloe-ih-a-his-tlon	weasel tied together
Australia	cha-yes-desi	rolled hat

Samples from the *Navajo Code Talkers' Dictionary,* Department of the Navy, Navy Historical Center, Washington, D.C. (declassified in 1968).

Army to provide the Allies with a language that the Germans could not decipher. He participated in the Normandy Invasion on D-Day. Like the Navajo Indians who served in the Pacific theater, the Comanches were called "Code Talkers." Chibitty was forbidden to speak his native language in school when he was growing up.

Gladys Iola Tantaquidgeon (b. June 15, 1899), the oldest Mohegan Indian, dies at the age of 106 in Uncasville, Connecticut, on November 1. Tantaquidgeon was a direct descendent of Uncas, the famed Mohegan chief who broke away from the Pequots around 1635 with other tribe members and sought to work with the first English settlers in the region now known as Connecticut. She received a traditional Mohegan upbringing, and was the third Medicine Woman of her tribe since 1859. Tantaquidgeon was an expert on ancient-culture preservation, collecting tribal correspondence and birth and marriage records that documented the tribe's history. Her efforts helped the dwindling Mohegans regain federal recognition in 1994. The 1,700-member tribe now runs the successful Connecticut casino Mohegan Sun.

R. C. Gorman dies on November 3. Gorman, a Navajo from Chinle, Arizona, was a foremost American Indian artist, painter, and printmaker. Born Rudolph Carl Gorman on July 26, 1931, Gorman was called by the *New York Times* the "Picasso of American Indian Art." He is best known for his paintings, sculptures, and lithographs depicting American Indian women, usually round, barefoot, and wrapped in shawls or blankets. His father was also a painter and a member of the Navajo code talkers in WWII.

Vine Deloria, Jr., dies on November 13 at age 72. The Sioux scholar and spiritual leader was born in 1933 in Martin, South Dakota, near the Pine Ridge Reservation. Deloria became a foremost Indian scholar, authoring 20 books including the influential best seller *Custer Died for Your Sins* (1969). He was heavily involved in Indian organizations, serving as the executive director of the National Congress of American Indians in 1964, and as a founding trustee of the National Museum of the American Indian. He was a powerful influence and major thinker on Indian rights and issues.

POLI. In October, two American Indian groups in South Carolina receive state recognition as tribes. The Waccamaw Indian People along the east coast of the state and the Pee Dee Nation of Upper South Carolina are granted recognition by the state Minority Affairs Commission. The Commission was given the power to recognize Indian tribes and groups by the state legislature last year. The Catawba Indian Nation is the only federally recognized tribe in South Carolina.

GLOSSARY

adobe. Sun-dried clay, often mixed with straw.

AD. Anno Domini. In the Gregorian calendar, AD is Latin for "in the year of our Lord," referring to Our Lord Jesus Christ. "AD 2000" literally means in the 2000th year since the birth of Christ. In this system, years after the traditional birth of Christ are prefixed with the letters AD.

AIM. American Indian Movement, an Indian activist organization founded in 1968 that organized many successful Indian protests in the 1970s.

Aleuts. The native peoples of the Aleutian Island chain stretching 1,400 miles off of the southwestern coast of Alaska. In this isolated setting, the Aleut developed a unique culture based on hunting sea otters and other water animals.

allotment. The federal government policy that divided communally-owned Indian land into 160-acre plots called allotments. Allotments were assigned to individual Indians as private property.

annuity. An annual payment due to a tribe according to the terms of a treaty with the U.S. government. Annuities were spent by the tribe as a whole or divided among tribal members.

BC. Before Christ. The years before the birth of Christ in the Gregorian calendar are followed by the letters BC.

BCE. Before the Common Era (or Before the Christian Era, or Before the Current Era). Eventually, BCE is expected to replace BC (Before Christ). The Common Era is the period beginning with the year 1 onwards. BC and BCE are identical in value.

Beringia. During one of the Earth's Ice Ages, water froze into glaciers, reducing the sea level 200 to 300 feet, exposing a subcontinent known as Beringia. This subcontinent connected Asia and North America and formed a migration route for hunters and animals searching for food.

BIA. Bureau of Indian Affairs. The part of the U.S. Department charged with overseeing the federal government's dealings with Indian groups.

cash crop. A crop such as cotton or tobacco that is produced mainly to be sold on the market rather than consumed as a staple crop.

cede. Regarding land cessions, to surrender possession of, to yield, or grant possession of to others. Indians ceded land to whites by treaties.

circa (ca. or c.). The Latin word literally meaning "about" is commonly abbreviated by c. or ca. This is often used to describe dates that are uncertain. It is used throughout the prehistoric period since the dates are estimates only.

clan. A group of people united by kinship, especially through a common ancestor.

colonialism. A political and economic system in which one country or nation sends settlers to occupy and control another country or region.

Confederate states. The Confederate states (or Confederacy) were the 11 southern states that seceded from the United States in 1860–1861.

Constitution. The document that states the fundamental laws of a nation and determines the powers of the government and rights of the people.

Dawes Act. Same as the *General Allotment Act of 1887* that called for the division of communally-held Indian lands into 160-acre plots called allotments.

epidemic. A contagious disease that spreads rapidly throughout a population.

ethnocentrism. The belief that one's own group is superior to another group.

federal recognition. The formal acknowledgement by the U.S. government that a group is an Indian tribe, and thus entitled to the services and benefits reserved for that group by the government.

Five Civilized Tribes. The Cherokee, Seminole, Creek, Choctaw, and Chickasaw tribes, whose original homelands were located in the Southeast United States. They were considered by whites to be more "civilized" than other Indians because of their early adoption of certain white customs.

Friends of the Indian. Non-Indian reformer groups that encouraged the U.S. government to adopt more benevolent policies toward Indians and to provide equal protection of the law, education, citizenship, and individual land title to Indians. These groups also proposed to remold Native Americans into mainstream citizens.

fur trade. A trade network through which Indian trappers obtained products from European traders in exchange for animal furs.

globalization. The process in which the flow of culture, trade, immigration, and communication is increased worldwide.

horticulture. The process and science of growing fruit, plants, and crops.

ideology. The objectives and ideas that influence a political group, nation, community, or culture.

imperialism. The practice of or belief in extending the power of a nation through territorial acquisition or gaining control over the political and economic life of another area.

Indian boarding schools. Boarding schools operated by the Bureau of Indian Affairs where Indian children were sent away from their parents and reservations to be indoctrinated in non-Indian customs while learning English and other academic subjects.

Indian Claims Commission (ICC). The commission formed by Congress in 1946 to review and resolve all outstanding land claims of Indian groups within the continental United States.

Indian Territory. This was the area west of the Mississippi River to which many eastern Indian groups were forced to relocate during the nineteenth century. By 1854, the area was roughly the same as present-day Oklahoma. When Oklahoma was admitted as a state into the Union in 1907, Indian Territory was dissolved.

Inuit. Best known as Eskimos, the Inuit are the native people of the arctic land stretching from central Alaska to the northern coast of Canada and onto the island of Greenland.

Iroquois Confederacy (Iroquois League; Six Nations). A confederacy of five powerful tribes (Cayuga, Oneida, Seneca, Mohawk, and Onondaga) native to what is today New York State. In 1722, a sixth tribe (Tuscarora) joined the confederacy.

Manifest Destiny. The belief that it was God's will that the United States occupy the whole continent between the Atlantic and Pacific Oceans.

Maritime. Pertaining to the navigation and commerce of the sea.

Mestizo. A person of mixed racial ancestry, particularly of mixed European and Native American ancestry.

Métis. A group of people in Canada of mixed Indian and European ancestry with a distinct culture.

missionary. One who seeks to convert others to a particular religion or doctrine.

monarchy. A political system whereby absolute sovereignty lies with a single individual who inherits the power.

myth. A traditional, typically ancient story that explains a world view, cultural mores, or natural phenomenon, and often involves supernatural beings, ancestors, or heroes.

National Congress of American Indians (NCAI). This pan-Indian organization was founded in 1944 in response to the federal government's policies of termination and assimilation forced upon tribal governments. It continues to be active today, representing 250 member tribes throughout the United States.

nationalism. A devotion to one's nation that often emphasizes the promotion of one's national culture and interests above other nations' cultures and interests.

New Amsterdam. The name the Dutch called Manhattan Island (New York) after acquiring the land from the Indians in 1626.

New France. The possession of land by France in North America from the sixteenth century to 1763, incorporating much of southeast Canada, the Great Lakes region, and the Mississippi Valley.

New Netherland. A colony founded by the Dutch on the east coast of North America in the seventeenth century which ended when the English took control of it in 1664, turning its capital, New Amsterdam, into New York City. The area extended from Albany, New York, in the north to Delaware in the south, encompassing parts of what today are the states of New York, New Jersey, Pennsylvania, Maryland, Connecticut, and Delaware.

New Spain. The former Spanish possession in the New World, including the southwest United States, Mexico, Central America north of Panama, South America (except Brazil), the West Indian islands, Florida, and the islands of the Philippines.

New World. The Western hemisphere; North and South America.

Northwest Passage. Spanish and British explorers sought a Northwest Passage—a water route from the Atlantic Ocean to the Pacific Ocean to the Indies through the Arctic Archipelago of northern Canada and along the northern coast of Alaska.

Northwest Territory. The Northwest Ordinance of 1787 allowed for the creation of as many as five states in the northwest portion of the Ohio Valley on lines originally laid out in 1784 by Thomas Jefferson. Known as the Northwest Territory (or Old Northwest), the new federal lands were east of the Mississippi and between the Ohio River and Great lakes.

Old Northwest. The area today covering the states of Ohio, Indiana, Illinois, Michigan, and Wisconsin. Also known as the Northwest Territory.

Old World. The Eastern hemisphere; Europe, specifically.

Plague. A highly contagious, usually pandemic disease.

Proselytize. The act of trying to persuade someone to join a particular religious faith.

Protestant. One of many Western Christian churches that developed after splitting from the Roman Catholic Church.

Puritanism. A religious movement of the sixteenth and seventeenth centuries based on the beliefs that hard work and self-control were important and that pleasure was unnecessary and wrong. The Puritans are the same group as the Pilgrims. In the seventeenth century, many Puritans emigrated from Europe to the New World.

Red Power Movement. The Indian activists movement of the late 1960s and early 1970s. Red Power groups, such as the American Indian Movement, used dramatic protests to draw attention to Indian issues.

Relocation. The federal Indian policy of the late 1940s and 1950s that encouraged and assisted Indians on reservations to move to cities for better jobs and housing.

Removal. The federal Indian policy that sought to extinguish Indian claims to lands in the eastern part of the United States and relocate the Indian groups to lands west of the Mississippi River.

repatriation. The return of Indian burial remains and artifacts to their tribes of origins.

secular. Related to worldly or temporal concerns as opposed to religious concerns.

self-determination. Federal Indian policy inaugurated in the 1970s that sought to give Indians more control over their political and economic affairs and promoted increased Indian involvement in government programs to improve their standard of living. This policy was a major change from the Termination and Relocation policies of the government from earlier years.

Seven Cities of Cíbola. Seven legendary golden cities in what is now the American Southwest. The myth was related by Indians, Spanish explorer Cabeza de Vaca and his companions in 1536, and by Spanish missionary Marcos de Niza in 1539 to Spaniards in Mexico City. The belief in these legendary cities of splendor and riches waiting to be discovered propelled Spanish conquistadors into the far reaches of New Spain.

Shaman. A Native American priest whose followers believe he or she can heal and affect events through magic or contact with the afterlife.

syncretism. An instance in which two or more religious traditions blend into a new practice.

wampum. Cylindrical white and purple beads made from quahog clam shells that northeastern Indian tribes strung on sinew to create beaded strings and belts. Traditionally, wampum was used in rituals and ceremonies, but after contact with whites, it was also used as a medium of exchange in the fur trade in the Northeast.

Westernization. The adoption of Western culture by non-Western peoples often involving loss of local cultures, dress, languages, and traditions.

BIBLIOGRAPHY

BOOKS, ARTICLES, AND GOVERNMENT REPORTS

Armstrong, Virginia Irving. *I Have Spoken.* New York: Pocket Books, 1972.

Axelrod, Alan. *Chronicle of the Indian Wars: From Colonial Times to Wounded Knee.* New York: Prentice Hall, 1993.

Barrett, Carole A., ed. *American Indian History.* 2 vols. Pasadena, Calif.: Salem Press, 2003.

Beauchamp, William M. *The History of the New York Iroquois.* New York: Charles Scribners, 1913.

Black Elk. *Black Elk Speaks: Being the Life Story of a Holy Man of the Oglala Sioux.* Lincoln: University of Nebraska Press, 1932.

Bonnichsen, Robson, and Karen L. Turnmire, eds. *Ice Age People of North America.* Corvallis: Oregon State University Press for Center for the Study of the First Americans, 1999.

Bonvillain, Nancy. *Hiawatha: Founder of the Iroquois Confederacy.* New York: Chelsea House Publishers, 1992.

Bragdon, Kathleen J. *Columbia Guide to American Indians of the Northeast.* New York: Columbia University Press, 2001.

Brito, Silvester J. *The Way of a Peyote Roadman.* American University Studies, series 21, Regional Studies, vol. 1. New York: Peter Lang, 1989.

Brown, Dee. *Bury My Heart at Wounded Knee.* New York: Hold, Rinehart & Winston, 1970.

Cantor, George. *North American Indian Landmarks: A Traveler's Guide.* Detroit: Visible Ink, 1993.

Catlin, George. *Letters and Notes on the Manners, Customs, and Condition of the North American Indians.* Vol. 2. New York: Dover, 1841.

Champagne, Duane, ed. *Chronology of Native North American History from Pre-Columbian Times to the Present.* Detroit: Gale Research, 1994.

Champagne, Duane, and Michael A. Paré, eds. *Native North American Chronology.* New York: UXL, 1995.

Chronology of the American Indian: A Guide to Native Peoples of the Western Hemisphere 25,000 B.C.–1994. Newport Beach, Calif.: American Indian Publishers, 1994.

Cwiklik, Robert. *Tecumseh, Shawnee Rebel.* North American Indians of Achievement Series. New York: Chelsea House, 1993.

Darst, Guy. "Reagan Calls Indian Life 'Primitive.'" *Seattle Times,* May 21, 1988.

Davis, Christopher. *North American Indian.* Feltman, England: Hamlyn House, 1969.

Declaration of Indian Purpose. Chicago: American Indian Chicago Conference, 1961.

Deloria, Vine, Jr. *Custer Died for Your Sins; An Indian Manifesto.* New York: MacMillan, 1969.

Del Testa, David W., Florence Lemoine, and John Strickland, eds. *Global History: Cultural Encounters from Antiquity to the Present. Vol. 3: The Age of Discovery and Colonial Expansion.* Armonk, N.Y.: Sharpe Reference, 2004.

Dennis, Henry C., ed. *The American Indian, 1492–1976: A Chronology & Fact Book.* Ethnic Chronology Series, No. 1. Dobbs Ferry, NY: Ocean Publications, 1977.

Eastman, Charles A. *Indian Boyhood.* Boston: Little, Brown and Co., 1930.

Encyclopedia of North American Indians. Boston: Houghton Mifflin, College Division, 1996.

Fee, Chester Anders. *Chief Joseph: The Biography of a Great Indian.* New York: Wilson-Erickson, 1936.

Francis, Lee. *Native Time: A Historical Time Line of Native America.* New York: St. Martin's, 1995.

Garland, Hamlin. *The Book of the American Indian.* New York: Harper, 1923.

Glaspell, Kate E. "Incidents in the Life of a Pioneer." *North Dakota Historical Quarterly,* 8 (1941), 184–190.

Grinde, Donald A., Jr., ed. *Native Americans.* Washington, D.C.: CQ Press, 2002.

Grinnell, George Bird. *The Fighting Cheyennes.* New York: Charles Scribner's Sons, 1915.

Hale, Lorraine. *Native American Education: A Reference Handbook.* Santa Barbara, Calif.: ABC-CLIO, 2002.

Hazen-Hammond, Susan. *Timelines of Native American History: Through the Centuries with Mother Earth and Father Sky.* New York: Berkley Publishing Group, 1997.

Heard, J. Norman. *Handbook of the American Frontier: Four Centuries of Indian-White Relationships.* 5 vols. Metuchen, N.J.: Scarecrow Press, 1987–1998.

Highwater, Jamake. *Many Smokes, Many Moons: A Chronology of American Indian History through Indian Art.* Philadelphia: J. B. Lippincott, 1978.

Hook, Jason, and Martin Pegler. *To Live and Die in the West: The American Indian Wars, 1860–90.* London: Fitzroy Dearborn, 2001. Oxford: Osprey, 1999.

Institute for the Development of Indian Law. *A Chronological List of Treaties and Agreements Made by Indian Tribes with the United States.* Washington, D.C.: Institute for the Development of Indian Law, 1973.

Irvine, Keith, ed. *Encyclopedia of Indians of the Americas.* 7 vols. St. Clair Shores, Mich.: Scholarly, 1974.

Jackson, Andrew. President Andrew Jackson's Message to Congress "On Indian Removal," December 6, 1830. Records of the United States Senate, 1789–1990, Record Group 46, National Archives.

Jane, Lionel Cecil, ed. and trans. *The Four Voyages of Columbus.* 2 vols. New York: Dover, 1988.

Jelks, Edward B., and Juliet C. Jelks. *Historical Dictionary of North American Archaeology.* Westport, Conn.: Greenwood, 1988.

Jennings, Francis. *The Invasion of America: Indians, Colonialism, and the Cant of Conquest.* New York: Norton, 1975.

Johansen, Bruce E. *Forgotten Founders: Benjamin Franklin, the Iroquois, and the Rationale for the American Revolution.* Ipswich, Mass.: Gambit, 1982.

Johansen, Bruce E., ed. *The Native Peoples of North America: A History, Volume 1.* Native America: Yesterday and Today Series. Westport, Conn.: Praeger, 2005.

Katz, William Loren. *Black Indians: A Hidden Heritage.* New York: Atheneum, 1986.

Keoke, Emory Dean, and Kay Marie Porterfield. *Encyclopedia of American Indian Contributions to the World: 15,000 Years of Inventions and Innovations.* New York: Facts on File, 2002.

Kessel, William B., and Robert Wooster, eds. *Encyclopedia of Native American Wars and Warfare.* New York: Facts on File, 2005.

Konstantin, Phil. *This Day in North American Indian History: Important Dates in the History of North America's Native Peoples for Every Calendar Day.* Cambridge, Mass.: Da Capo, 2002.

Lane, Campbell. "The Sun Dance of the Cree Indians," *Canadian Record of Science,* 2 (1887): 22–26.

Leitch (LePoer), Barbara A. *Chronology of the American Indian.* St. Clair Shores, Mich.: Scholarly, 1975.

MacLeod, William Christie. *The American Indian Frontier.* New York: Alfred A. Knopf, 1928.

Magnusson, Magnus and Herman Palsson. The Vinland Sagas: the Norse Discovery of America. Graenlendinga Saga and Erik's Saga. Harmondsworth, Middlesex, England: Penguin, 1965.

Manypenny, George W. *Our Indian Wards.* New York: Da Capo, 1972. First published Cincinnati: R. Clarke, 1880.

Matthews, Leonard, Geoffrey Campion, and Arlene C. Rourke. *Indians.* Vero Beach, Fla.: Rourke Publications, 1989.

Mays, Dorothy A. *Women in Early America: Struggle, Survival, and Freedom in a New World.* Santa Barbara, Calif.: ABC-CLIO, 2004.

Melmer, David. "Judge Takes Charge: Lamberth Puts BIA Trust Minders on 5-Year Probation." *Indian Country Today,* January 5, 2000.

Morris, Roy, Jr. *Sheridan: The Life and Wars of General Phil Sheridan.* New York: Crown, 1992.

The New Encyclopaedia Brittanica. Chicago: Encyclopaedia Brittanica, 2005.

Nies, Judith. *Native American History: A Chronology of the Vast Achievements of a Culture and Their Links to World Events.* New York: Ballantine Books, 1996.

O'Driscoll, Patrick. "Crazy Horse's Eyes Again Watching Over His Land." *USA Today* [final edition], June 3, 1998.

Olson, James S., Mark Baxter, Jason M. Tetzloff, and Darren Pierson, eds. *Encyclopedia of American Indian Civil Rights.* Westport, Conn.: Greenwood, 1997.

O'Sullivan, John L. "Annexation." *The United States Magazine and Democratic Review,* 17, no. 85–86 (July-August 1845), 7.

Pratt, Richard. "Kill the Indian, and Save the Man." Paper presented at the Nineteenth Annual National Conference of Charities and Correction, Denver, Colo. *Official Report of the Nineteenth Annual National Conference of Charities and Correction,* 1892.

Radin, Paul. *The Story of the American Indian.* New York: Boni & Liveright, 1927.

Rajtar, Steve. *Indian War Sites: A Guidebook to Battlefields, Monuments, and Memorials, State by State, with Canada and Mexico.* Jefferson, N.C.: McFarland, 1999.

Remini, Robert V. *Andrew Jackson & His Indian Wars.* New York: Viking, 2001.

Rose, Cynthia, and Duane Champagne, eds. *Native North American Almanac.* Detroit UXL, 1994.

Saraband, Inc. *Illustrated Atlas of Native American History: Traces the Movement of North America's Native Peoples from Prehistoric Times to the Present Day.* Edison, N.J.: Chartwell Books, 1999.

Sell, Henry Blackman, and Victor Weybright. *Buffalo Bill and the Wild West.* New York: Oxford University Press, 1955.

Sonneborn, Liz. *Chronology of American Indian History: The Trail of the Wind.* New York: Facts on File, 2001.

The Sovereignty & Goodness of God, Together with the Faithfulness of His Promises Displayed; Being a Narrative of the Captivity and Restoration of Mrs. Mary Rowlandson and Related Documents. Boston: Bedford Books, 1682.

Swisher, Karen Gayton, and AnCita Benally. *Native North American Firsts.* Detroit: Gale, 1998.

Taylor, Joseph Henry. *Frontier and Indian Life.* Washburn, N.Dak.: Washburn's Fiftieth Anniversary Committee, 1932.

Thomas, Kevin. "Movie Review; An Affirming Journey in 'Fancydancing.' " *Los Angeles Times,* October 25, 2002.

Thompson, William N. *Native American Issues: A Reference Handbook.* Santa Barbara, Calif.: ABC-CLIO, 1996.

Thorgilsson, Ari. *Islendingabók: The Book of the Icelanders.* Edited and translated by Halldór Hermann Sson. Ithaca, N.Y.: Cornell University Library, 1930.

Trager, James, ed. *The People's Chronology: A Year-by-Year Record of Human Events from Prehistory to the Present.* Rev. and updated ed. New York: Holt, Rinehart and Winston, 1992.

Trigger, Bruce G., and Wilcomb E. Washburn, eds. *Cambridge History of the Native Peoples of the Americas—North America, Vol. 1.* Cambridge: Cambridge University Press, 1996.

U.S. Commissioner of Indian Affairs. *Annual Report, 1875.* Washington, D.C.: Office of Indian Affairs, 1875.

Vogel, Virgil J. *This Country was Ours: A Documentary History of the American Indian.* New York: Harper & Row, 1972.

Waldman, Carl. *Timelines of Native American History.* New York: Prentice-Hall General Reference, 1994.

Waldman, Carl, and Molly Braun, Illust. *Atlas of the North American Indian.* Appendix A: Chronology of North American Indian Prehistory and History. New York: Facts on File/Checkmark Books, 2000.

Weatherford, Jack M. *Indian Givers: How Indians of the Americas Transformed the World.* New York: Crown, 1988.

Welch, James, and Paul Stekler. *Killing Custer: The Battle of the Little Big Horn and the Fate of the Plains Indians.* New York: W. W. Norton, 1994.

Wetmore, Charles A. *Report of Mission Indians of Southern California.* Washington, D.C.: GPO, 1875.

Wheeler, Homer W. *Buffalo Days.* Indianapolis, Ind.: The Bobbs-Merill Company, 1925.

Wildenthal, Bryan H. *Native American Sovereignty on Trial: A Handbook with Cases, Laws, and Documents.* Santa Barbara, Calif.: ABC-CLIO, 2003.

WEB SITES

American Indian Civics Project. *American Indian Issues: An Introductory and Curricular Guide for Educators.* W. K. Kellogg Foundation, Native American Higher Education Initiative. 1997–2001. http://sorrel.humboldt.edu/~go1/kellogg/NativeRelationship.html.

American Indian Heritage Month. *American Indians in World War II.* http://www.defenselink. mil/specials/nativeamerican01/wwii.html.

Burke Museum of Natural History and Culture. *Ancient People in the Americas.* Seattle: University of Washington, 2004. http://www.washington.edu/burkemuseum/kman/ancient-peoples.htm.

Carter, Nancy Carol. *Chronology of the Indigenous Peoples of San Diego County.* San Diego, Calif.: University of San Diego School of Law, 2004. http://www.sandiego.edu/nativeamerican/chronology.html.

Ferguson, Bob. *Choctaw Chronology.* Choctaw, Mississippi: Mississippi Band of Choctaw Indians, 2004. http://www.choctaw.org/history/chronology.htm.

First People. Simon Pokagon—Potawatomi Chief. http://www.firstpeople.us/FP-html-Wisdom/SimonPokagon.html (accessed June 20, 2006).

Fussichen, Kenneth. *U.S. History before 1700 Chronology.* http://users.commkey.net/fussichen/otdU16.htm.

Hendrix, Levanne R. *American Indian/Alaska Native Chronology of Selected Historical Events.* Appendix A of Health and Health Care of American Indian and Alaska Native Elders. San Francisco: University of California, San Francisco. http://www.stanford.edu/group/ethnoger/americanindian.html#appA.

Infobase Ventures. *Native American—WorldHistory.com.* http://www.worldhistory.com/wiki/N/Native-American.htm.

Legends of America. *Native American Legends: First Owners of the American West.* http://www.legendsofamerica.com/NA-NativeAmericans.html.

Mayer, Eric. *Emayzine.com. Dr. E's Social Science Webzine.* Chronology 1776–1830, and Chronology 1830–1890. Victorville, Calif.: Victor Valley College. http://www.emayzine.com.

Minnesota State University, Mankato. Emuseum. *Minnesota History: A Chronology,* 2005. http://www.mnsu.edu/emuseum/history/mnstatehistory/timeline.html.

Native Wire: American Indians in the News. Falls Church, Va.: American Indian Heritage Foundation. http://www.indians.org/NativeWire/nativewire.html.

Osborn, Tracey. *Native American History and Culture.* http://www.teacheroz.com/Native_Americans.htm.

Pearson Education. *American Indian Glossary—InfoPlease.* http://www.infoplease.com/spot/aihmglossary1.html.

Public Broadcasting Service. *The Gold Rush.* PBS, 1997. http://www.pbs.org/goldrush/.

Rogers, Will. *Will Rogers Home Page.* http://willrogers.org.

Rogers, Will. *Will Rogers Today.* November 15, 2002. www.willrogerstoday.com.

Schacht, Miriam. *Native American Literature Chronology to 1969.* Austin: University of Texas, 2002. http://www.cwrl.utexas.edu/~schacht/e314v/chrono.html.

Southern Ute Indian Tribe. *Ute Indian Chronology.* Southern Ute Indian Cultural Center. http://www.utelegacy.org/pages/chrono.html.

Strom, Karen M. *Timeline of Events Relevant to the Northern Plains Tribes.* http://www.hanksville.org/daniel/timeline2.html.

White, Jenny L. *How the West was Won (or Lost): The Frontier in American Literatures and Cultures.* Berkeley: University of California, 2003. http://ist-socrates.berkeley.edu/~jwhite/Spring2003/chronology.html.

WorldHistory.com. *Native American.* http://www.worldhistory.com/wiki/N/Native-American.htm.

INDEX

About the Author

PHILLIP M. WHITE is Reference Librarian and Bibliographer for American Indian Studies, San Diego State University Library. His extensive list of published work includes *Bibliography of Native American Bibliographies* (2004), *Peyotism and the Native American Church: An Annotated Bibliography* (2000), *The Kickapoo Indians, Their History and Culture: An Annotated Bibliography* (1999), and *The Native American Sun Dance Religion and Ceremony: An Annotated Bibliography* (1998), all available through Greenwood Press. He is also author of *California Indians and Their Reservations: An Online Dictionary* (1999–present).